IMAGES
of America

DEVON HORSE SHOW AND COUNTRY FAIR

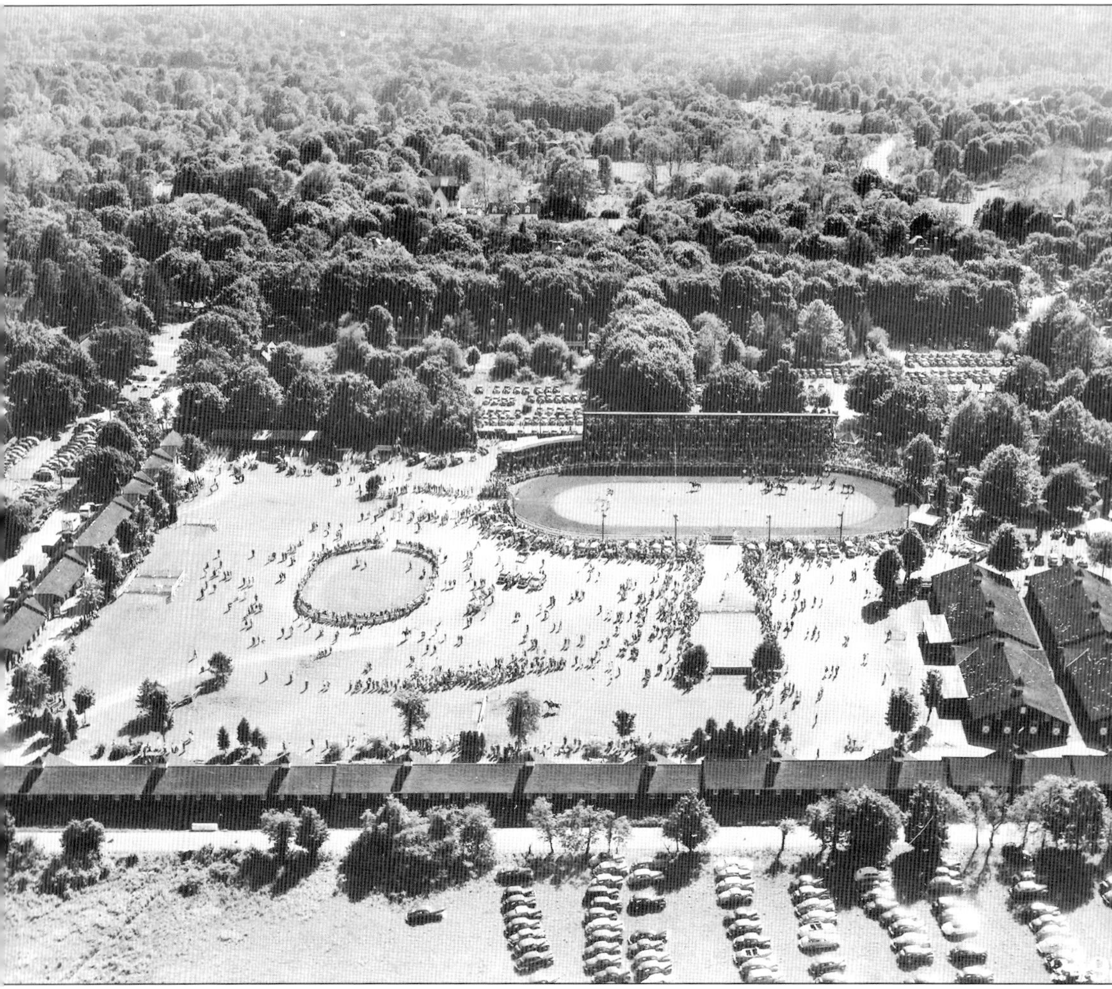

This 1930 aerial image of the Devon Horse Show and Country Fair on its present grounds facing west depicts the expansion of grandstands, stables, and fairgrounds since the first 1896 show. The Devon Inn, where the shows were held between 1898 and 1900, no longer appears in the far left of this image. It was destroyed by fire in 1929. (Courtesy of the Hagley Museum and Library.)

On the Cover: In 1898, the show was moved to the Devon Inn so that guests could enjoy the event from the sprawling porches, windows, and back lawn of the elegant hotel. Spectators and carriages lined the rail as judges determined the winner of the children's pony class on June 21, 1898. (Courtesy of the Devon Horse Show and Country Fair Archives.)

IMAGES
of America

DEVON HORSE SHOW AND COUNTRY FAIR

Charlene Keller Fullmer and Kathryn Elizabeth Brown

ARCADIA
PUBLISHING

ISBN 978-1-4671-0619-1

Published by Arcadia Publishing
Charleston, South Carolina

Printed in the United States of America

Library of Congress Control Number: 2020950543

For all general information, please contact Arcadia Publishing:
Telephone 843-853-2070
Fax 843-853-0044
E-mail sales@arcadiapublishing.com
For customer service and orders:
Toll-Free 1-888-313-2665

Visit us on the Internet at www.arcadiapublishing.com

This book is dedicated to the volunteers who have supported and enriched the Devon Horse Show and Country Fair for the last 125 years. Champions will always meet at Devon.

All royalties from this book benefit the Devon Horse Show and Country Fair Foundation.

Contents

ACKNOWLEDGMENTS

In trying to capture the indomitable spirit of the 125-year institution that is Devon, we were limited in time and text. We regret that we could not honor all of the champions whose countless contributions have placed Devon in a class by itself. We are indebted to Claire Costello and Evan Brazunas, who cheerfully spent weekends with us in the archives, scanned hundreds of images, and then scanned hundreds more, sharing history along the way. We strived to be as accurate as possible, and we thank Peter Doubleday and David Distler for their encyclopedic knowledge of the sport. Thanks to the Devon faithful who shared their reflections, knowledge, insights, and photographs, including Kathy Schwartz, Dolly Somers, Karen Meyers, Ginni Vosburg, Gail McCarthy, and Helen and Eric Corkhill. Michael Criscuolo provided valuable resources and documents from the Bryn Mawr Hospital Archives. Veronica Finkelstein provided excellent content for Chapters 4 and 5. The photographs tell the story, and to that end, we thank show photographer Brenda Carpenter for her creativity, dedication, and support. The Engraver graciously shared vintage photographs from the early years. The Philadelphia Evening Bulletin Photograph Collection, courtesy of the Special Collections Research Center (SCRC), Temple University Libraries, Philadelphia, Pennsylvania, was a treasure trove, and we thank the archivists for their assistance.

Except where noted, all images are courtesy of the Devon Horse Show and Country Fair Archives. Photographers highlighted are, among others, Axt, Budd, Freudy, Hass, Hood-Weintraub, MacGregor, Reily & Way, Reuss, Schreiber, and Steinmetz. The sources of written history are *A Week Down in Devon: A History of the Devon Horse Show*, by Christopher S. Hyde; *The Bryn Mawr Hospital: 1893–1968* and *The Bryn Mawr Hospital Centennial 1893–1993: A Country Doctor's Dream*, by Theodore J. Berry, MD; *Down Through the Years . . . 1896–1946: A Short History of Devon*, by Raymond S. Cox; *"My Dear, There Are Horses Here, Too!": A Chronological and Cultural History of the Devon Country Fair*, by Edwina L. Kerr; the *Philadelphia Inquirer*; the *New York Times*; *Main Line Times*; *Suburban and Wayne Times*; the *Chronicle of the Horse*; the personal reflections of Richard E. Kurtz, Esq., plus many scrapbooks, yearbooks, handbooks, and newspapers from the Devon and Bryn Mawr Hospital Archives.

We are grateful to our families for their unwavering love and guidance throughout this project and their support of all things Devon.

—CKF & KEB

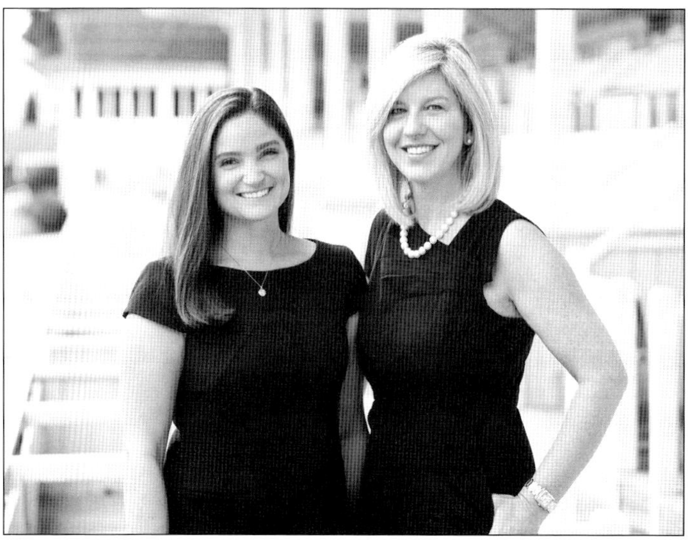

Pictured are authors Kathryn Elizabeth Brown (left) and Charlene Keller Fullmer (right). Brown is an officer of Devon Country Fair, and Fullmer is on the board of directors of the Devon Horse Show and Country Fair Foundation. They both serve on the executive committee of Devon Country Fair, where they have a combined 45 years of Devon experience. (Courtesy of Brenda Carpenter Photography.)

INTRODUCTION

As we begin our 2021 season of the Devon Horse Show and Country Fair, we take this time to celebrate 125 years of what is arguably the most exciting event in equestrian sports. Devon holds the distinction of being the oldest outdoor, multi-breed horse show in North America and to date has an annual spectator base of approximately 126,000 people during an 11-day event. On this commemoration of our 125th anniversary, I like to think that our history is just beginning, the future is bright, and Devon will exist for at least 125 more years.

Devon's legacy has been grounded in tradition. Generational families of founders such as the Wanamakers, Dixons, and Strawbridges, to name a few, have supported Devon since its inception and remain loyal boxholders today. The same can be said of our volunteers! The multigenerational families who work each year in support of the show share their memories of selling lemon sticks in the Candy Booth or tea sandwiches in the Tea Cart when they were children. Now, their grandchildren carry on the tradition. Even our competitors have legacies across the Devon disciplines. With this base of multigenerational support, it is no wonder that our motto "Where Champions Meet" applies to every category of contributor to the show.

Devon's philanthropy has enjoyed an equally storied history. After World War I and its support of the war efforts, the Devon Horse Show realized its potential for service in the community, and the Devon Horse Show and Country Fair Inc. as we know it today was born. Devon has cherished a very special relationship with our beneficiary, Bryn Mawr Hospital, which began in 1919 and remains a key member of our organization.

Each year, Devon draws new volunteers, supporters, and competitors. This volunteerism is critical to our show, and today we have over 2,500 volunteers on the grounds. Nothing compares to Devon, and that is the perception of our reputation on the international stage of equestrian sports. The proximity of the crowd to the quality of competition that occurs, the size and enthusiasm of our spectators, the unique reliance upon volunteers within our organization, and the quality of shopping, dining, entertainment, and activities all contribute a lasting memory for everyone who enters our gates. And it is this unique experience that draws back each person to this event, year after year.

Devon Horse Show and Country Fair takes the reader through the early years of the show, beginning with its inception on the lawn of the Devon Inn in 1896. By 1914, it had become the largest outdoor horse show in the entire country. The show was nearly cancelled in 1918 due to World War I. Instead, the decision was made to hold a scaled-down version of the show as a charity fundraiser for the war efforts. Shortly thereafter, Devon decided that it would incorporate a country fair, the profits of which would support its beneficiary on the Main Line, Bryn Mawr Hospital. To this day, the charitable focus of the show distinguishes the Devon Horse Show from other equestrian events around the country. Since its initial donation of $26,000 in 1919, the Country Fair averages an annual gift of $400,000, and we are proud to say that our donations to the hospital have exceeded $18 million.

The Devon Horse Show started as a one-day event that consisted of approximately 30 classes. Over the years, various disciplines were added, and classes now include hunters, jumpers, Saddlebreds, Hackneys, and roadster and harness ponies. We are now recognized in the National Show Hunter Hall of Fame. Grand Prix night continues to draw record crowds and today features $250,000 in prize money. The coaching, carriages, and pleasure horses remain popular events and time-honored traditions. A few years ago, arena eventing was added to the program, which further increased attendance and excitement. As a premier international equestrian event, Devon has included several Olympian exhibitors and attracted national figures, from presidents to celebrities, who have spectated, competed, or otherwise enjoyed 11 days in May.

Since our 100th anniversary in 1996, we have made many significant improvements to the grounds with a focus on preserving and improving our facilities. The construction of the Devon Club and the new Exhibitors Lounge have enhanced the Devon experience for competitors and spectators alike. The barns were renovated and rebuilt, and new footing was installed in the Dixon Oval to ensure safety for the riders and horses. Many other renovations to support our facilities have been implemented, and while less noticeable, they are critical to the infrastructure of the show. In the past five years, the Devon Horse Show and Country Fair has seen tremendous growth. Through the strength and commitment of our board of directors, we will ensure a legacy for generations to come.

This book is designed to memorialize the past and preserve some of our magnificent history and traditions for future generations to enjoy and reflect. Just as the cancellation of the show during World War II infused new life into this organization, we return in 2021 grounded in our history with a renewed purpose to make Devon the ultimate experience for our competitors, volunteers, supporters, and spectators. Devon will go on. Our future is bright and our traditions remain strong. Please join us in celebrating our history and our future on this wonderful 125th anniversary.

—Wayne W. Grafton
Chairman and CEO, Devon Horse Show and Country Fair

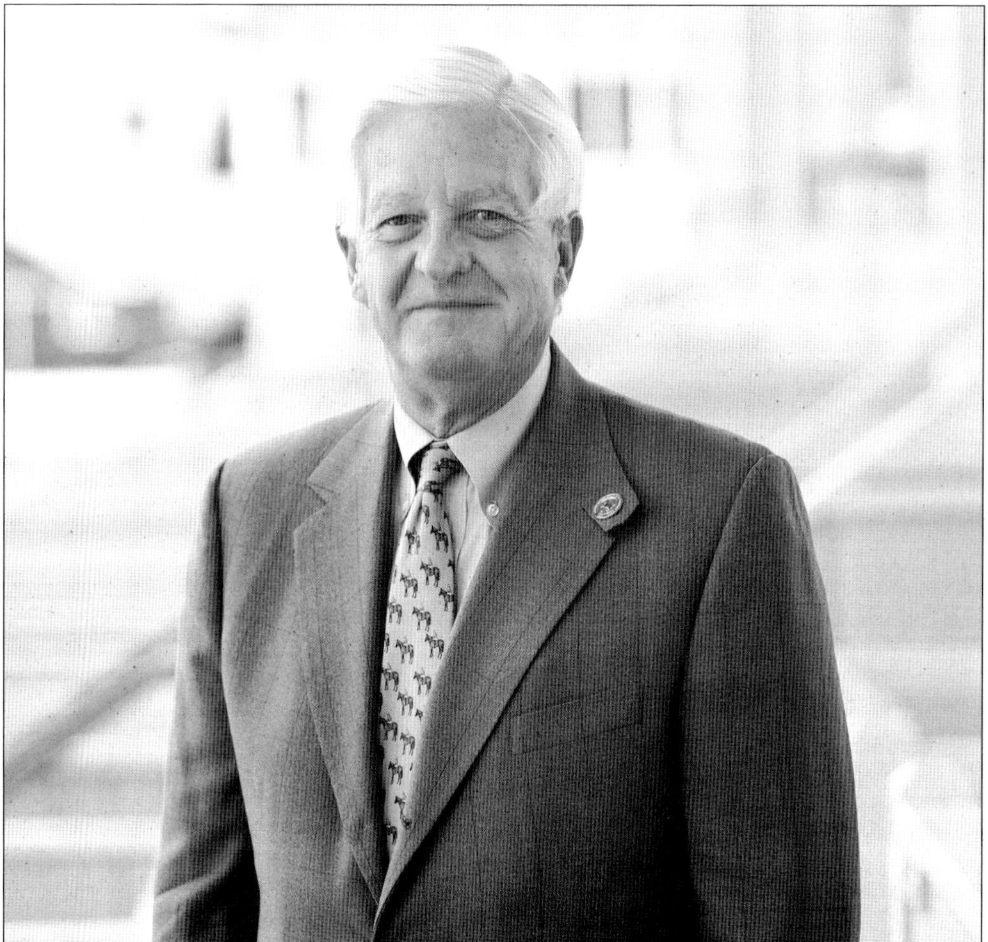

Wayne W. Grafton has served as chairman and chief executive officer of both the corporate board of the Devon Horse Show and Country Fair Inc. and the Devon Horse Show and Country Fair Foundation Board since 2015. He has been a boxholder and competitor in the singles and pairs coaching division at Devon for over 40 years. (Courtesy of Brenda Carpenter Photography.)

One

The Devon Horse Show Begins

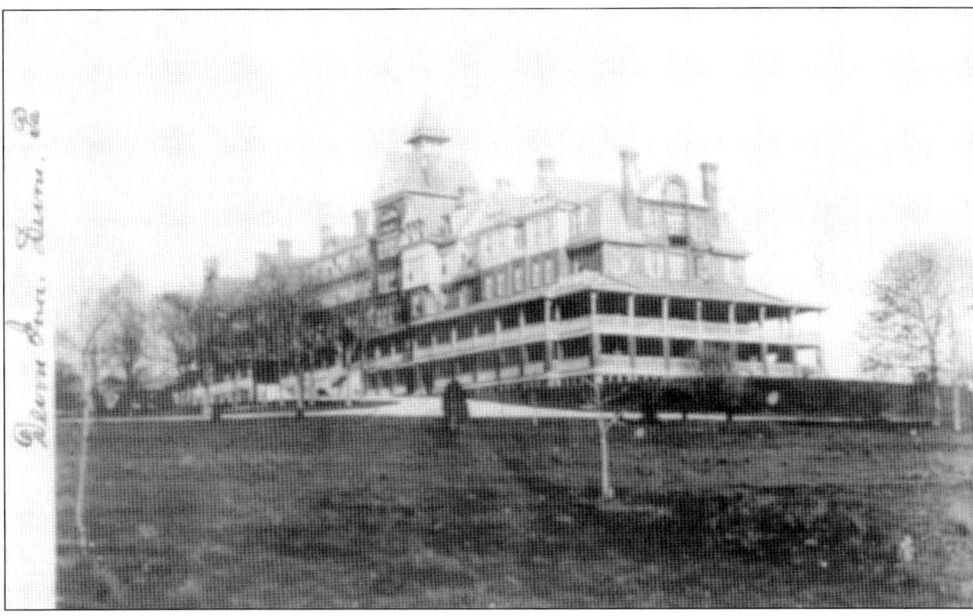

In the late 1800s, the Pennsylvania Railroad sought to market its route along the western suburbs of Philadelphia known as the "Main Line." To entice wealthy Philadelphians to escape humid city summers for the bucolic countryside, hotels were built in Bryn Mawr and Devon near the train stations. The Devon Inn was at the height of its glory as a grand resort to which urbanites flocked from late spring through summer. (Courtesy of The Engraver.)

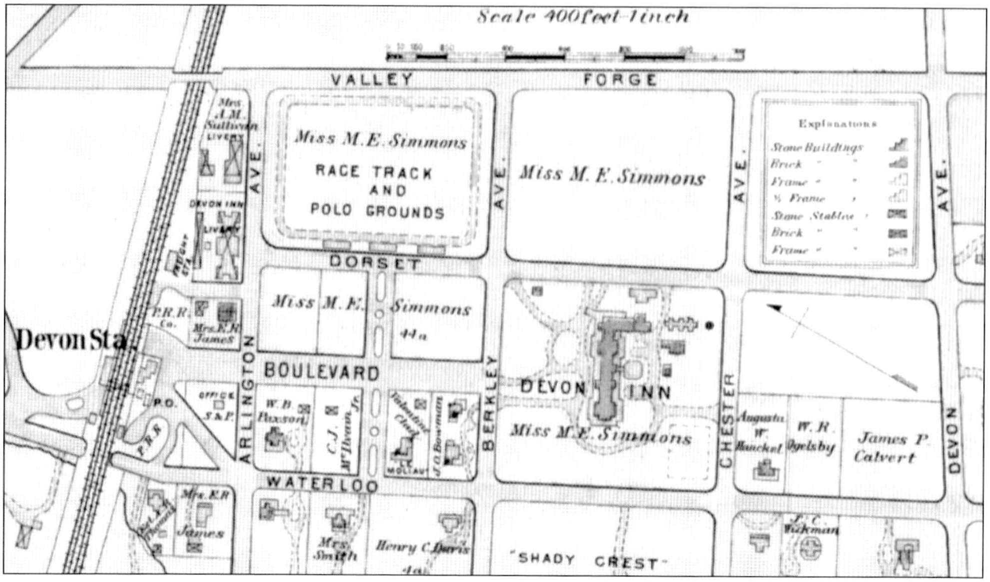

DEAR SIR:

In order to effect an organization for the purpose of holding a Horse Show at Devon, a meeting of gentlemen, interested in the breeding, showing and ownership of horses, is called for Friday Evening, May 22, 1896, eight o'clock, at Devon Inn.

Please attend and invite others who may be interested.

Signed,

HENRY T. COATES
C. DAVIS ENGLISH
HENRY M. WARREN
GEORGE H. EARLE, JR.
JOHN W. PATTON
D. B. SHARP
LEM. COFFIN ALTEMUS
JOSEPH F. PAGE
R. PENN SMITH
E. B. COLKET
JAMES W. PATTERSON
E. W. TWADDELL

With the horse as the primary mode of transport from train stations to Main Line country houses, demand grew for lighter, faster horses suitable for harness instead of the plow horses bred by local Welsh farmers. In May 1896, country gentlemen from Chester County invited other prominent gentry to meet at the Devon Inn "in order to effect an organization for the purpose of holding a Horse Show at Devon." The objective of the newly formed Devon Horse Show Association was to promote the breeding of Saddlebred and Hackney horses for driving and to improve the local hunter stock. Its first order of business was to sponsor a one-day horse show on July 2, 1896, at the Devon Race Track and Polo Grounds, the present location of the Devon Horse Show. (Above, courtesy of The Engraver.)

The 1896 show had nearly 30 classes and 100 entries to interest local farmers as well as gentry. The committee encouraged local breeders "to bring stock to the notice of city people who have money to buy them with little trouble and expense." Ribbons and prizes of $10 and $5 for first and second places were awarded for each event. Classes included "Farmer-Owned Yearlings," "Hackney Brood Mares with Foal at Foot," and "Stallions Suitable for Getting the General Purpose Horse."

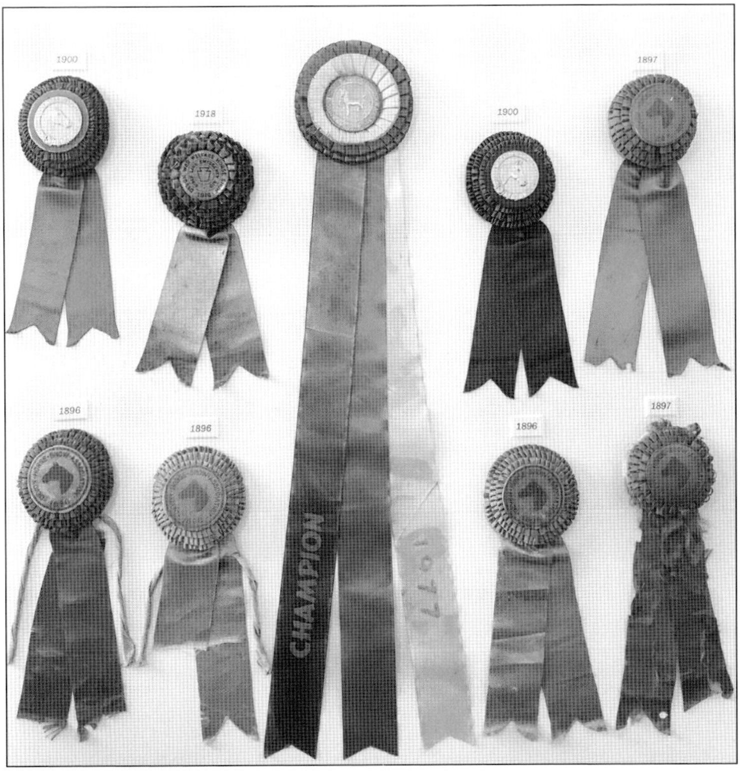

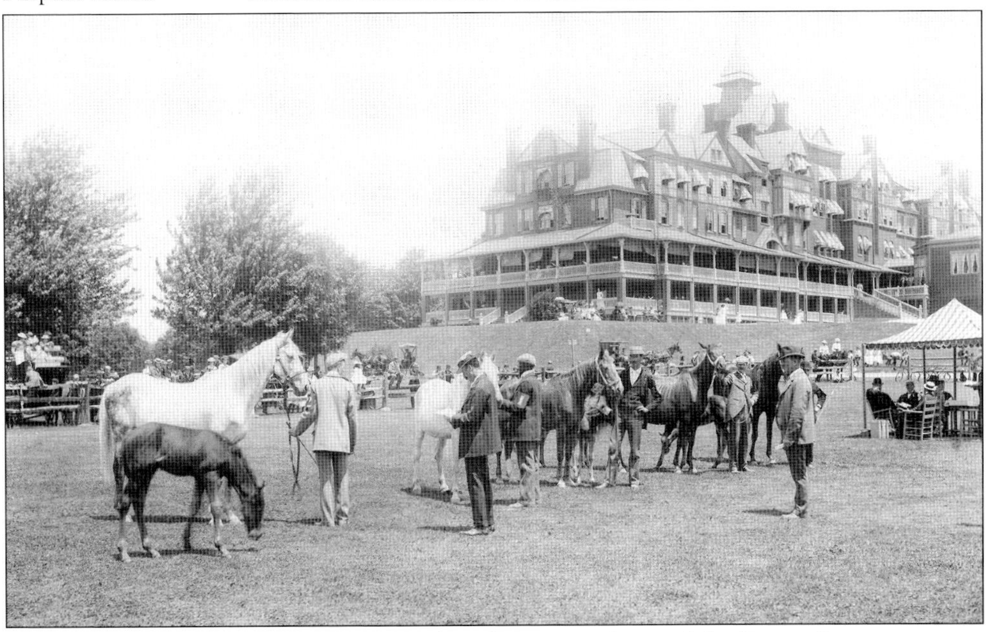

From 1898 to 1900, the show was moved to the 13-acre lawn of the Devon Inn to increase attendance. With the Devon station nearby, railroad executives suggested the move so that the summer resort guests could watch from the sprawling porches and windows. The 1898 show was held on June 21 and 22 and became "quite a feature of the season of this eminently fashionable summer resort," as reported in the *Philadelphia Times*.

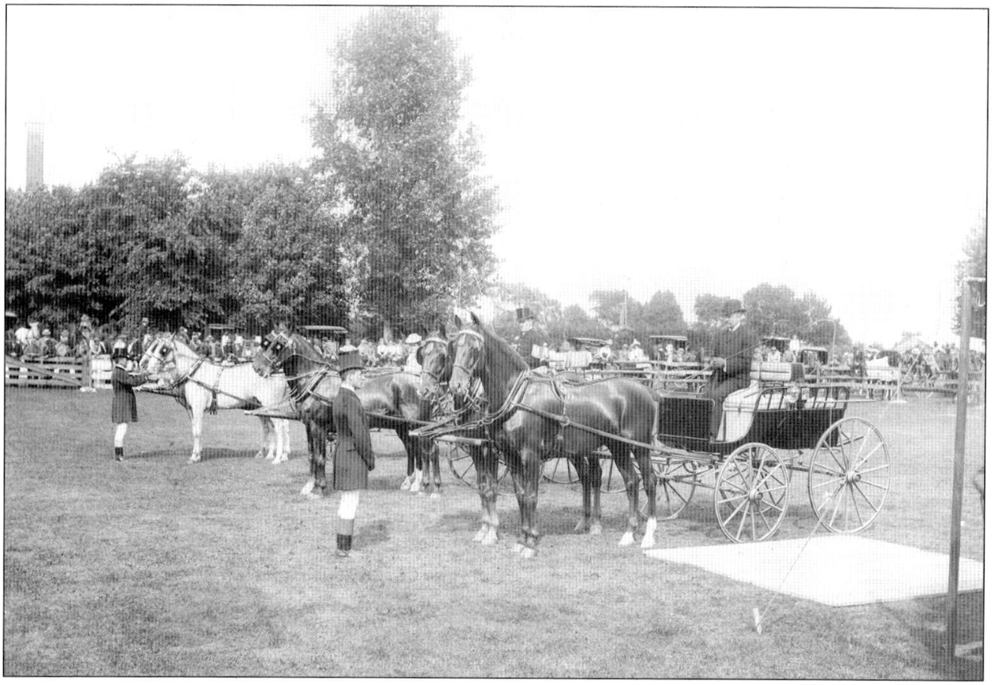

Nearly 3,000 people attended the 1898 show consisting of 36 classes. Harness horses, Saddlebreds, Hackneys, and Hunters were shown. Children participated in pony classes, and ladies competed in riding and driving classes. As detailed in the June 22, 1898, edition of the *Philadelphia Inquirer*, "the quarter-of-a-mile ring was surrounded by a three-rail fence, around which tally-hos, tandems, and every conceivable shape of a single team was tied. There was a distinguished assemblage. Lovers of the sport were prominent."

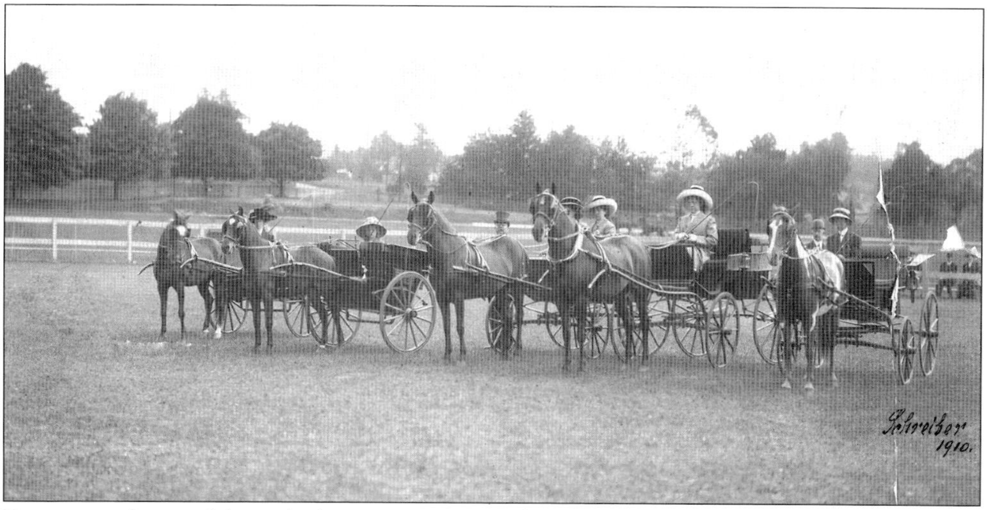

Devon was designed from the beginning to appeal to many classes of society and was open to all participants. Devon not only brought together prominent Philadelphia names including Wanamaker, Clothier, du Pont, and Cassatt, it also encouraged local farmers to attend and breed proper stock for riding, driving, coaching, hunting, and polo playing. The broad mixture of classes, breeds, and participants in the early shows would distinguish Devon and brand its appeal for the next 125 years.

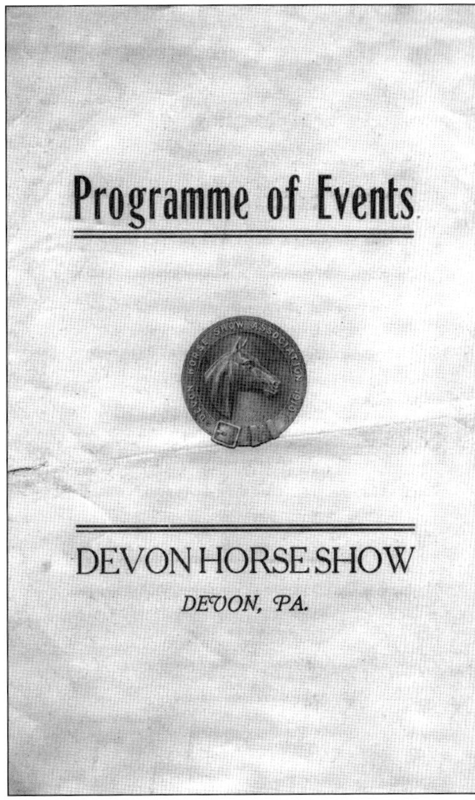

Programme of Events

DEVON HORSE SHOW

DEVON, PA.

After 1900, the Devon Horse Show did not take place for nearly 10 years. Loss of financial backing, competition from other local horse shows, and area residents heading to beaches for the summer ended the Devon Horse Show for a decade. In 1910, William T. Hunter revived the show on its present grounds, and it became a six-day event with 146 horses competing for a total of $20,000 in prizes. That same year, the show was first mentioned in *The Horse Show Blue Book*, which listed the results of major national shows. By 1914, Devon had 1,000 entries. Devon had become the largest outdoor horse show in the country. (Both, courtesy of The Engraver.)

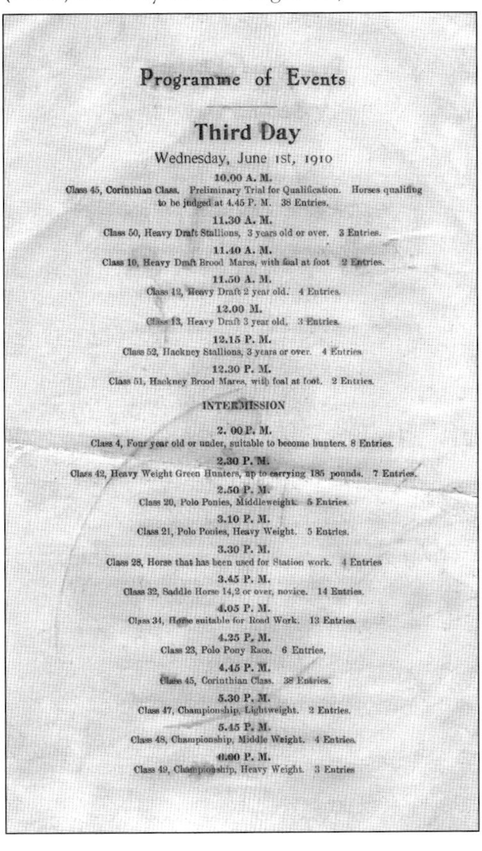

Programme of Events

Third Day

Wednesday, June 1st, 1910

10.00 A. M.
Class 45, Corinthian Class. Preliminary Trial for Qualification. Horses qualifing to be judged at 4.45 P. M. 38 Entries.

11.30 A. M.
Class 50, Heavy Draft Stallions, 3 years old or over. 3 Entries.

11.40 A. M.
Class 10, Heavy Draft Brood Mares, with foal at foot 2 Entries.

11.50 A. M.
Class 12, Heavy Draft 2 year old. 4 Entries.

12.00 M.
Class 13, Heavy Draft 3 year old. 3 Entries.

12.15 P. M.
Class 52, Hackney Stallions, 3 years or over. 4 Entries.

12.30 P. M.
Class 51, Hackney Brood Mares, with foal at foot. 2 Entries.

INTERMISSION

2. 00 P. M.
Class 4, Four year old or under, suitable to become hunters. 8 Entries.

2.30 P. M.
Class 42, Heavy Weight Green Hunters, up to carrying 185 pounds. 7 Entries.

2.50 P. M.
Class 20, Polo Ponies, Middleweight. 5 Entries.

3.10 P. M.
Class 21, Polo Ponies, Heavy Weight. 5 Entries.

3.30 P. M.
Class 28, Horse that has been used for Station work. 4 Entries

3.45 P. M.
Class 32, Saddle Horse 14,2 or over, novice. 14 Entries.

4.05 P. M.
Class 34, Horse suitable for Road Work. 13 Entries.

4.25 P. M.
Class 23, Polo Pony Race. 6 Entries,

4.45 P. M.
Class 45, Corinthian Class. 38 Entries.

5.30 P. M.
Class 47, Championship, Lightweight. 2 Entries.

5.45 P. M.
Class 48, Championship, Middle Weight. 4 Entries.

6.00 P. M.
Class 49, Championship, Heavy Weight. 3 Entries

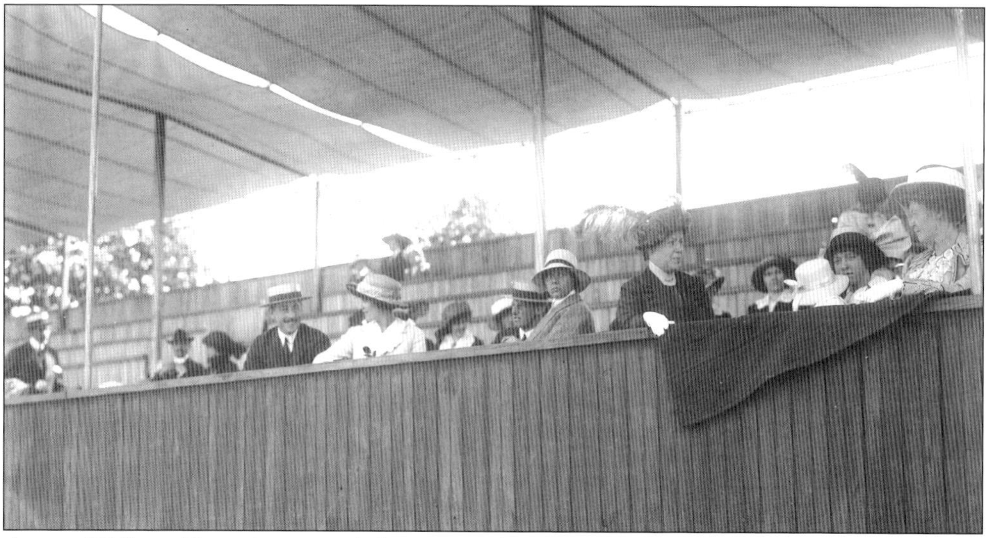

Among William Hunter's accomplishments as chairman of the show from 1910 until 1916 was the construction of grandstands and a boardwalk. Forty-six boxes covered by canvas awnings and a bandstand for musicians were assembled for the 1910 show. Boxholders included Ambassador William Christian Bullitt Jr., Gov. George Howard Earle III, the Cassatts, the Van Rensselaers, the Pews, the Drexels, and the du Ponts.

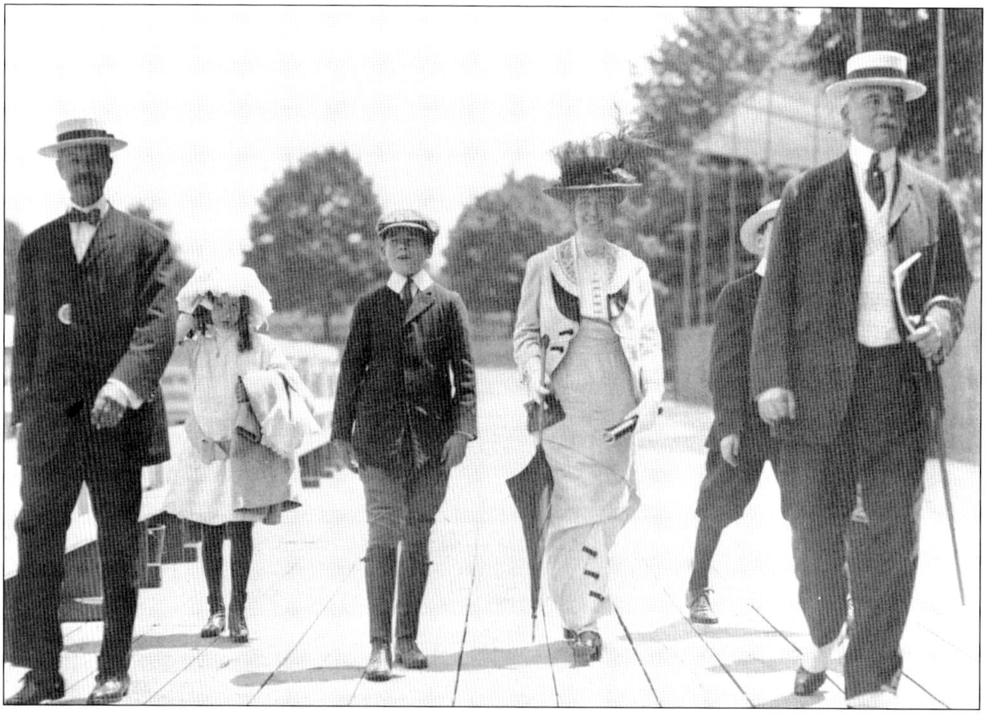

Dressed for the show, the family of Edward Brinton Smith, whose Philadelphia investment banking firm was the predecessor of Smith Barney & Co., strolls in front of the grandstands in 1913 after Geoffrey Smith's (center) performance in the children's class. Devon's wooden boardwalk kept spectators' feet, trousers, and dresses dry during muddy downpours but also served as a promenade for the latest fashions.

Preliminary Financial Statement Devon Horse Show Association

November 1st, 1915, to December 31st, 1916

Receipts	Amount
Cash on hand November 1st, 1915	$ 411.62
Received for dues	2418.00
" " entry fees	4703.00
" " stabling	5338.80
" " boxes	3357.00
" " catalogue advertising	1431.27
" " sale of catalogues	343.00
" " gate tickets and parking spaces	2830.75
" " cups and prizes	1588.30
" " refunds	604.49
" " interest on deposit account	38.12
	$23,064.35

Disbursements	Amount
Postage	$ 472.19
Printing and stationery	1969.65
Labor and wages	1480.89
Incidental and sundry expenses	1034.15
Salaries, office force	309.55
Feed and stabling	3703.86
Judges, ring supervision and assistants	505.80
Policing	221.03
Cups and prizes	7566.60
Music	219.50
Newspaper advertising	623.49
Commissions on catalogue advertisements	280.00
Insurance premiums	159.25
Refunds	635.80
Refreshments, liquid	381.71
Refreshments, caterer	525.44
Lumber, hardware, etc., etc., purchased for Capital Account	1850.63
Prize ribbons	602.70
Tents	102.73
Charity donations	152.50
Cash on hand December 31st, 1916	266.88
	$23,064.35

Estimated value of outstanding accounts December 31st, 1916

Bills receivable	$1250.00
Bills payable	0.
Estimated profits of 1916 show	3000.00

Charles M. Lea,
Treasurer

The Devon 1916 Financial Statement reflects that feed and stabling costs were $3,703.86. The show had no stables, requiring local liveries or the Devon Inn to serve as temporary quarters for horses. William Hunter turned out horses on his nearby farm to provide stabling, grain, and hay for $3 a day. Most exhibitors rode to Devon in the early morning and left by evening.

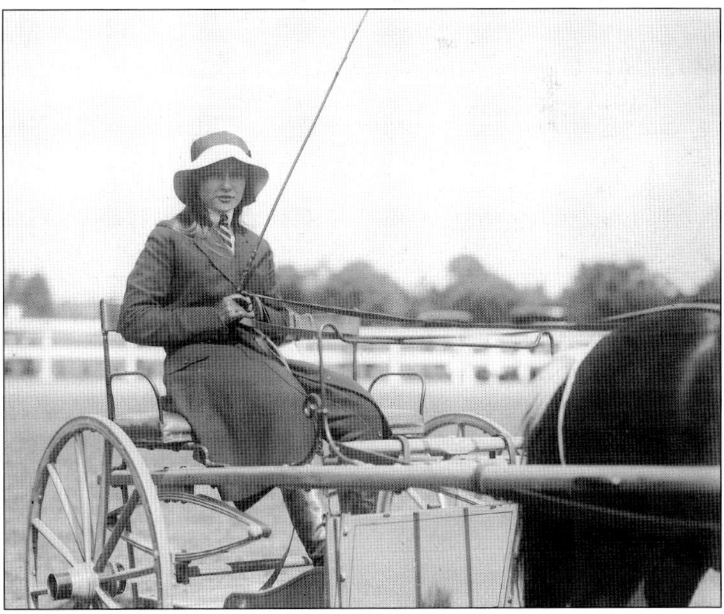

Gladys Earle, daughter of Philadelphia lawyer George H. Earle Jr., one of the horse show's founders, competed in the 1916 roadster class. Beginning in 1912, for one day of the show, prominent horsewomen judged saddlers, ponies, hunters, and harness horses, and the class caller and veterinarian were women. Women competitors also steadily increased during these years.

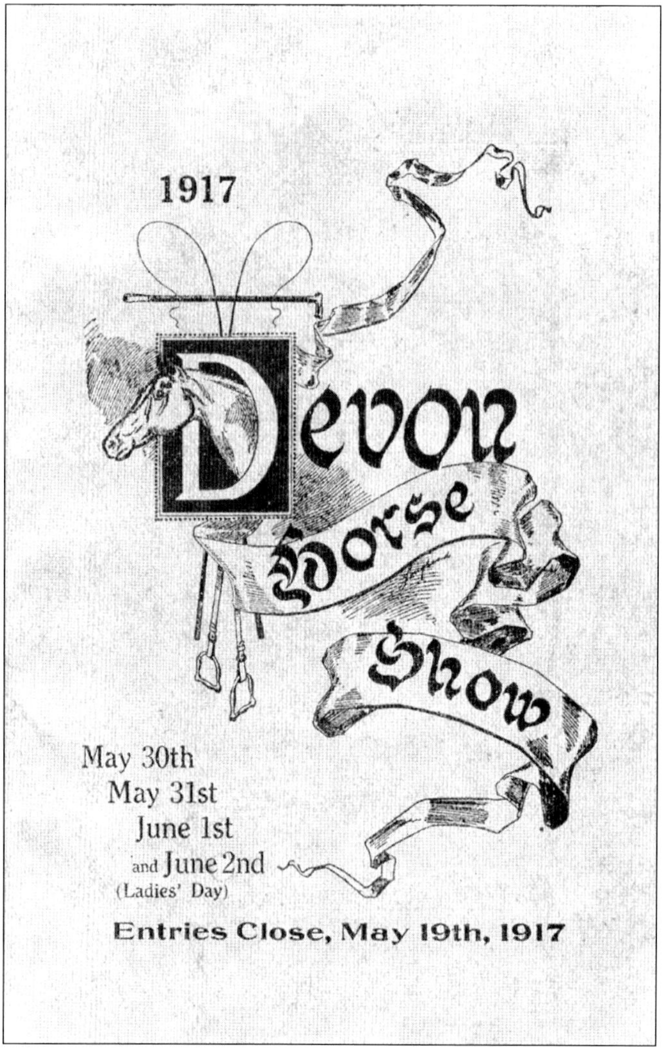

The Devon Horse Show was one of the charter members of the American Horse Shows Association, established in 1917. The original managers of Devon sought to cancel the event in 1918 after the country's entry into World War I. Dr. Thomas G. Ashton and William H. Wanamaker intervened, adamant that enough support could be mustered if the show's profits were to benefit a wartime charity. They asked Anna Coxe Yarnall, chair of the Main Line branch of the Emergency Aid, to encourage her organization to serve as beneficiary. Wanamaker's daughter, Isabella, and Jean Liseter Austin assisted in the process. The Devon War Relief Horse Show was a success, although on a much smaller scale than past shows. The show donated $9,000 to Emergency Aid. (Left, courtesy of The Engraver.)

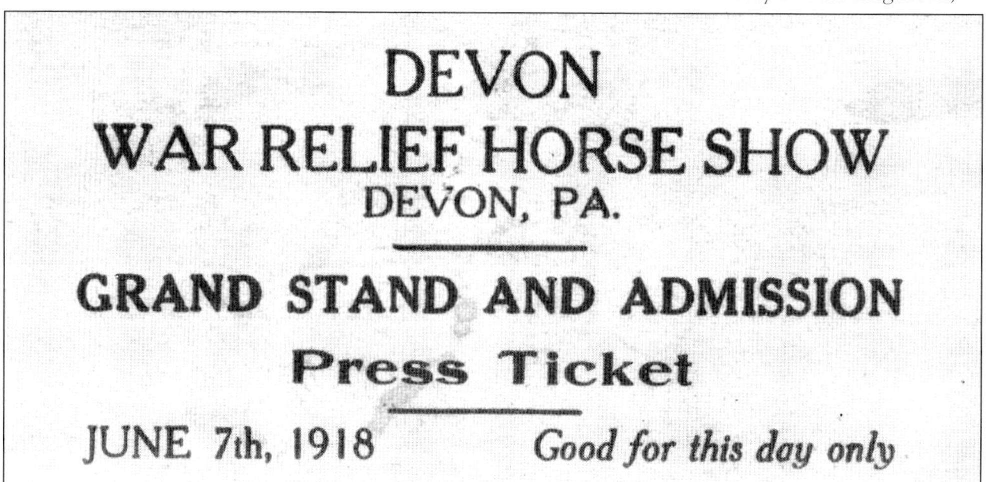

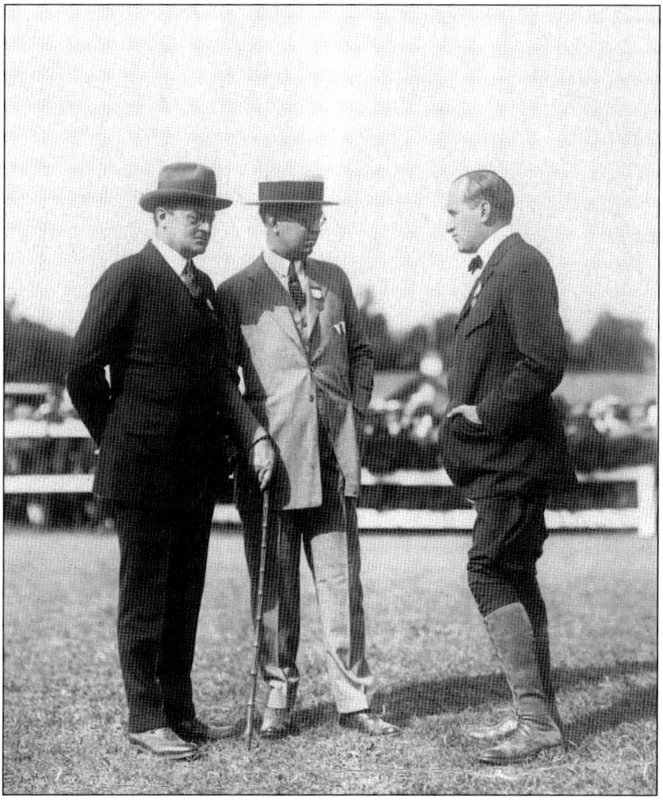

Encouraged by these philanthropic efforts, Chairman Thomas G. Ashton (left), William H. Wanamaker, and Isaac H. Clothier Jr. (right) decided to hold a show to benefit Bryn Mawr Hospital, where Dr. Ashton practiced. The committee secured a charter and incorporated the Devon Horse Show and Country Fair Inc. The officers included T. Dewitt Cuyler, president; Archibald Barklie, vice president; Edward Illsley, secretary; and Dr. Ashton, treasurer. Barklie's wife, Isabel Armstrong Barklie, served as the first chair of the Country Fair. She was one of the main forces behind the incorporation, aided by the wives of the prominent men associated with the show.

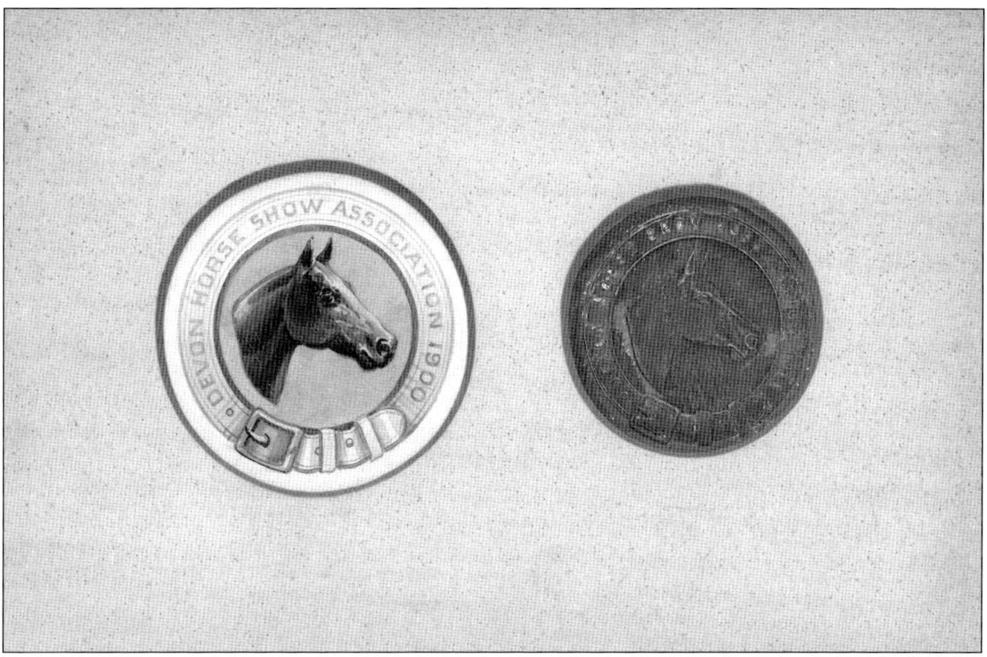

Thomas G. Ashton, who would serve as an officer of the show until 1932, lent his champion Hackney Wynnewood as the silhouette model for the official Devon logo that is still in use today. From 1900 to 1918, the Hackney head on the show ribbons faced right, and after 1919, it faced left.

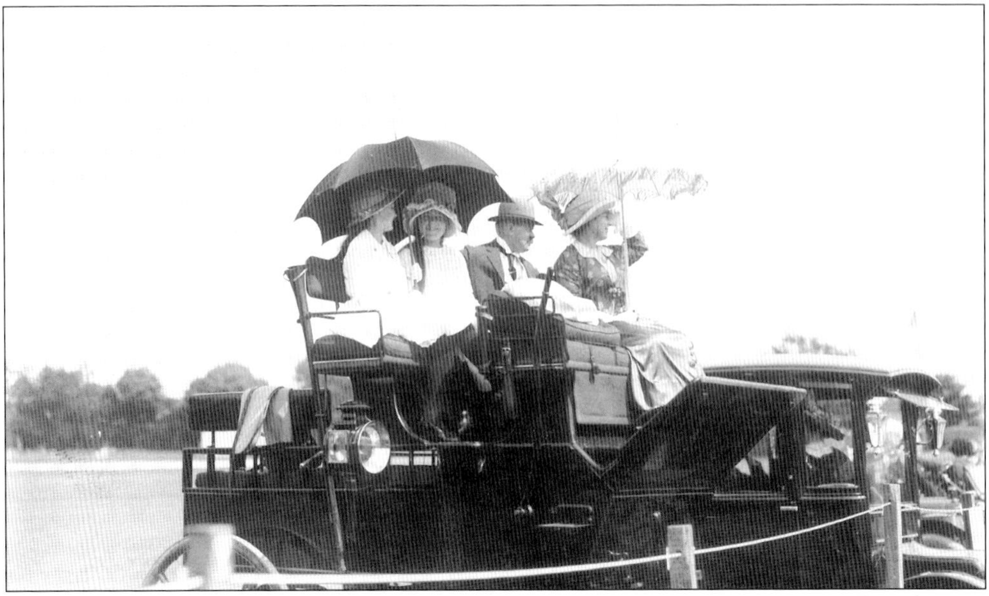

Spectators came in carriages, coaches, and motors, on bicycles and on foot, surrounding the ring to observe the show. The Pennsylvania Railroad promoted frequent train service to Devon for families from Philadelphia. The first day of the 1920 show, held on Wednesday, was Novice Day for the debut of young horses and ponies, saddled, harness, or hunter. The second and third days were Hunter and Hackney Days, respectively. Saturday morning classes on the fourth day were devoted to young riders, also known as Pony Day. The last day of the show, held on Memorial Day Monday, was Governor's Day, in honor of military and armed forces.

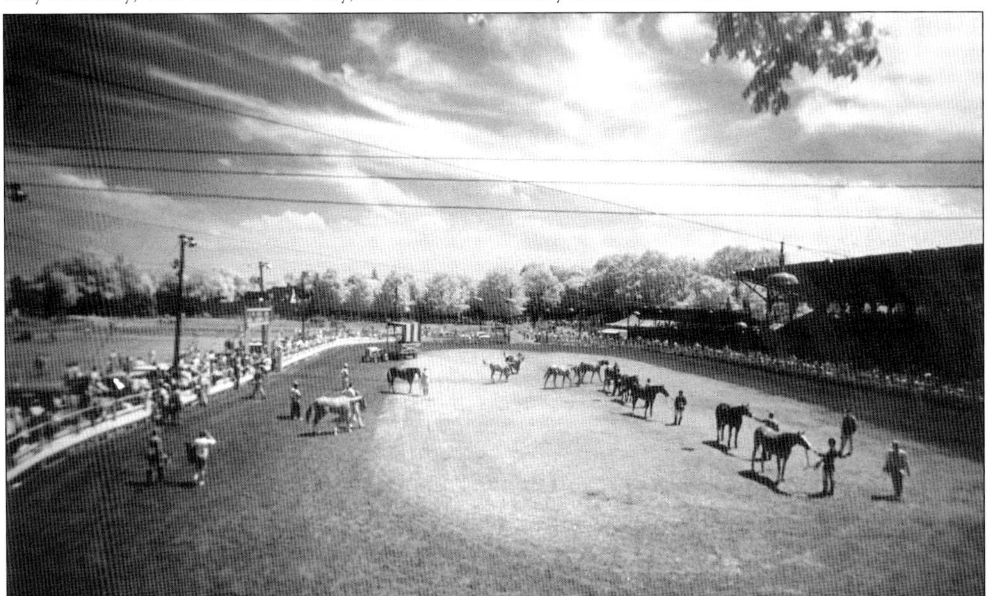

This wide-angle photograph of the showgrounds depicts horses showing on the line during the 1920s. The fenced main ring was expansive for a show at this time and was constructed on grass. Devon soon established its reputation as a place "where equine bluebloods gathered for judgment," as the *Philadelphia Inquirer* aptly described the scene.

Dog shows at the Devon Horse Show date back as far as 1914 and were sanctioned by the American Kennel Club. Although the show did not take place during World War II, it reserved its customary dates and retained its standing with the American Horse Show Association. In order to continue to benefit Bryn Mawr Hospital, the Devon Country Fair held dog shows over Memorial Day weekend in 1943 and 1944, with over 3,000 entries. The country fair chairs were performing war relief work, so the planning and execution fell to society debutantes. (Below, courtesy of The Engraver.)

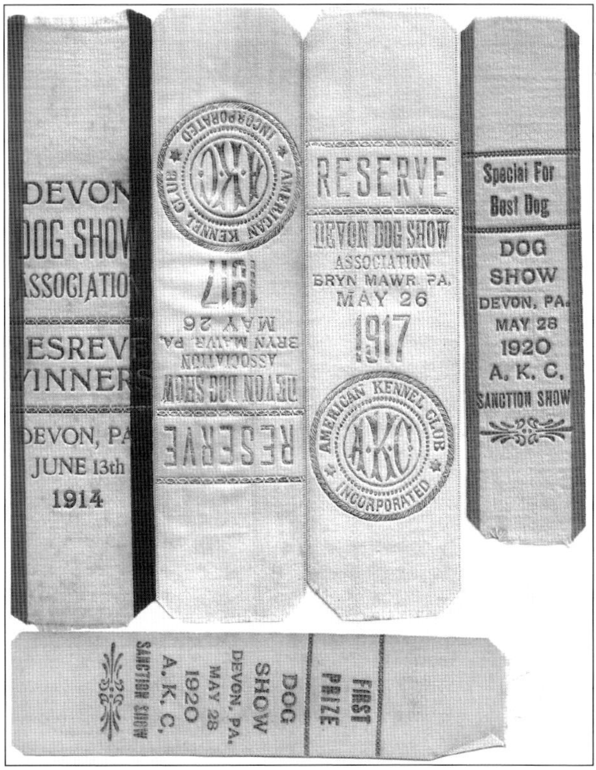

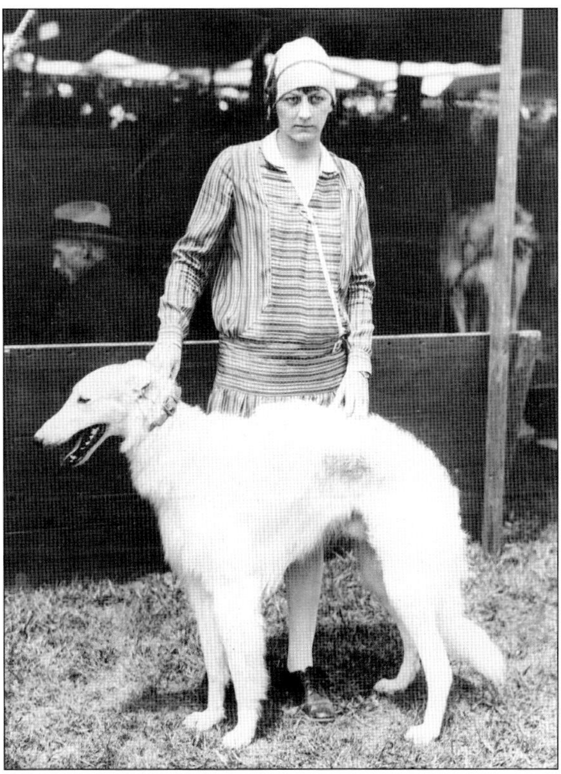

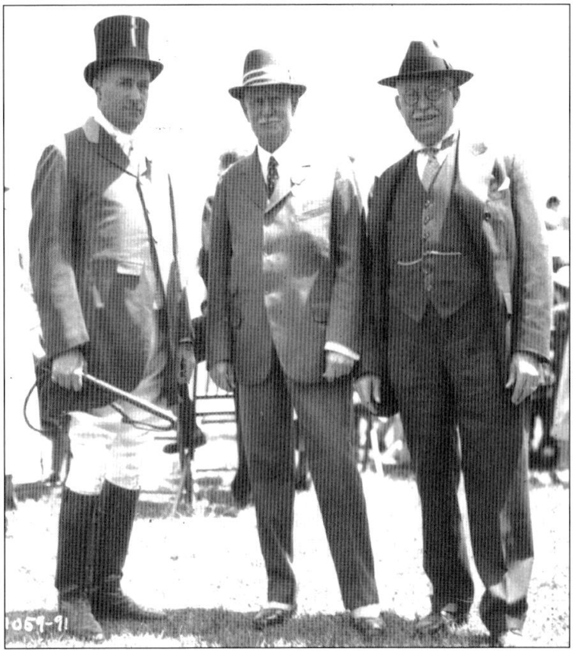

Isaac H. Clothier Jr. (left), an accomplished exhibitor and financial supporter of Devon, is shown here with show officials in 1922. That year, his aged chestnut gelding Durward Roberts was named by Devon judges as the Champion Hunter of the show. Only those hunters who had won the blue ribbon in hunting and jumping events were eligible to be judged for champion. Clothier and his horse won the $750 free-for-all hunter stake as well as the Sunnybrook Challenge Trophy.

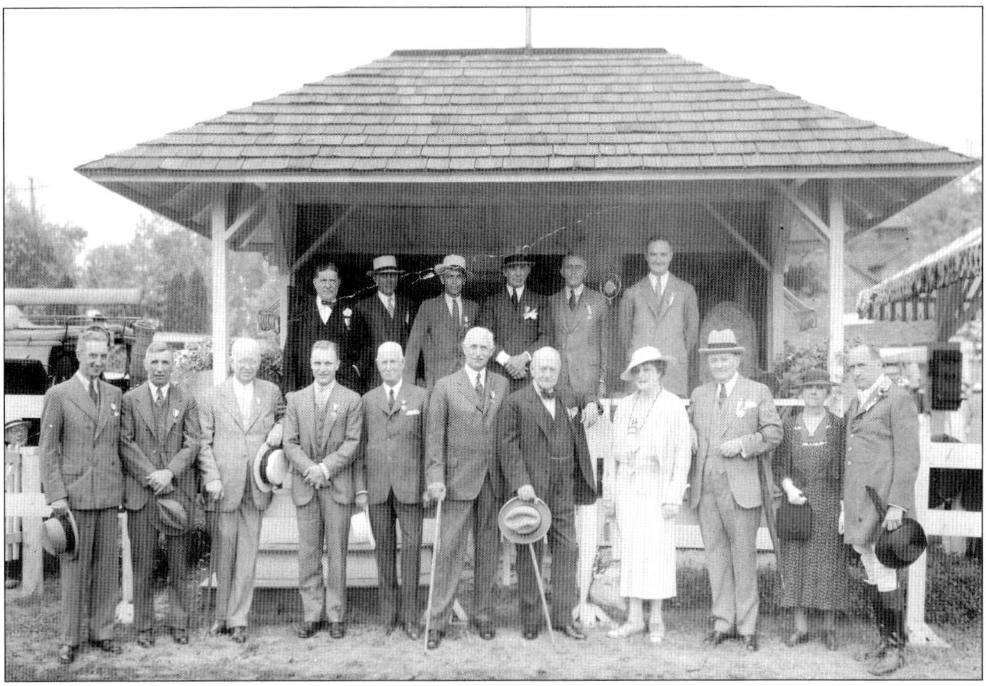

In 1920, the Devon grounds were purchased for $22,500 to give the show permanency, and a horse show committee was formed comprised of 25 influential gentlemen. Among those reported as horse show committee members for the early years were Henry T. Coates, president, and members Lemual C. Altemus, C. Davis English, J.W. Patten, A.B. Coxe, R. Penn Smith, D.B. Sharp, John H. Barnes, Charles E. Coxe, George W. South, Joseph H. Coates, William Wayne Jr., John T. Windrim, Hutchinson Galloney, George W. Kendrick III, A.E. Kennedy, W.N. Wilbur, and Isaac H. Clothier Jr.

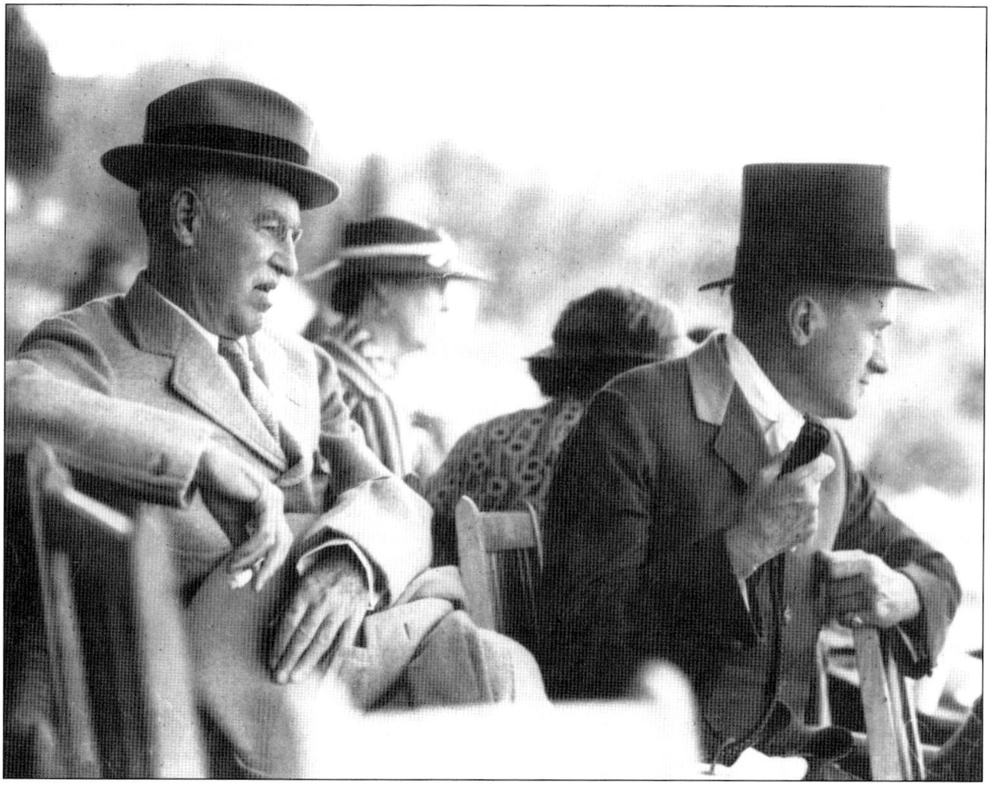

Brig. Gen. William Wallace Atterbury (left) joins Isaac H. Clothier Jr. (right) in the grandstands. A decorated World War I veteran, Atterbury began his career with the Pennsylvania Railroad in 1886 and returned after his military service to become its 10th president. He was instrumental in reorganizing railroad traffic for more efficient transportation of troops and supplies for the American Expeditionary Forces in France.

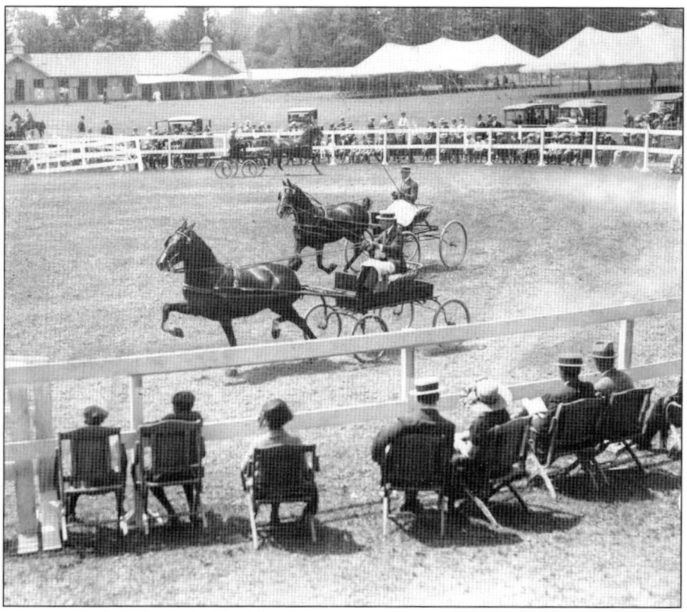

Spectators watch the 1923 Harness Singles Pleasure class at the Devon Horse Show and Country Fair, continuing the tradition of viewing the classes at the rail of the main ring. In the background, barns have been constructed by the exhibitors. The first barns were financed by William du Pont Jr. Other exhibitors followed suit, building their own structures and forming two lines of barns on the northeast corner of the property. (Courtesy of the SCRC, Temple University.)

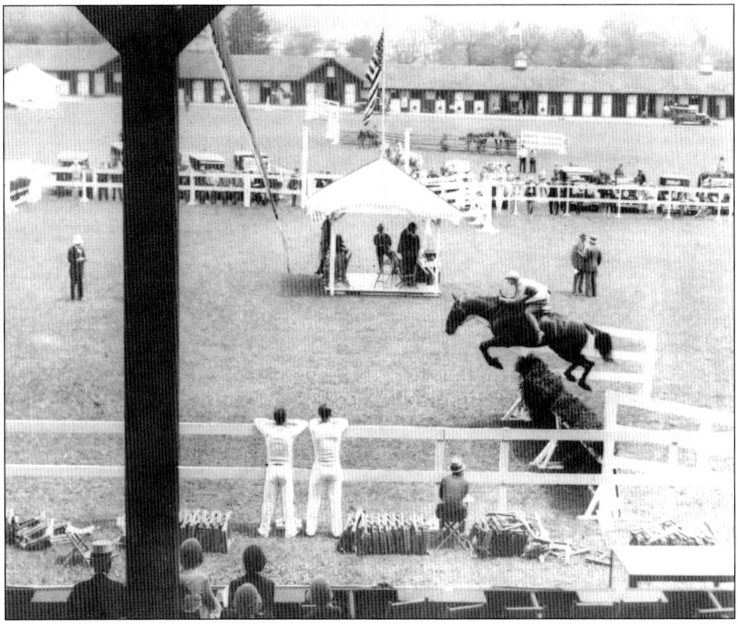

Peggy Cortwright rides Chase in class 145 of the program, a jumping class for green hunters, as the judges and officials sit in a gazebo in the center of the ring. The 1929 event was won by du Pont's Ruby Rose from Foxcatcher Farms. A large crowd turned out to see the opening day's events, and more than 2,000 entrants registered in the show. (Courtesy of the SCRC, Temple University.)

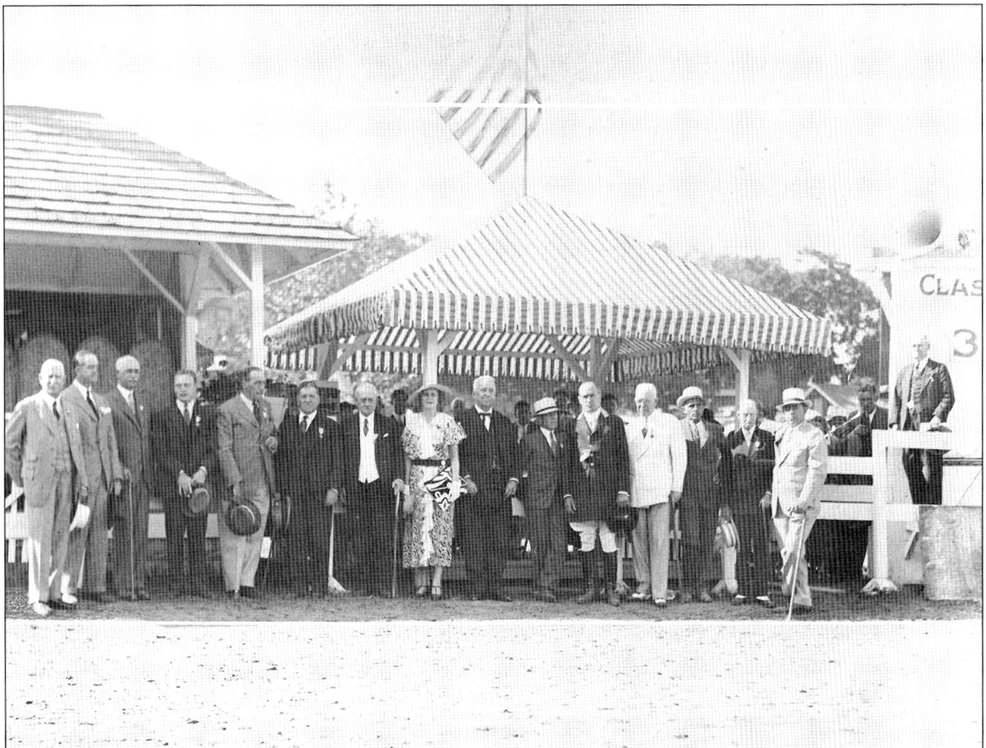

The Devon Horse Show committee and judges pose in the ring at the 1934 show. From left to right are Edward Ilsey; Rufus Finch; William M.M. Robinson; Charles C. Harrison Jr.; Gen. C.R. Peter Winser, DSO; William H. Ashton; Edward F. Beale; Eleanor Morris Lloyd; Samuel M. Vauclain; Henry V. Colt; Isaac H. Clothier Jr.; William H. Wanamaker Jr.; R.R.M. Carpenter; Louis Haight; and Thomas Clark.

Edgar and Helen Hope Montgomery Scott, wed in 1923, were legendary fixtures at Devon for 70 years. An heir to the Pennsylvania Railroad fortune, Scott joined his father-in-law, Robert Leaming Montgomery, to form the investment firm Montgomery Scott & Company, now known as Janney Montgomery Scott. The Scotts were life-long supporters of Devon, where Montgomery Scott began competing at a young age. An accomplished equestrian who retired many Devon trophies, she would frequently ride her mounts to Devon from Ardrossan, her family's estate in Villanova.

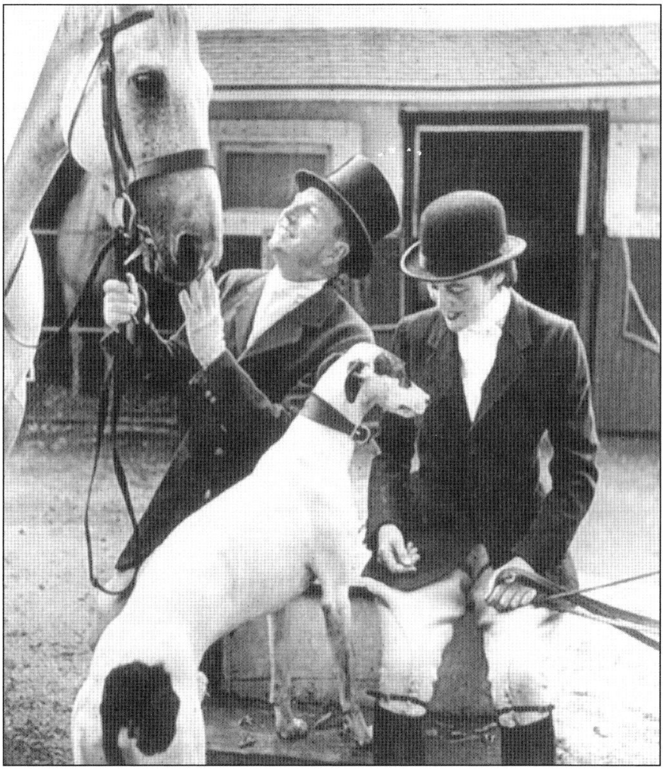

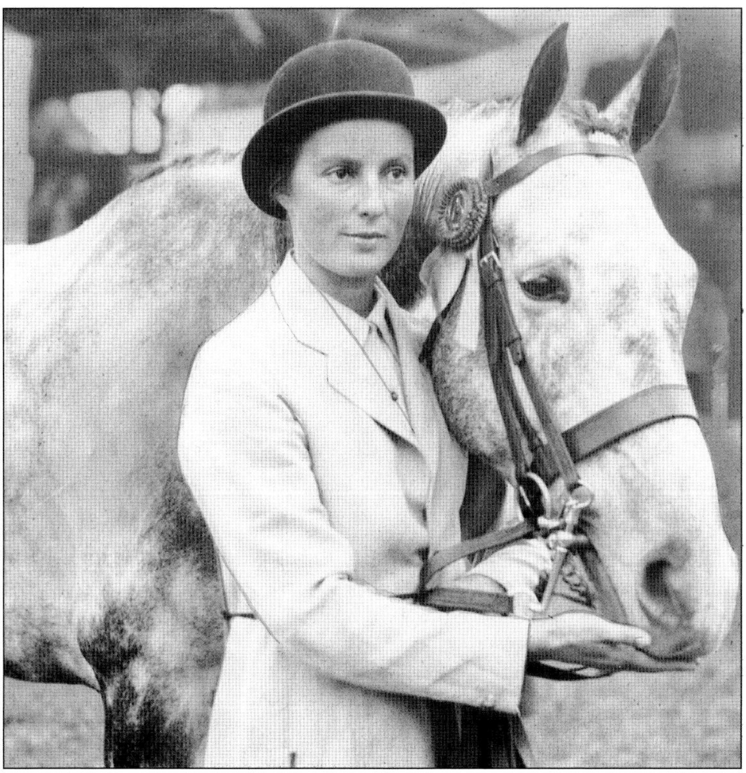

Mary Elizabeth Altemus Whitney won the Model Lightweight Hunters class in 1933 with her horse Gray Knight. Ladies traditionally rode sidesaddle in equestrian events until around 1915, when it was acceptable to ride astride the horse. (Courtesy of the SCRC, Temple University.)

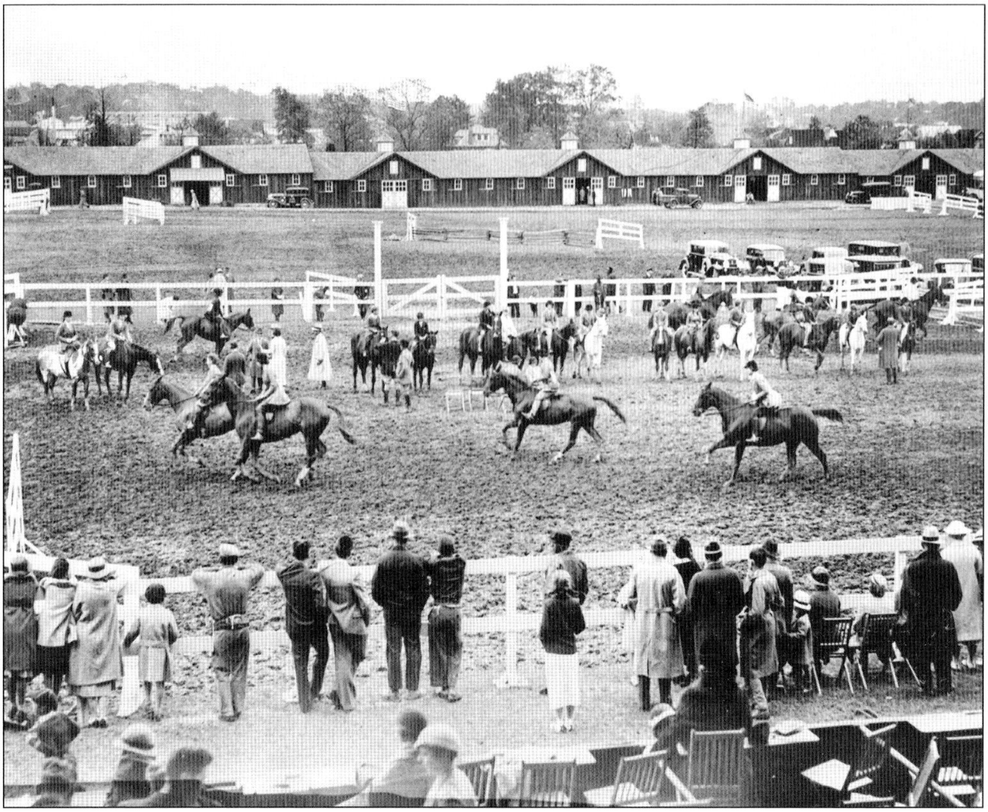

An unusually large number of entrants participated in the 1934 Children's Riding class event. Over 40 contestants under the age of 18 entered and showed. By 1935, the show featured 500 Thoroughbreds from Canada and 17 states as attendance records reached an all-time high of more than 50,000.

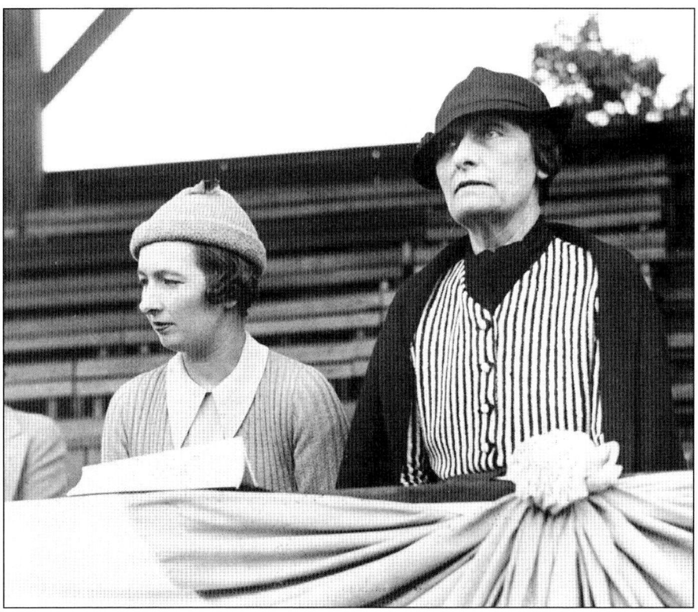

Despite the Depression, Devon was approaching 20 years of incorporation between the horse show and country fair. Ethel Dorrance Colket and her mother, Ethel Mallinckrodt Dorrance, wife of John T. Dorrance, of the Campbell Soup Company, enjoy the show from their box on May 24, 1935. The Dorrances and Colkets were supporters of Devon for generations and remain so today. (Courtesy of The Engraver.)

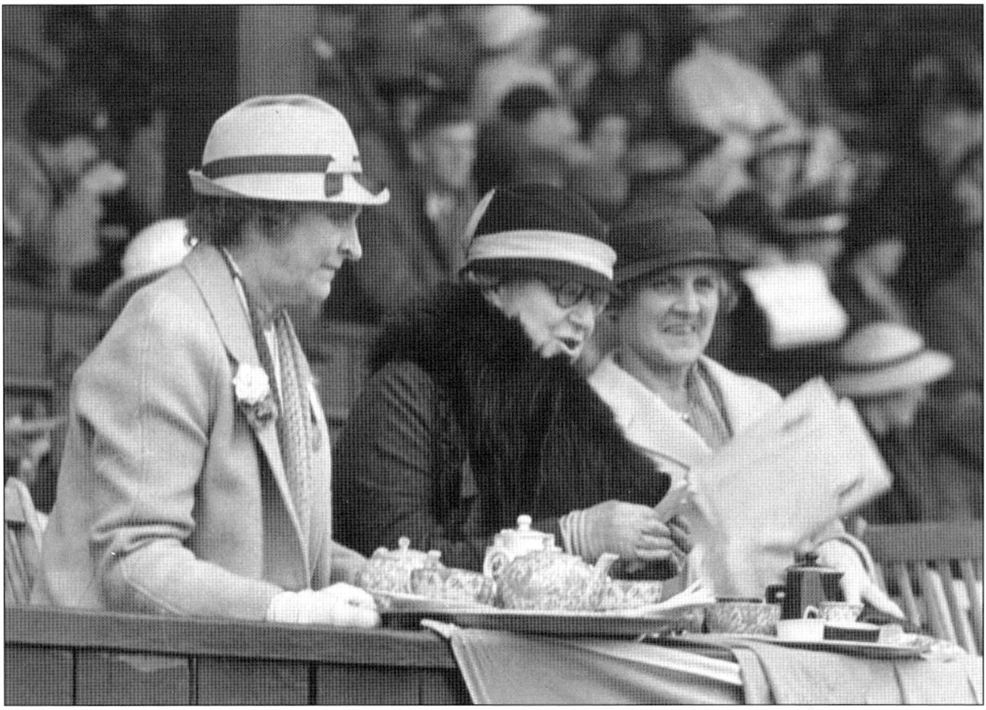

Above, on May 26, 1934, Eleanor Morris Lloyd (left), Amy Lewis Hutchinson (center), and Frances Fox Brockie (right) review the upcoming classes in the program over afternoon tea served in their grandstand box. Lloyd's corsage denotes her as a chair of the country fair, a tradition that continued into the 2000s. After serving as the fourth chair in the history of the country fair, Lloyd became the first director of the American Red Cross Allied Prisoner of War Food Packing Service, for which she earned the 1944 Gimbel Award for America's outstanding woman. At right, Lloyd welcomes Samuel M. Vauclain to the 1934 show. Vauclain was the former president of Baldwin Locomotive Works, an affiliate of the Pennsylvania Railroad and the president of Bryn Mawr Hospital.

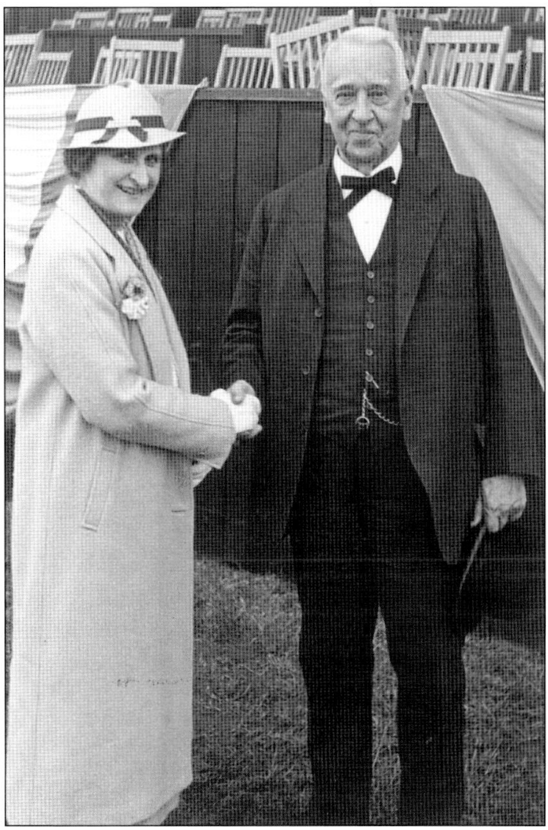

Old Days at Devon

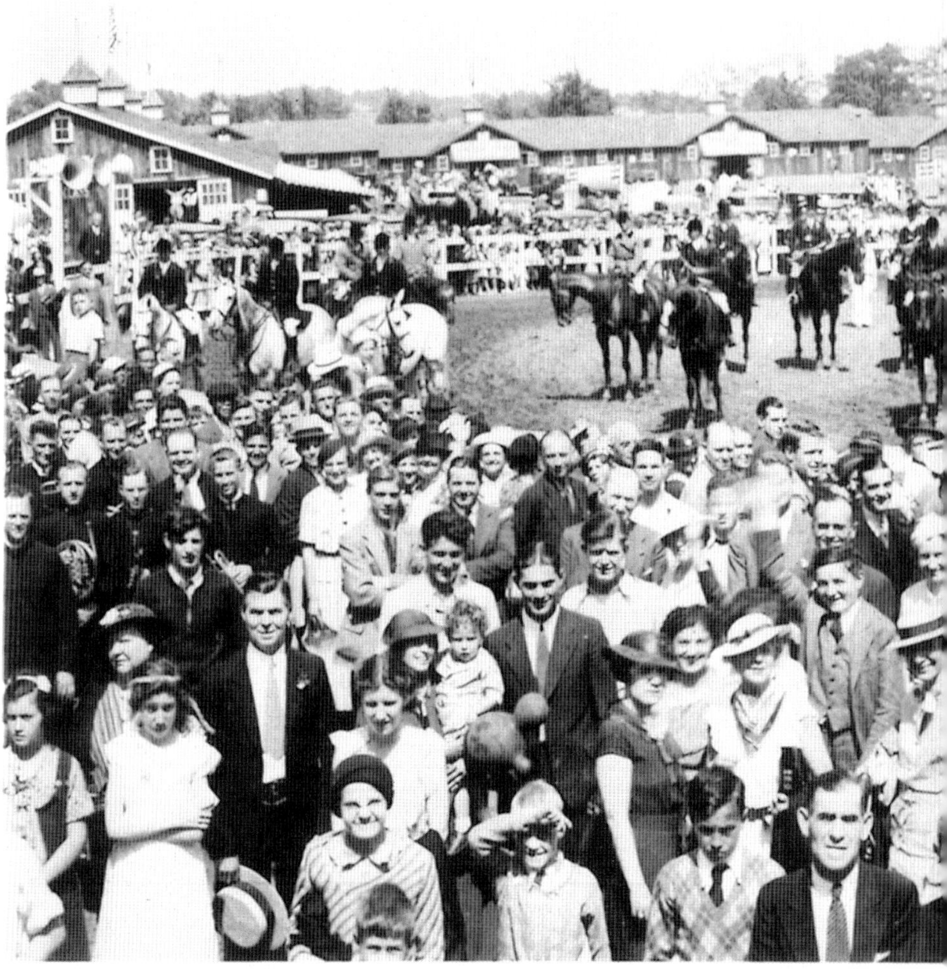

In 1939, Dorothy James, daughter of Gov. Arthur H. James, dedicated the Wanamaker Oval. Commemorating the 20th anniversary of the incorporation of the Devon Horse Show and Country Fair Inc., a bronze plaque bearing the names of the founders Dr. Thomas G. Ashton,

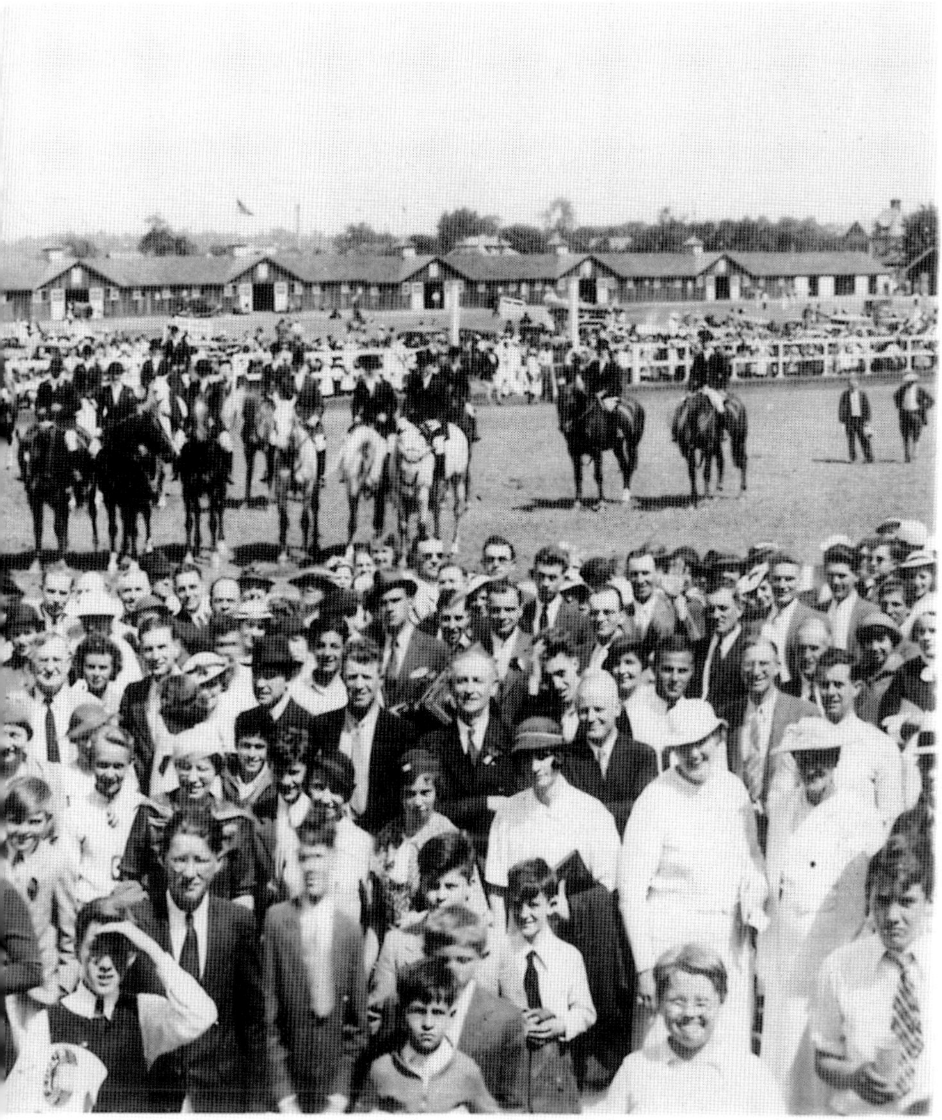

The Wanamaker Oval

William H. Wanamaker Jr., and Isabel Armstrong Barklie was unveiled by the board of directors as an expression of appreciation for their vision. Today, it remains prominently displayed on the main grandstand under Box 1. (Courtesy of The Engraver.)

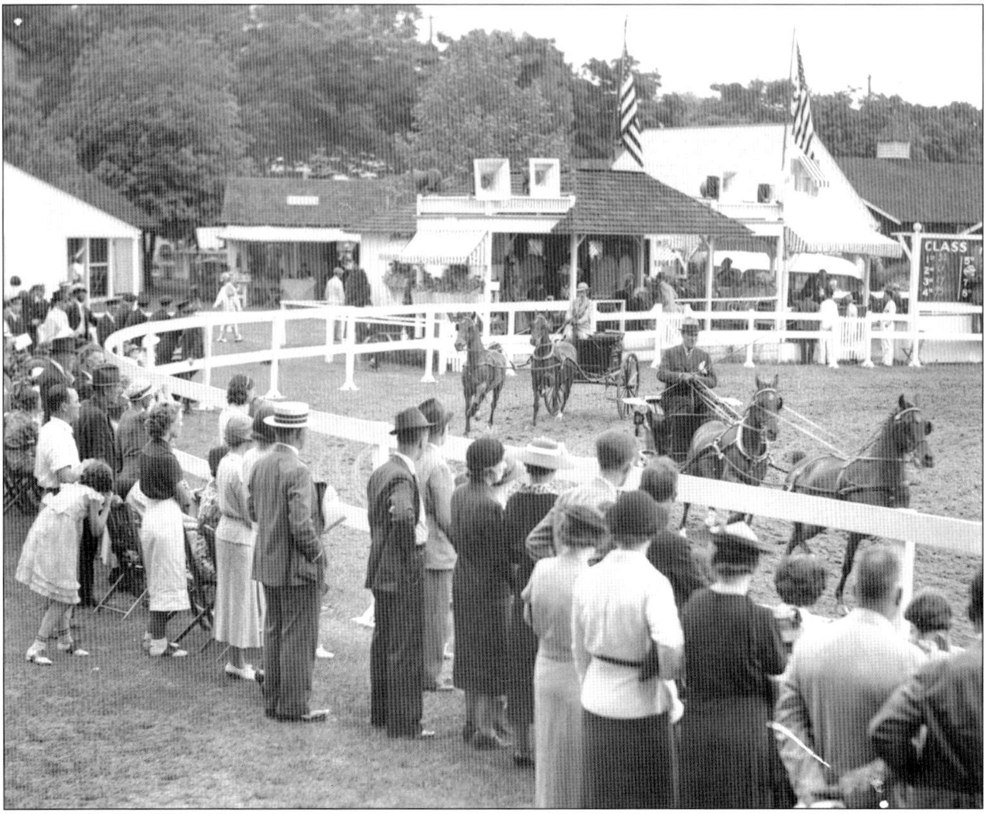

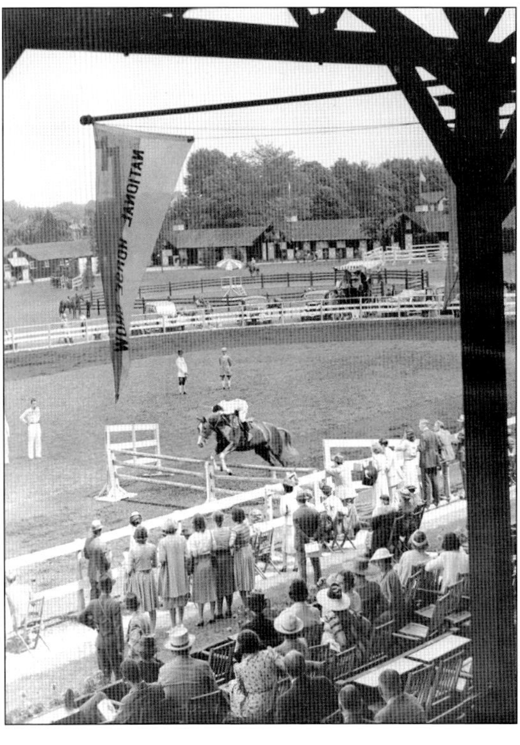

Spectators gather along the rail above to observe the 1937 Hackney Pony Tandem class performance. With the Devon railroad station a few hundred feet from its gate across Lancaster Avenue, exhibitors from all over the Eastern Seaboard could easily come to Devon to show champion horses. At left is a 1939 hunter class. The hunter course expanded from the main oval to the adjacent field, with competitors jumping over obstacles spanning the two areas, including water jumps and stone walls. Spectators had a habit of walking across the course during hunter classes, and it became a hazard. The committee dismantled the outside course in 1968, constructing the new Gold Ring with the generosity of Jean Ellen DuPont McConnell. (Left, courtesy of The Engraver.)

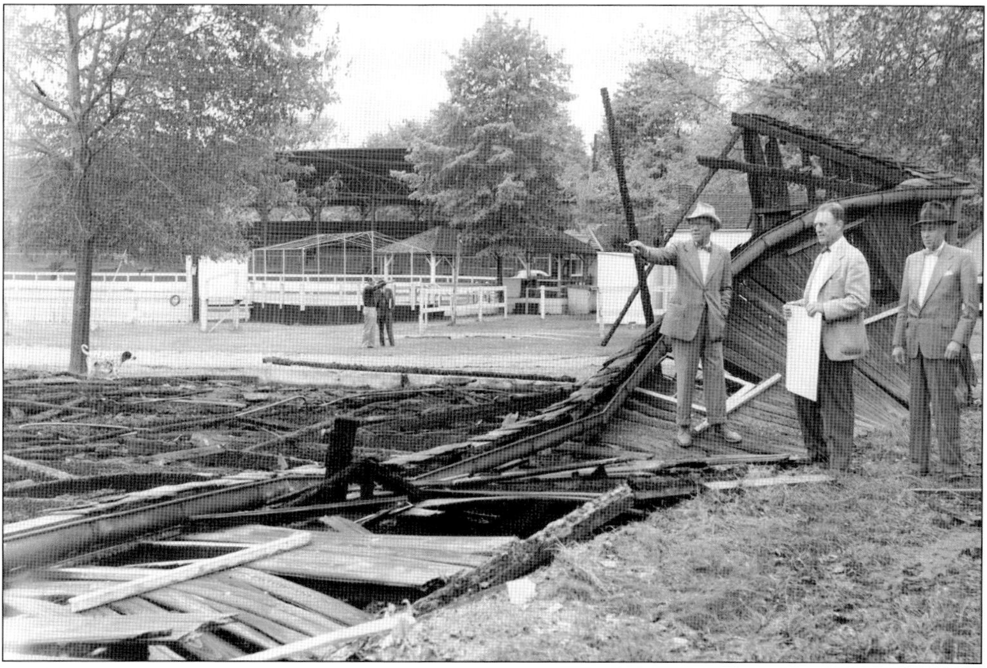

On May 7, 1952, three weeks before the show, a fire spread across the showgrounds. It started in a refuse pile. A strong wind carried the 100-foot-high blaze, which completely destroyed the permanent stables along Valley Forge Road, damaging more than 270 stalls. In the foreground of the above photograph, the grounds are inspected by, from left to right, Fred Pinch, show manager; William Ashton, chairman of the show committee; and Ward Sullivan, show secretary. After the debris was removed, temporary tent stalls were pitched near the grandstand and along Berkley and Valley Forge Roads. Fortunately, no horses were on the grounds during the fire, and the show opened as planned.

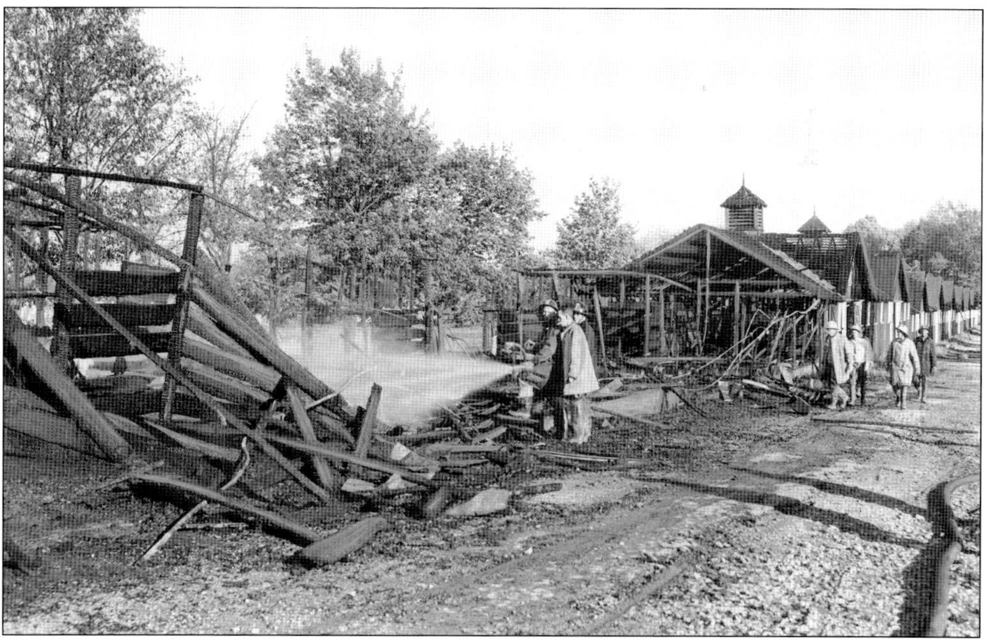

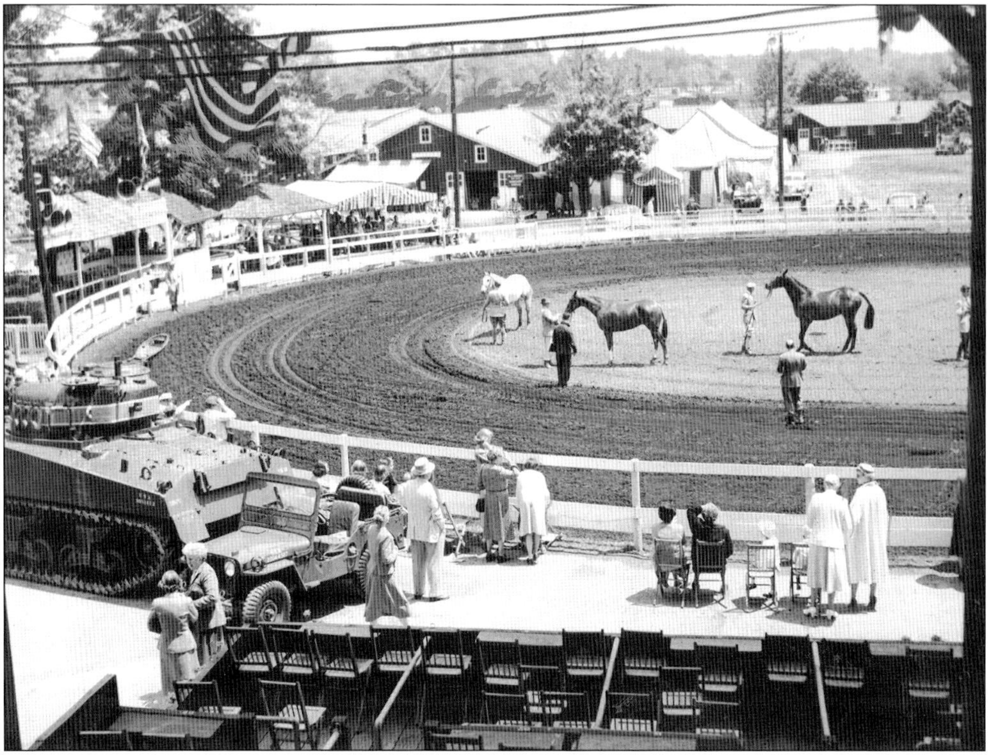

In the early 1950s, the number of exhibitors began to fall drastically. Only 300 exhibitors sent in advanced registrations until a telephone campaign salvaged the numbers. While the country fair's donations to Bryn Mawr increased, attendance was down. Reasons for the decline were attributed to the Cold War and Korean War. Here, at the 1953 show, a US tank and Jeep are displayed on the showgrounds, signaling the end of the Korean War. The Hunters-in-Hand class is shown in Wanamaker Oval. (Courtesy of the SCRC, Temple University.)

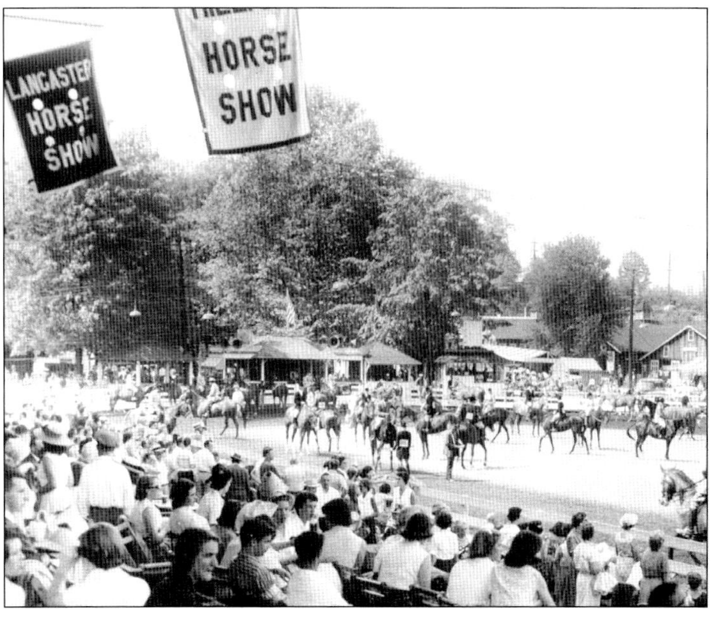

By the late 1950s, a new era of Devon unfolded. To attract spectators and competitors alike, the show attempted to eschew its perceived exclusivity as a mere society event. It introduced special events and exhibitions using television, radio, and newspapers to advertise popular classes and highlight celebrity events to elevate its attendance while maintaining its unique status as a national horse show.

Two

FOR THE BENEFIT OF BRYN MAWR HOSPITAL

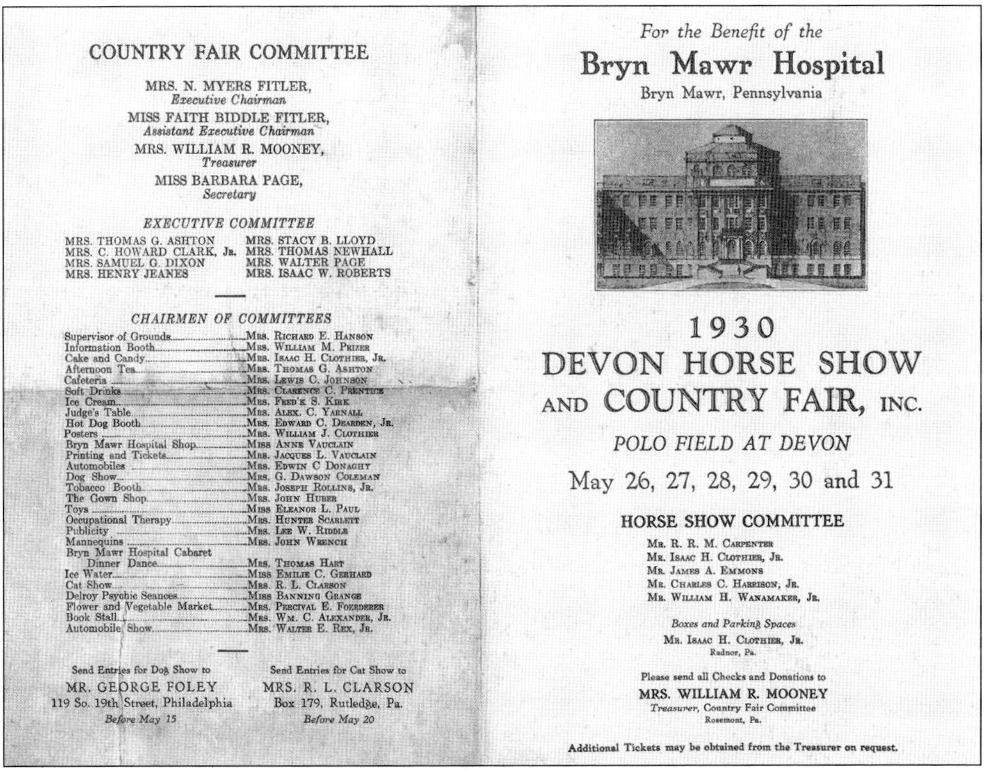

COUNTRY FAIR COMMITTEE

MRS. N. MYERS FITLER,
Executive Chairman

MISS FAITH BIDDLE FITLER,
Assistant Executive Chairman

MRS. WILLIAM R. MOONEY,
Treasurer

MISS BARBARA PAGE,
Secretary

EXECUTIVE COMMITTEE

MRS. THOMAS G. ASHTON
MRS. C. HOWARD CLARK, JR.
MRS. SAMUEL G. DIXON
MRS. HENRY JEANES
MRS. STACY B. LLOYD
MRS. THOMAS NEWHALL
MRS. WALTER PAGE
MRS. ISAAC W. ROBERTS

CHAIRMEN OF COMMITTEES

Supervisor of Grounds	Mrs. Richard E. Hanson
Information Booth	Mrs. William M. Prizer
Cake and Candy	Mrs. Isaac H. Clothier, Jr.
Afternoon Tea	Mrs. Thomas G. Ashton
Cafeteria	Mrs. Lewis C. Johnson
Soft Drinks	Mrs. Clarence C. Prentice
Ice Cream	Mrs. Fred'k S. Kirk
Judge's Table	Mrs. Alex. C. Yarnall
Hot Dog Booth	Mrs. Edward C. Dearden, Jr.
Posters	Mrs. William J. Clothier
Bryn Mawr Hospital Shop	Miss Anne Vauclain
Printing and Tickets	Mrs. Jacques L. Vauclain
Automobiles	Mrs. Edwin C Donaghy
Dog Show	Mrs. G. Dawson Coleman
Tobacco Booth	Mrs. Joseph Rollins, Jr.
The Gown Shop	Mrs. John Huber
Toys	Miss Eleanor L. Paul
Occupational Therapy	Mrs. Hunter Scarlett
Publicity	Mrs. Lee W. Riddle
Mannequins	Mrs. John Wrench
Bryn Mawr Hospital Cabaret Dinner Dance	Mrs. Thomas Hart
Ice Water	Miss Emilie C. Gerhard
Cat Show	Mrs. R. L. Clarson
Delroy Psychic Seances	Miss Banning Grange
Flower and Vegetable Market	Mrs. Percival E. Foerderer
Book Stall	Mrs. Wm. C. Alexander, Jr.
Automobile Show	Mrs. Walter E. Rex, Jr.

Send Entries for Dog Show to
MR. GEORGE FOLEY
119 So. 19th Street, Philadelphia
Before May 15

Send Entries for Cat Show to
MRS. R. L. CLARSON
Box 179, Rutledge, Pa.
Before May 20

For the Benefit of the
Bryn Mawr Hospital
Bryn Mawr, Pennsylvania

1930
DEVON HORSE SHOW
AND COUNTRY FAIR, INC.

POLO FIELD AT DEVON

May 26, 27, 28, 29, 30 and 31

HORSE SHOW COMMITTEE

Mr. R. R. M. Carpenter
Mr. Isaac H. Clothier, Jr.
Mr. James A. Emmons
Mr. Charles C. Harrison, Jr.
Mr. William H. Wanamaker, Jr.

Boxes and Parking Spaces
Mr. Isaac H. Clothier, Jr.
Radnor, Pa.

Please send all Checks and Donations to
MRS. WILLIAM R. MOONEY
Treasurer, Country Fair Committee
Rosemont, Pa.

Additional Tickets may be obtained from the Treasurer on request.

George S. Gerhard, MD, recognizing the need for a community hospital in the Philadelphia countryside, founded Bryn Mawr Hospital, the Devon Horse Show's chosen beneficiary. Gerhard strongly believed that medical expertise and community care together would improve the health and quality of life of Main Line residents. He persuaded other like-minded, influential men to support his cause. On October 3, 1893, Bryn Mawr Hospital opened with accommodations for 12 ward patients and 8 private patients. Major expansions occurred in 1929, 1965, and 2018.

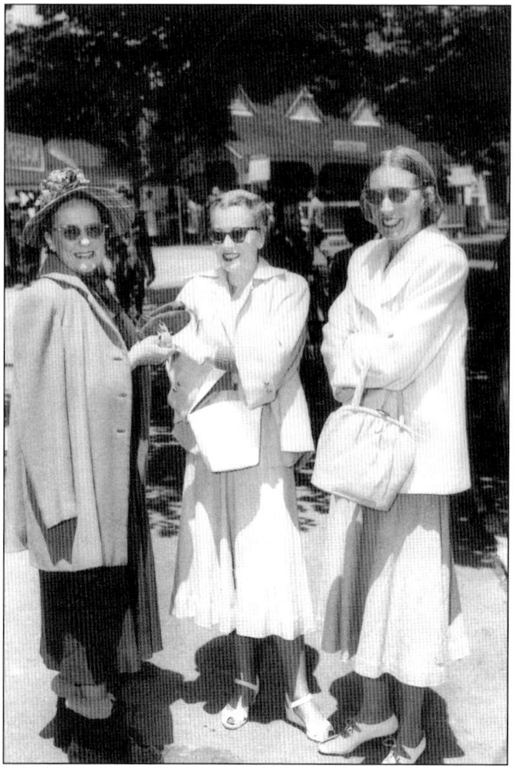

Bryn Mawr Hospital Women's Board members Georgiana "Sam" Wetherill Lewis and Katherine "Kit" Chase Warden and Devon Country Fair cochair Catharine Clothier Grange gather on the grounds around 1948. A longtime chair of the Bryn Mawr Hospital Women's Board, Lewis was one of the first women elected to the Bryn Mawr Hospital Board of Directors. Lewis served as chair of the Devon Country Fair from 1948 to 1950 and again in 1953.

Bryn Mawr Hospital nurses and physicians staffed the first aid station tucked away under the east grandstand, where they volunteered their time in five-hour shifts. Injuries included corneal abrasions, headaches, bumps, bruises, sunburns, and dog bites from free roaming stable dogs. In addition to suturing and dispensing medications and tetanus boosters, they handled all emergencies ranging from overheated spectators to a young woman sent to the hospital for an appendectomy.

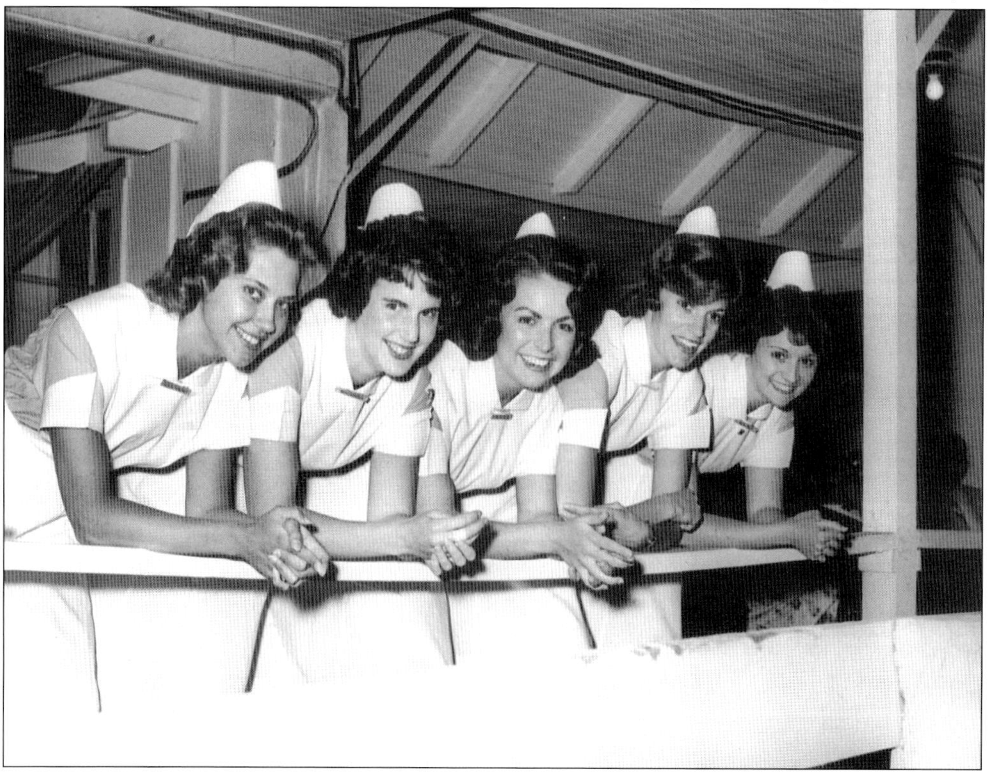

Chairs of the Devon Country Fair enjoy a strong relationship with the leadership at Bryn Mawr Hospital. From developing pre-events to the execution of the 11-day show, both organizations share goals of maximizing donations to the beneficiary and supporting the community. As is the tradition since 1919, the cochairs of the Devon Country Fair serve for a two-year period and oversee the various booths and operations of the fair to ensure smooth transition and execution. Pictured at right are members of the women's committee for the Devon Horse Show in 1936, Harriett Walker Kennedy, Margaret Schick LeMaistre, Edith Rumpf Fitler, and Isobel Rogers Dice. Pictured below in 1992 are the Devon Country Fair cochairs during the years 1990–1992. From left to right are Ginni Vosburg, Jane McCombs, Dolly Somers, and Deborah Martin. (Right, courtesy of the SCRC, Temple University.)

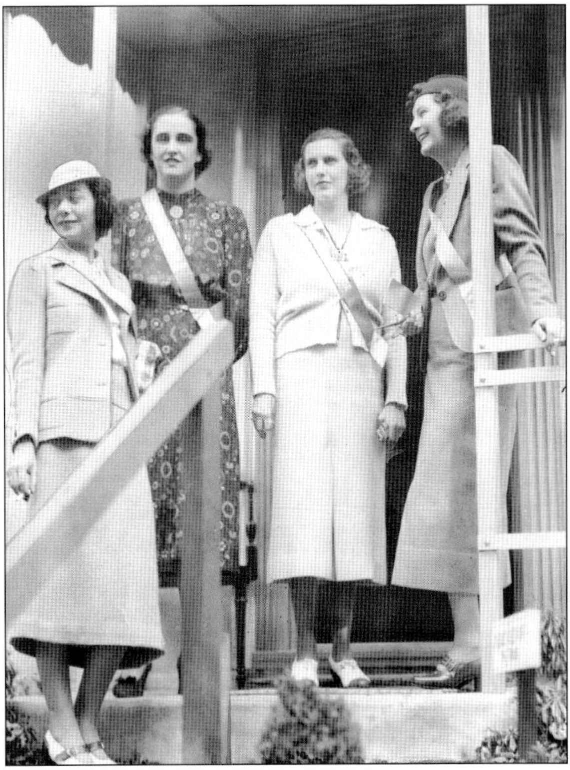

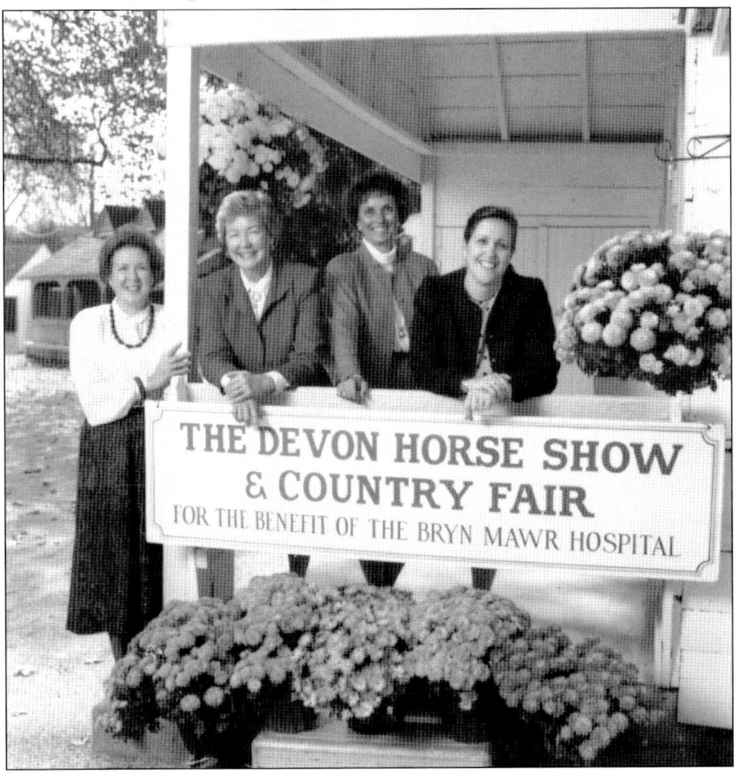

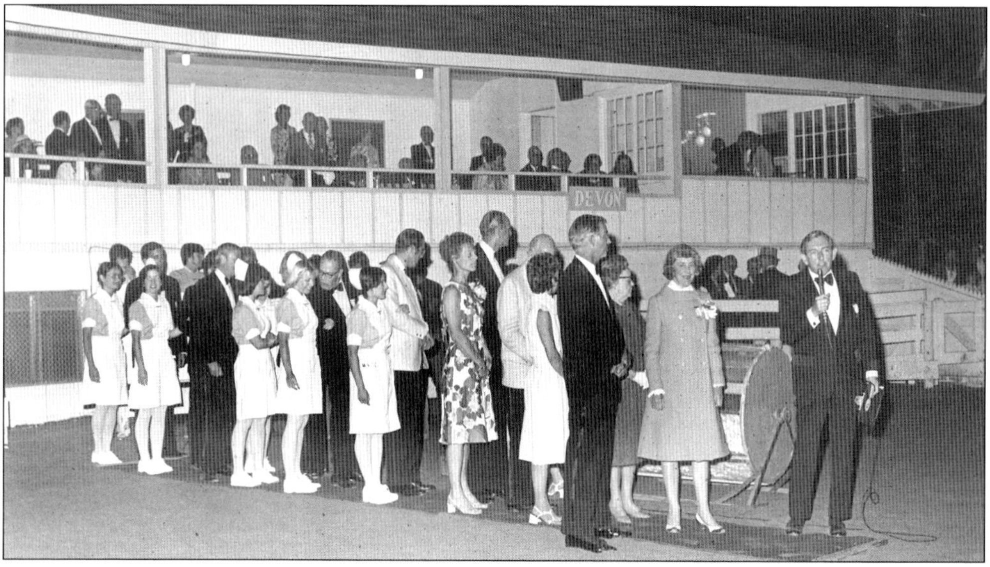

Bryn Mawr Hospital staff, doctors, and executives are encouraged to volunteer, participate, and attend Devon every year. One of Devon's highlights is the handing over of a key to a cherished prize on the final night of the show. A hush falls over the ring, a ticket is drawn from the Devon Derby drum, and the person with the matching stub receives the key to a new car. For many years, nurses were invited to draw the winning ticket for the Devon Derby raffle. Chances for the raffle are sold at the Bryn Mawr Hospital during the months leading up to the show, and often hospital staff are the lucky winners.

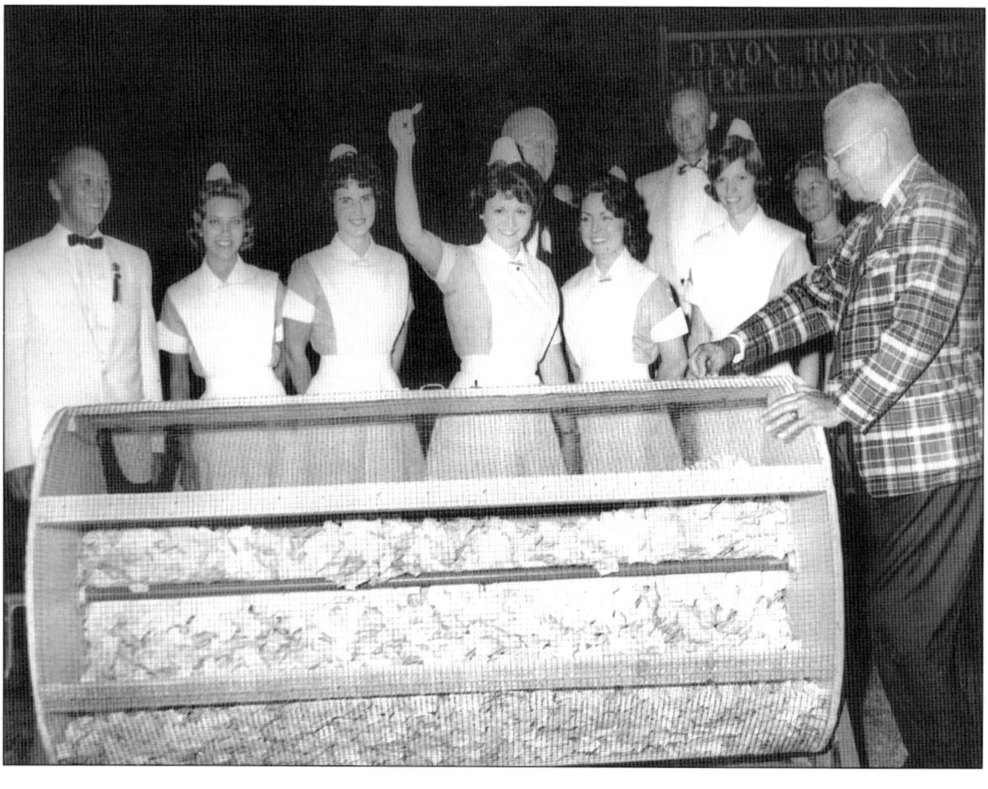

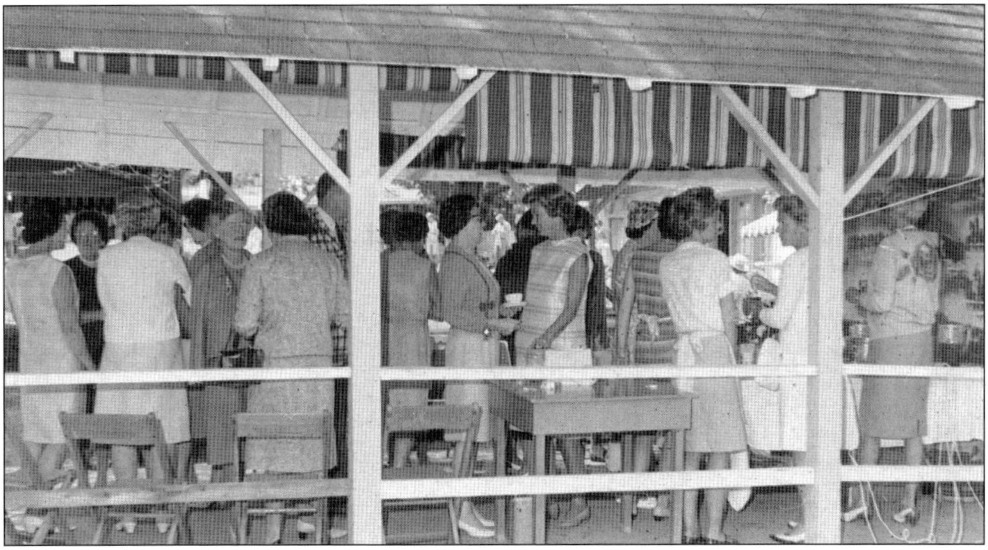

On the Wednesday before Devon's opening day, Bryn Mawr Hospital hosts a luncheon on the grounds to honor the Devon Country Fair chairs for their dedication and volunteerism. Above, chairs gather in the Devon pavilion before the luncheon in 1967 to kick off a successful show. Below, Bryn Mawr Hospital president Andrea "Andi" Gilbert addresses the chairs at the annual luncheon in the same pavilion 50 years later in 2017. Gilbert, a Devon board member and loyal supporter, can be seen actively volunteering at the country fair during the 11-day show. Under Gilbert's leadership, Bryn Mawr Hospital established several important facilities and patient care services utilizing the donations from the Devon Country Fair. She retired in January 2021 after more than 20 years of outstanding service to the Main Line Health community. (Below, courtesy of Brenda Carpenter Photography.)

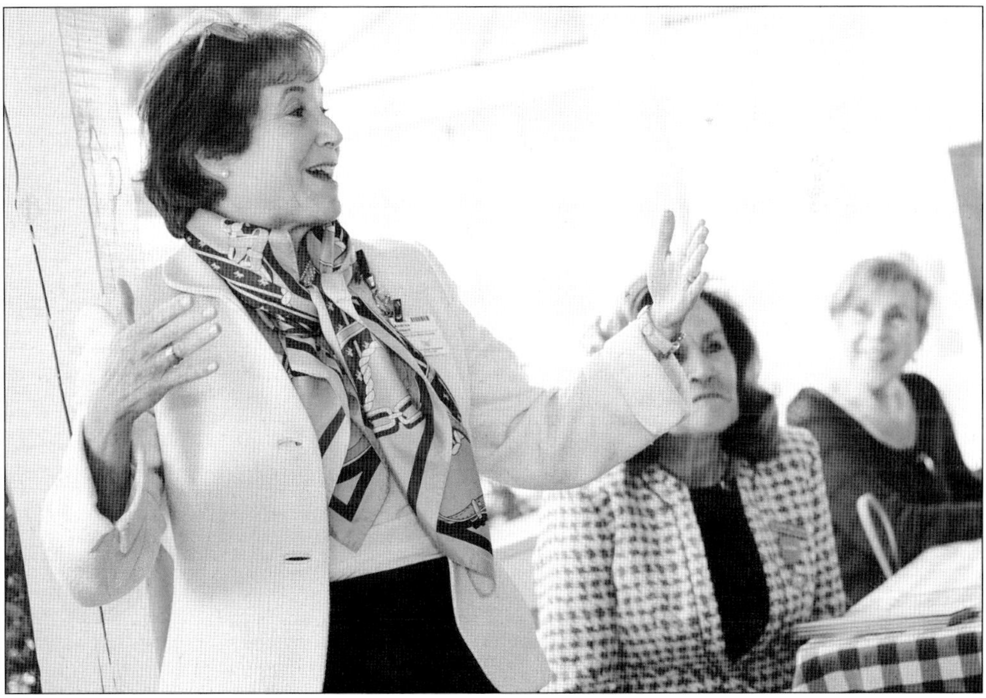

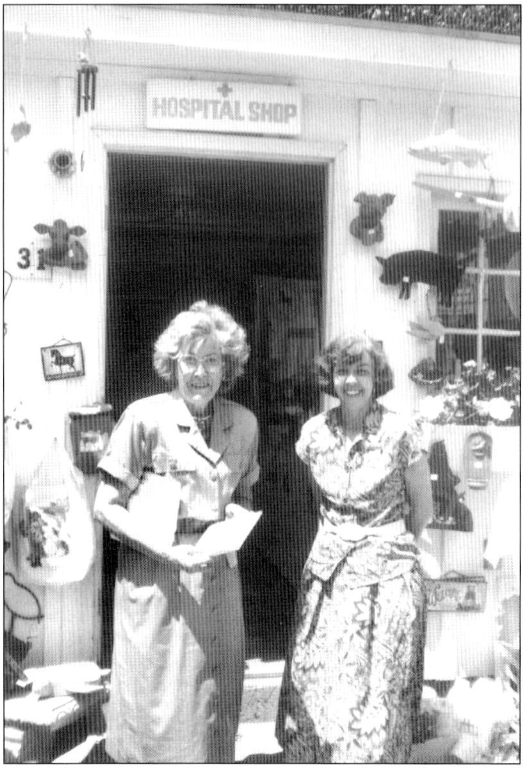

In 1925, the Bryn Mawr Hospital Women's Board voted to open the Bryn Mawr Hospital Shop at the country fair. Merchandise on display included decoupage, needlepoint, tote bags, place mats, knitted goods, woven baskets, pocketbooks, dresses and aprons, damask tablecloths, Devon Program covers, and golf bags. Representatives for the Bryn Mawr Hospital Women's Board would regularly join Devon chairs on this committee work year-round to create handmade crafts. The booth was discontinued in 2005.

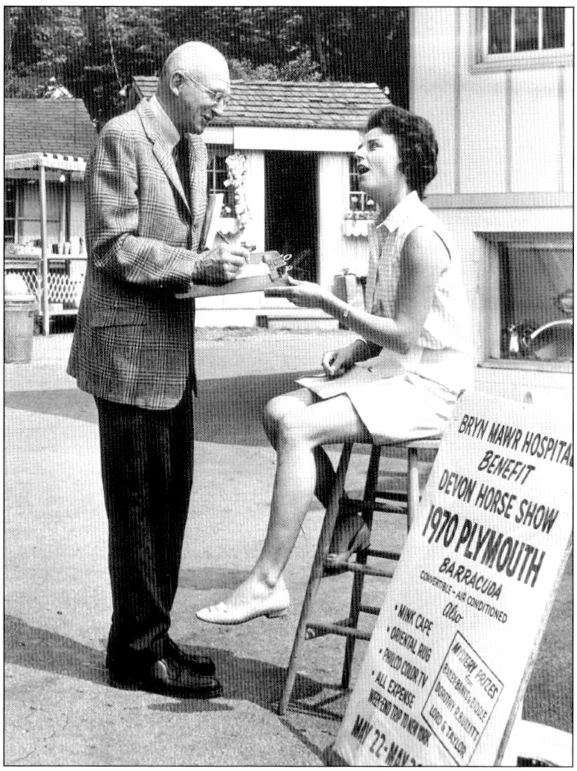

Devon Country Fair chair Kathy Schwartz, whose husband, Dr. Robert Schwartz, practiced at Bryn Mawr Hospital, persuades a Bryn Mawr administrator to try his luck at a Devon Derby chance for a 1970 Plymouth Barracuda. Other prizes that year included a mink cape, silk rug, Philco color television, an all-expenses-paid trip to New York, and "mystery prizes" from Bailey, Banks & Biddle, Dorothy R. Bullitt, and Lord & Taylor. Schwartz, her children, and her grandchildren continue to serve Devon as chairs today.

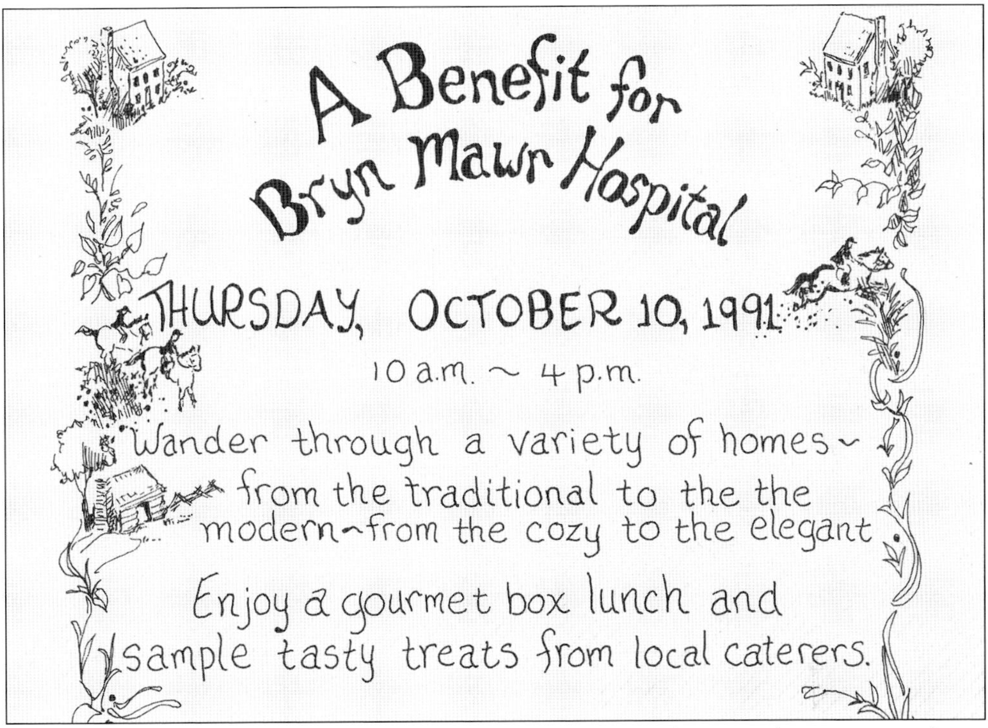

The Fall Festival of Homes, also known as the House Tour, was a long-standing Devon tradition and a fundraiser for Bryn Mawr Hospital. Various homes would be showcased along the Main Line with a luncheon provided. The house below on Conestoga Road in Wayne, Pennsylvania, was featured on the House Tour in its early years and was owned by Dr. Harold Ellis Farmer and his wife, Agnes Cherrington Speck Farmer, a prized orchid grower and Devon supporter. Farmer opened his practice in 1934 in Bryn Mawr, making house calls throughout the Main Line and as far as Coatesville. A Harvard University and University of Pennsylvania graduate and professor at Penn Medical School, he became the first African American doctor admitted to practice at Bryn Mawr Hospital in 1955.

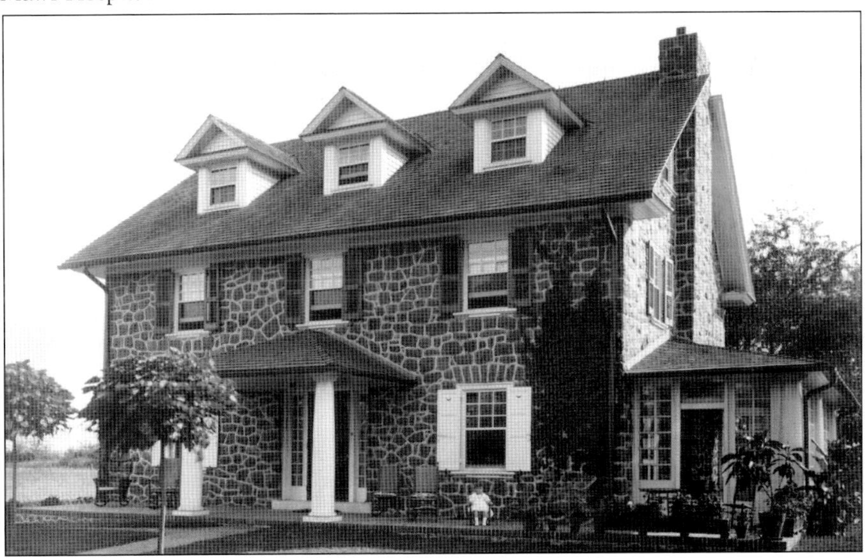

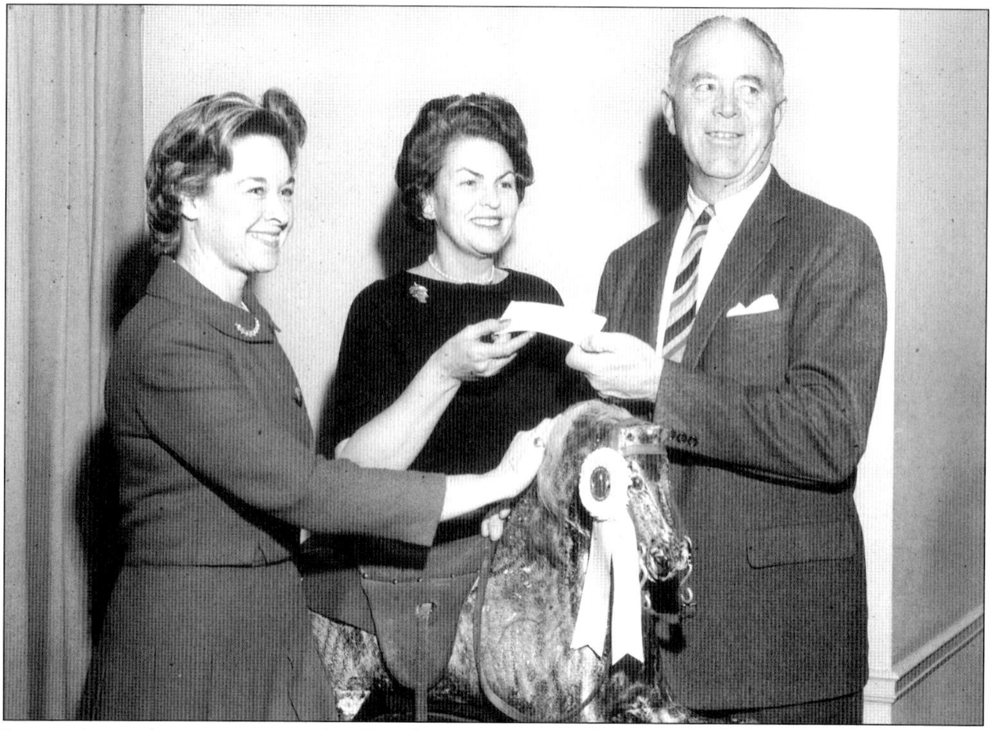

In a tradition that continues to this day, the Devon Horse Show and Country Fair presents a check to the Bryn Mawr Hospital for its annual donation. The culmination of thousands of volunteer hours by Devon committee members, the annual check presentation ceremony is attended by executive committee members of the Devon Country Fair, the board of directors of the horse show, medical staff executive committee members, and representatives of administration and various committees and departments of the hospital. Above, Devon Country Fair cochairs Lois Bromley (left) and Bunny Warburton (center) present a check to Bryn Mawr Hospital president Clarence A. Warden Jr. for proceeds from the 1962 show. Below, Bromley presents a check to Warden in 1963. External defibrillators like the one shown here were purchased with donations from the Devon Country Fair.

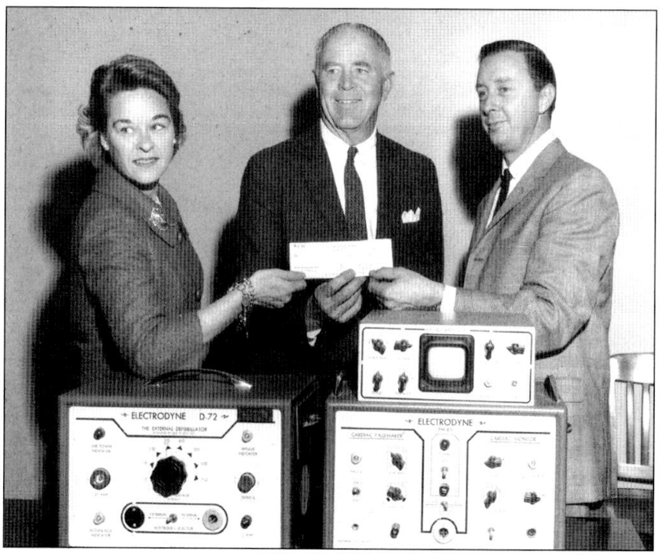

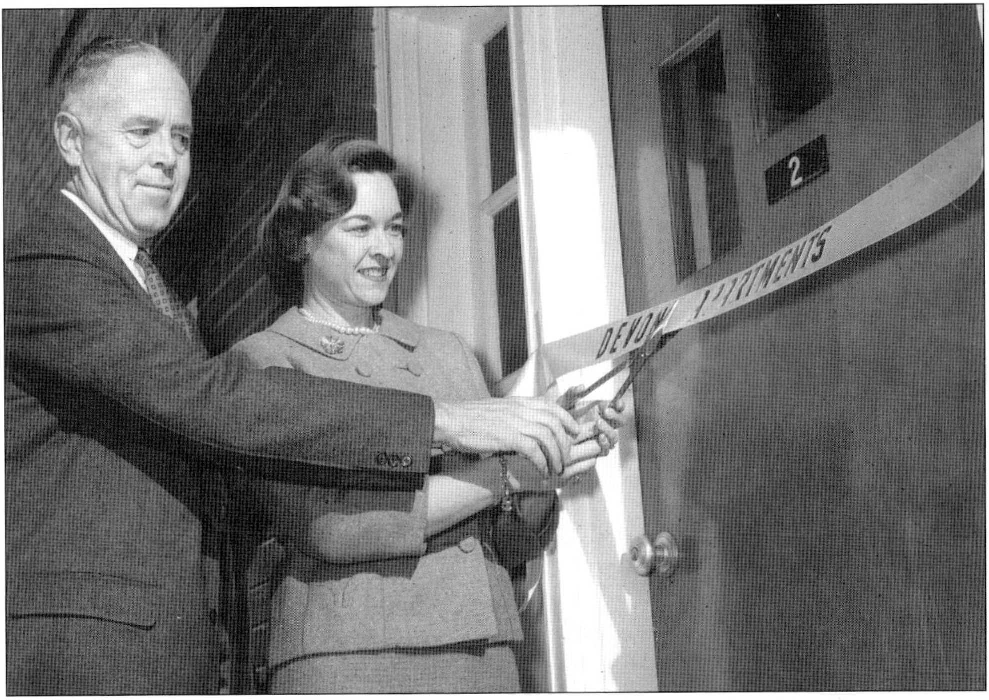

Above, Lois Bromley, cochair of the 1962 Devon Country Fair, cuts the ribbon for the Devon Apartments on Old Lancaster Road in Bryn Mawr with the assistance of Clarence A. Warden, president of Bryn Mawr Hospital. Proceeds from former shows helped to purchase and furnish the apartments, which were built to house married interns and residents of Bryn Mawr Hospital. Below, cochairs Margaret Peter Fritz (left) and Roxy Stull Willcox (right) pose with Warden in front of new facility construction in 1965, made possible by donations from Devon.

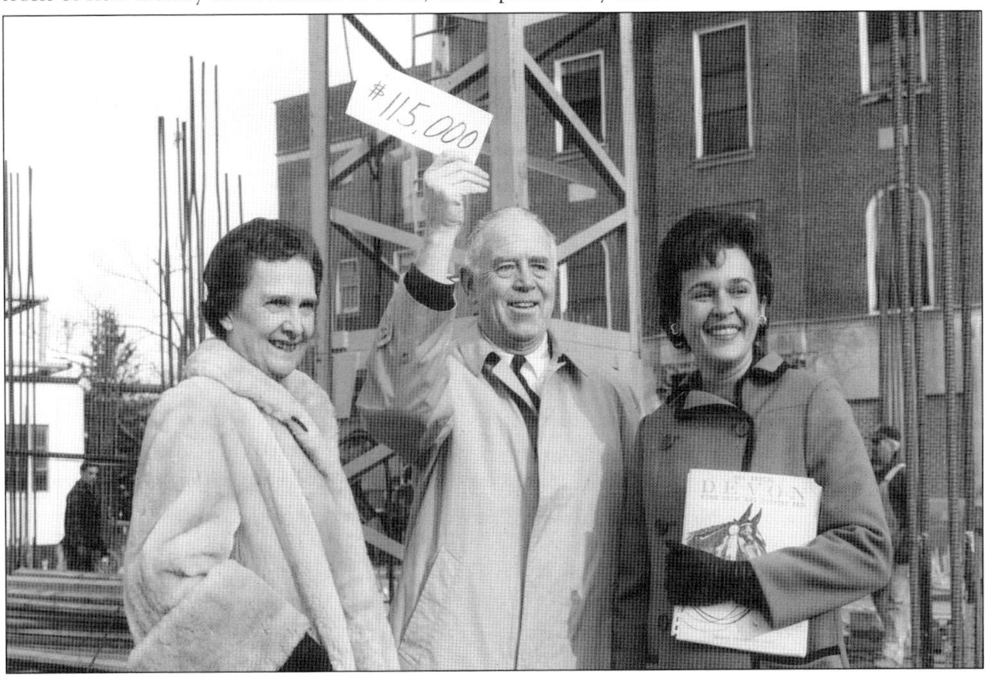

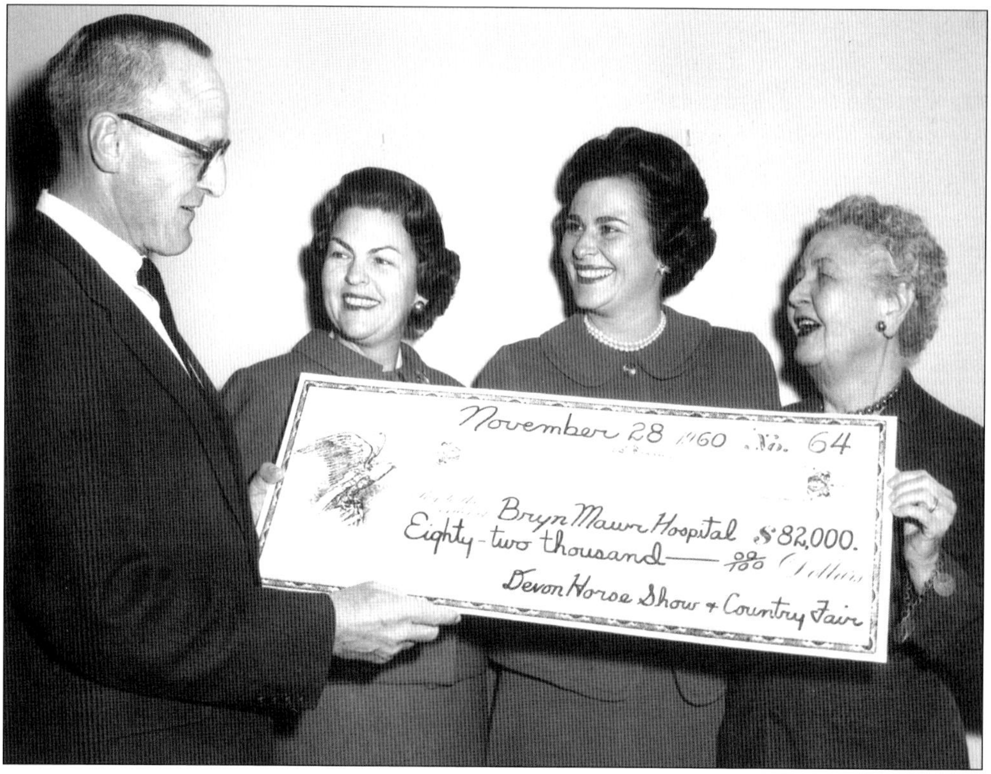

The donation amounts to Bryn Mawr increased significantly in the 1960s and 1970s, reflecting successful volunteer efforts. Above, Devon Country Fair cochairs Jane "Bunny" Warburton (left) and Kathleen Stull Smith (center) present a check for $82,000 to director J. Randolph Burke in 1960. Below, Sally Warden Stone (left) and Jo Ballengee (right), executive committee cochairs of the 1973 Devon Country Fair, present a check to Carl I. Bergkvist, president of the Bryn Mawr Hospital, for $138,000. The major portion of this amount was designated for the improvement fund and the balance for specific projects. At that time, the Devon Horse Show and Country Fair had donated almost $3 million to Bryn Mawr Hospital.

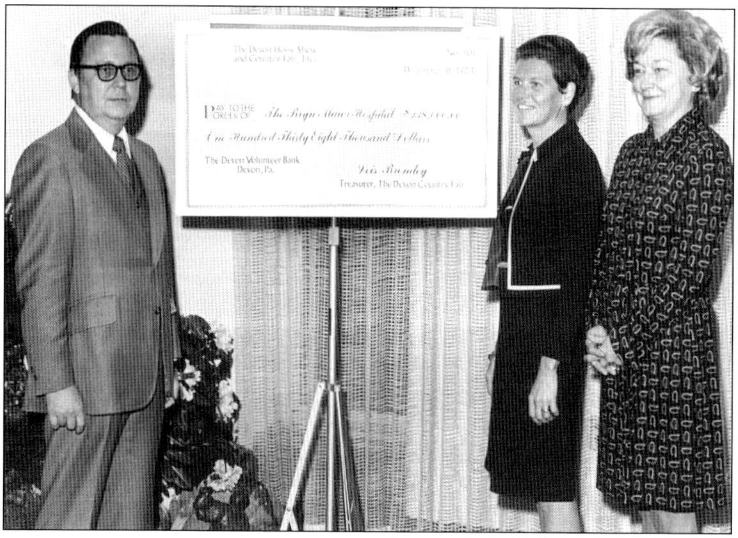

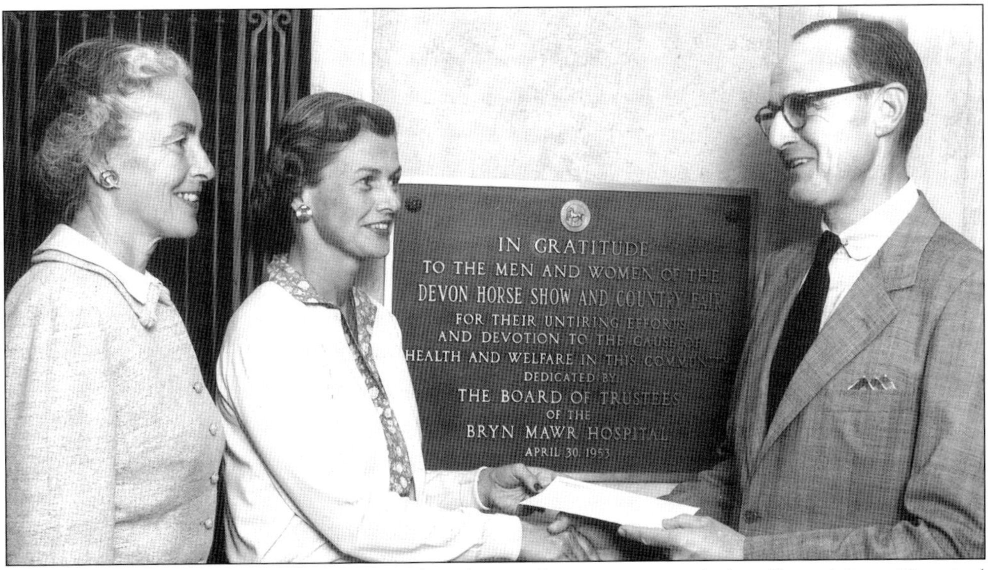

Honoring a decades-long partnership, the plaque above was unveiled at Bryn Mawr Hospital during the annual check presentation. It reads, "In gratitude to the men and women of the Devon Horse Show and Country Fair for their untiring efforts and devotion to the cause of health and welfare in this community. Dedicated by the Board of Trustees of the Bryn Mawr Hospital, April 30, 1953." Pictured here are Suzanne Matthews (left) and Lolly Davis (right), Devon Country Fair cochairs, presenting Bryn Mawr managing director J. Randolph Burke with a $65,000 donation in 1956, surpassing the $1-million mark of total donations to Bryn Mawr Hospital since the beginning of its partnership.

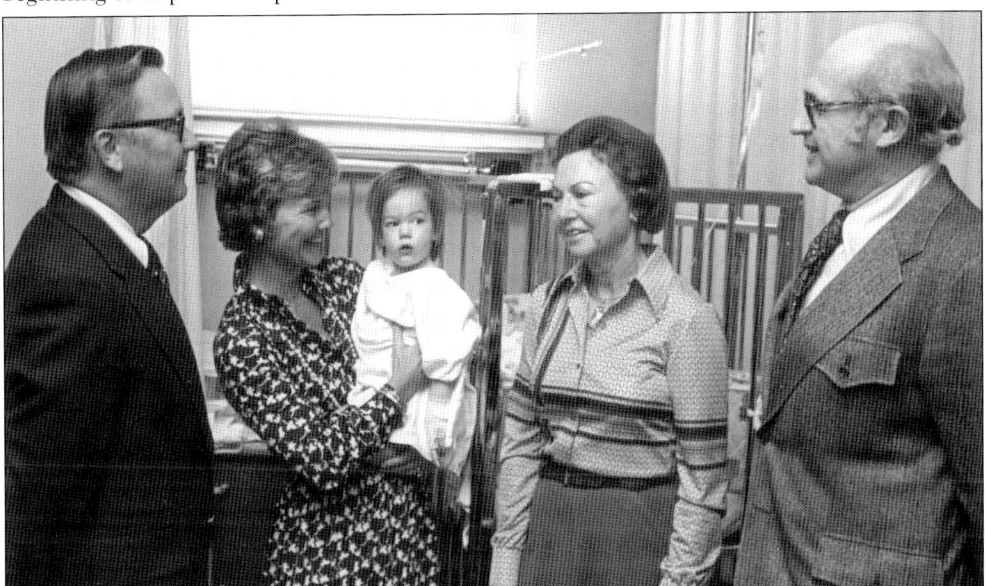

Visiting Sara Cornelius, daughter of Dr. and Mrs. Chalmers E. Cornelius II, are, from left to right, Carl I. Bergkvist, Bryn Mawr Hospital president; Sydney Davis Stevens and Sue Welch Clader, cochairs of the Devon Country Fair; and Robert F. Plotkin, director of pediatrics. The 1975 Devon Country Fair donation, totaling $145,000, was used to purchase monitoring equipment for the newly renovated pediatric department at Bryn Mawr Hospital.

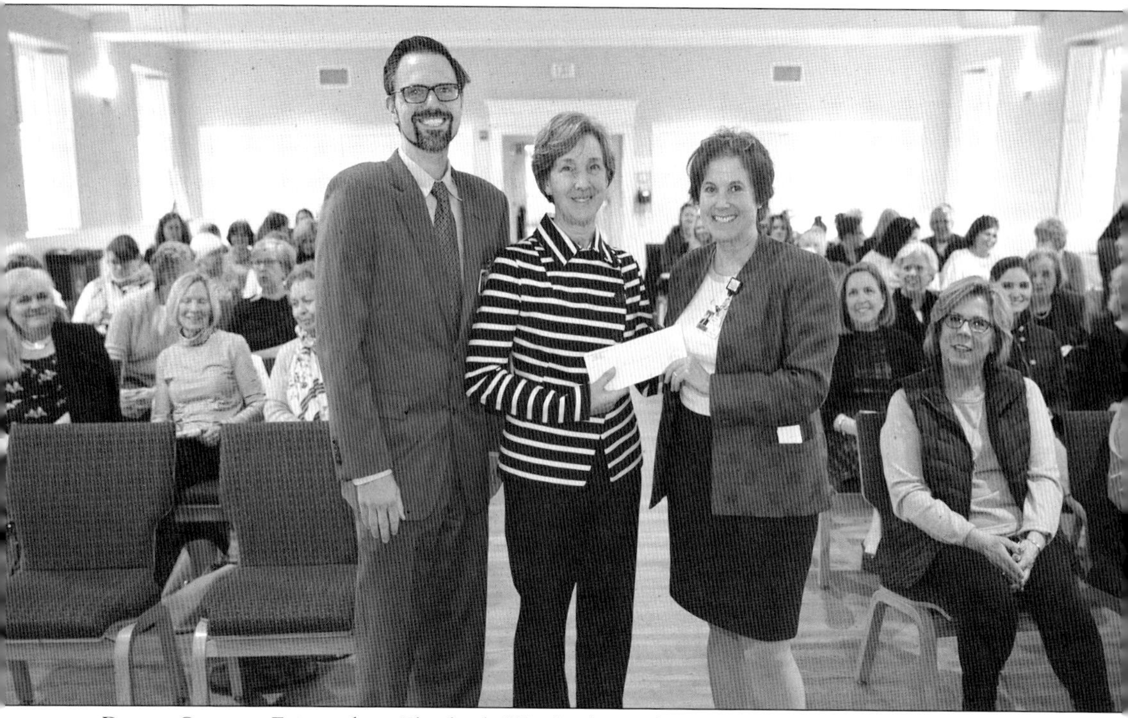

Devon Country Fair cochair Elizabeth Wright (center) presents a check to Bryn Mawr Hospital president Andrea Gilbert (right) and executive director of development Michael Criscuolo (left) in 2018. Behind them are the many chairs who make the Devon Country Fair possible. The over-100-year relationship between the Devon Horse Show and Country Fair and Bryn Mawr Hospital has enabled more than $18 million in donations to the hospital. Projects funded by Devon have included neonatal intensive care unit (ICU) respiration monitors, neuro-cardiac ICU beds, improvements in the cardiac catheterization lab, expansion of a comprehensive breast center, an infant abduction system for the nursery, an emergency department expansion, and pediatric emergency equipment. A recent $2-million pledge funded a 2019 ICU in the new patient pavilion named for Devon. Another $2 million will fund an inpatient behavioral health unit that will open in 2022. (Courtesy of Brenda Carpenter Photography.)

Three

THE COUNTRY FAIR

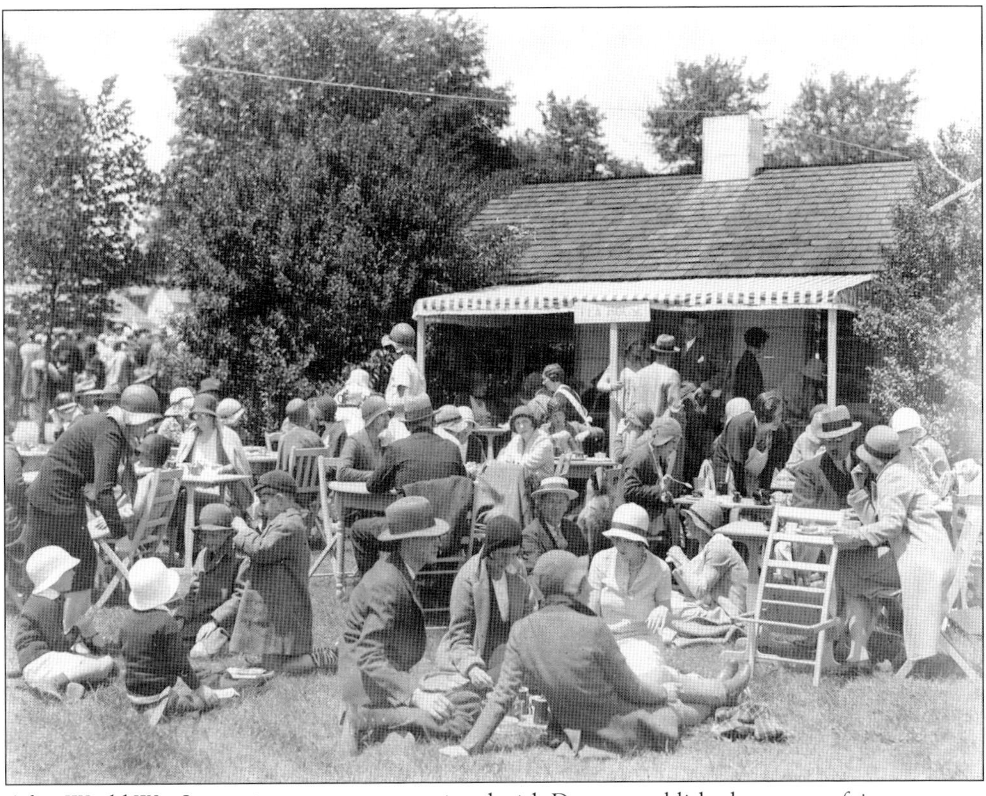

After World War I, prominent women associated with Devon established a country fair to support Bryn Mawr Hospital. Led by Isabel Armstrong Barklie, the country fair created its first committee, the Tea House. Outfitted in hats, dresses, and gloves, ladies served tea and other refreshments to spectators and exhibitors. The event was officially known as the Devon Horse Show and Country Fair Inc., sealing an indelible partnership for 100 years and counting. (Courtesy of The Engraver.)

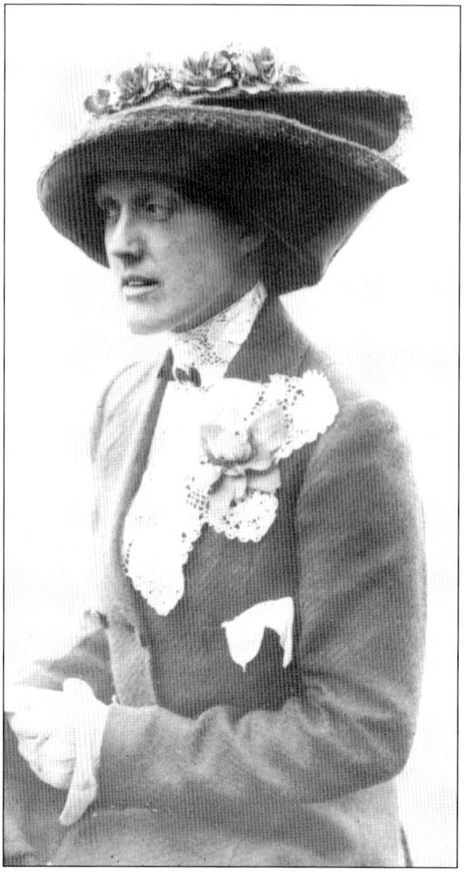

Women played an important role in Devon from its inception. Devon introduced Ladies' Day not only to encourage women to display the latest fashions but also to highlight their expertise and skill as the judges of the show classes. Mrs. William Hurst, shown at left, was a prominent Devon hunter judge who was photographed for *American Horse* magazine. With the passage of the 19th Amendment looming on the national stage, women at Devon were a force of their own. They mobilized during this time to create committees that increased revenue and saved the organization from dissolution, a fate met by other local horse shows during this time. Today, Ladies' Day remains a popular event showcasing fashions and millinery with a hat contest and luncheon. (Below, courtesy of The Engraver.)

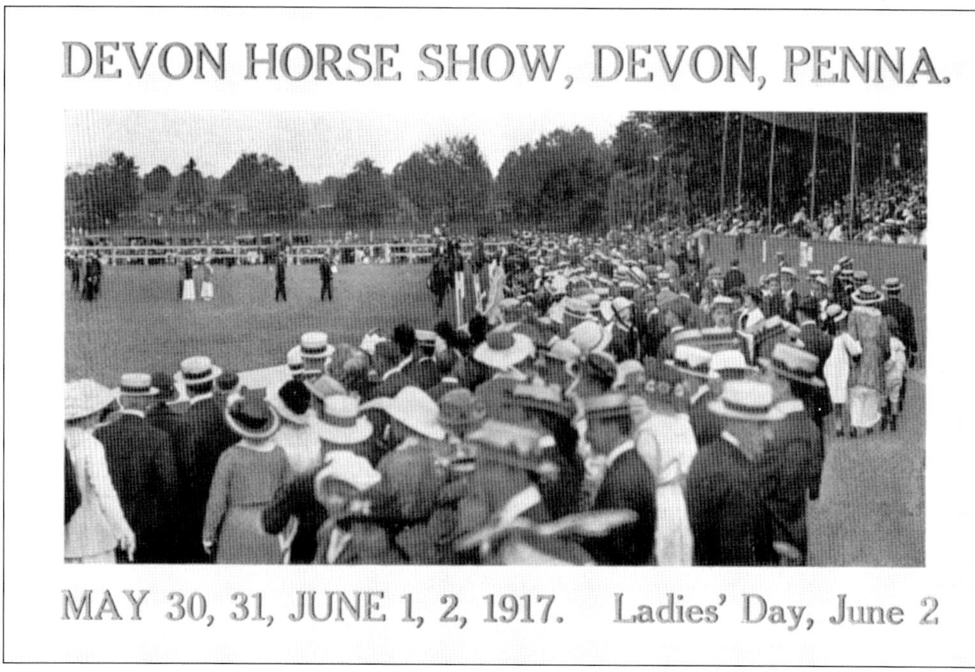

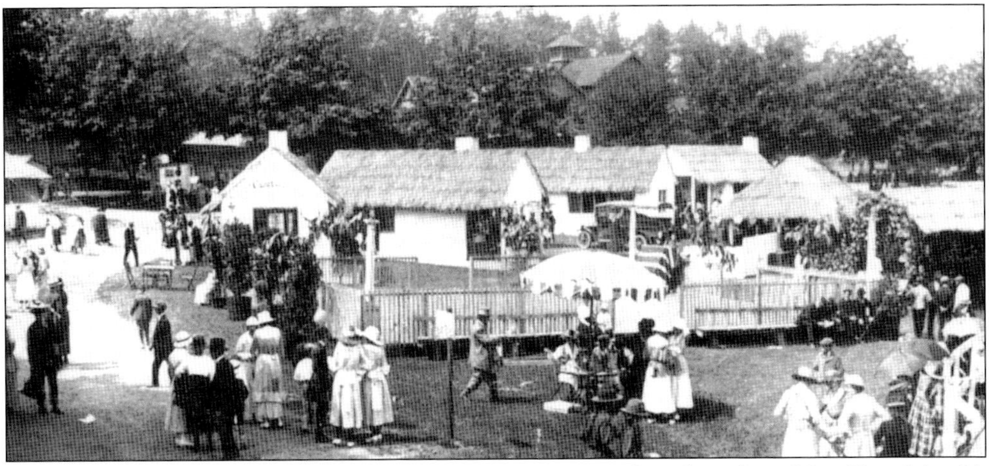

The first Devon Horse Show and Country Fair in 1919 was four days, from May 28 to May 31. Its worthy charity, Bryn Mawr Hospital, received $26,000 that year. Afternoon tea and dancing were provided in the pavilion, with a jazz band for entertainment. The Tea House served tea with sugar syrup, mint leaves, and lemons. Ladies brought their own lace tablecloths, sterling silver urns, and china cups to provide fresh-baked tea cakes and other refreshments. Known as the Country Village, the quaint, thatched-roof cottages that lined either side of the promenade of "Easy Street" sold cigarettes, ice cream, sandwiches, and rummage items to tempt equestrian spectators. The country fair returned in 1920 with the adoption of blue and white as the official colors of the show. As reported in the May 16, 1920, *Philadelphia Inquirer*, nationwide exhibitors "expressed surprise at the magnitude of the enterprise," recognizing that nearly 350 society women comprising the committees "worked tirelessly for months" to establish it as "one of the most elaborate outdoor affairs ever staged." (Below, courtesy of The Engraver.)

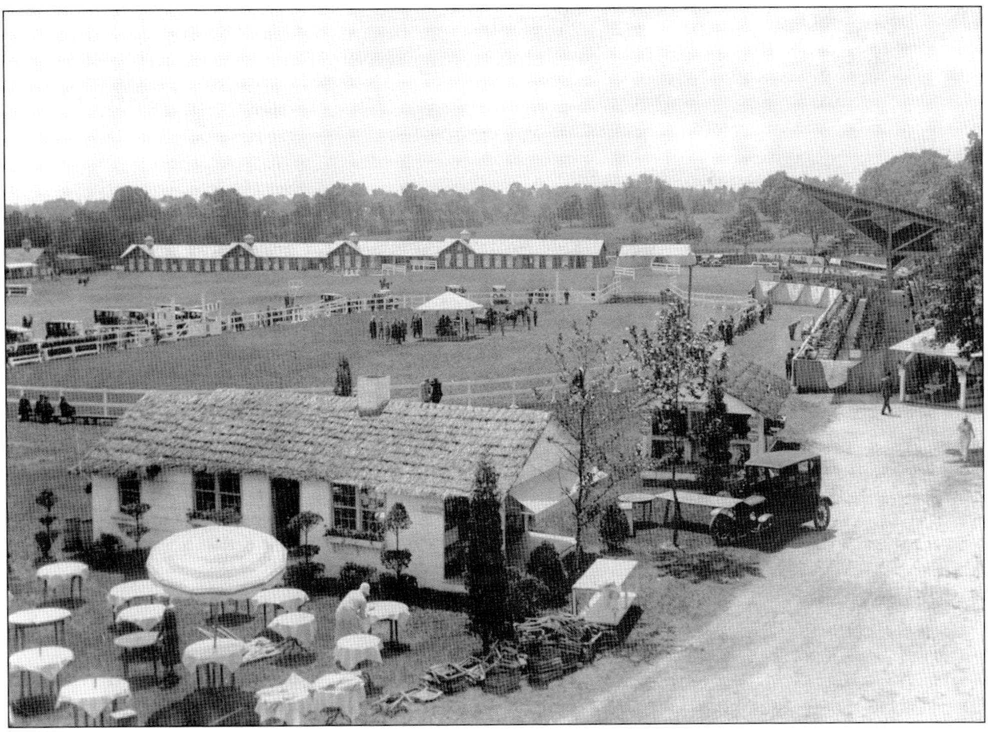

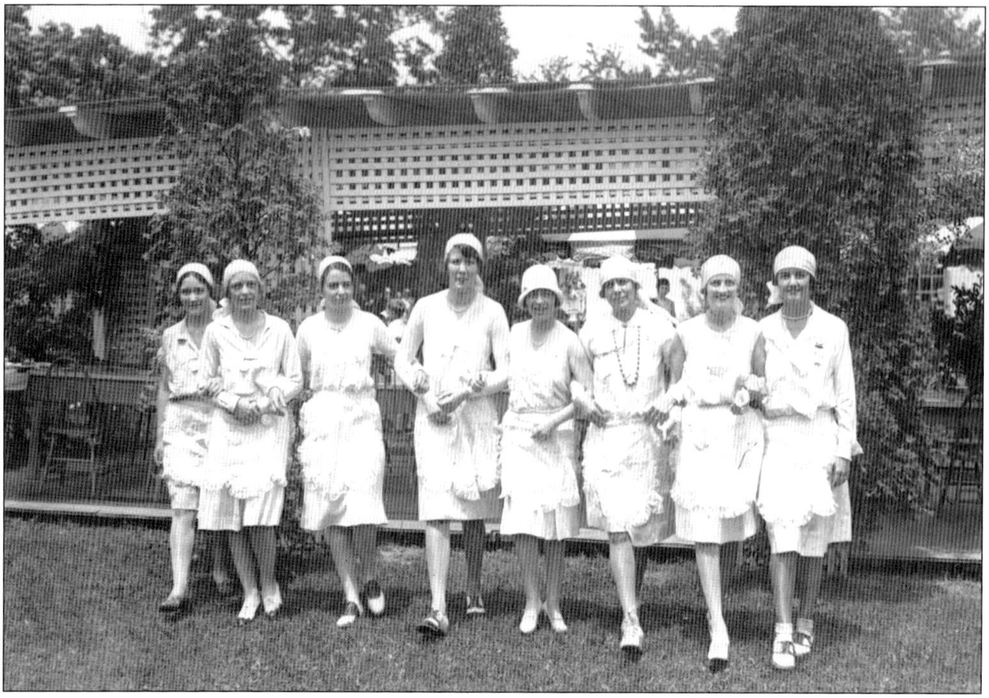

Socially prominent women, many of whom were the wives of men associated with the horse show or hospital, served as volunteers for the country fair. Strict dress code required volunteers to dress in all white, from hats to shoes. In the 1929 photograph above are, from left to right, Marion Galey, Rosina Malpass, Polly Brinley, Mary Law Starr, Madeleine Holden, Eleanor Rulon-Miller, Marion Moll Rollins, and Elise Hopkins Yarnell. Below, "Devon Beer Maids"—Priscilla DeCosta, Ann Schwartz, Elizabeth McElroy Stout, and Delores McElroy—pose in the Beer Garden at Devon on May 24, 1933. Prohibition did not end until the 18th Amendment was repealed on December 5, 1933, but libations freely flowed at Devon, despite a federal Prohibition raid and arrest of a Philadelphia man operating a speakeasy in one of the stalls on the grounds. (Above, courtesy of the SCRC, Temple University; below, courtesy of The Engraver.)

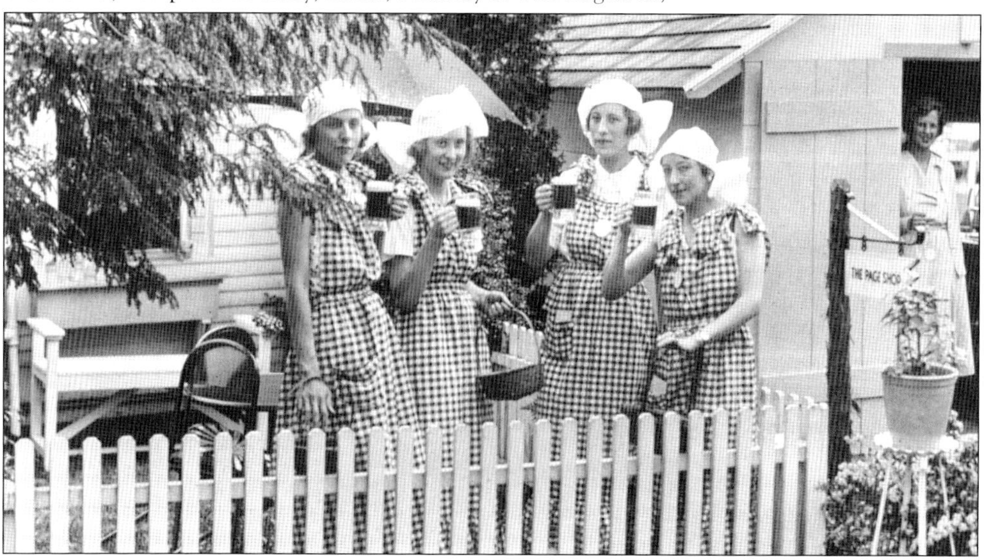

Children's Day is a long-standing Devon tradition, with activities such as pony and goat rides. The Swiss pony cart at right explored the grounds in the 1940s, selling posies and other gifts. Below, Charlotte Marquissee (left) and Mary Dickinson (right) cart around the Klapp children. Billy the Goat would take children around the showgrounds for 10¢ a ride. Children today still enjoy a dedicated day of activities on the grounds during the last Saturday of Devon. There is an Itty Bitty Hat parade in which children decorate their own hats and parade around the grounds to show off their crafts as local musicians provide the beat. A popular event is the Children's Tea Party with additional crafts, activities, and visits from pet lambs and dogs. (Both, courtesy of The Engraver.)

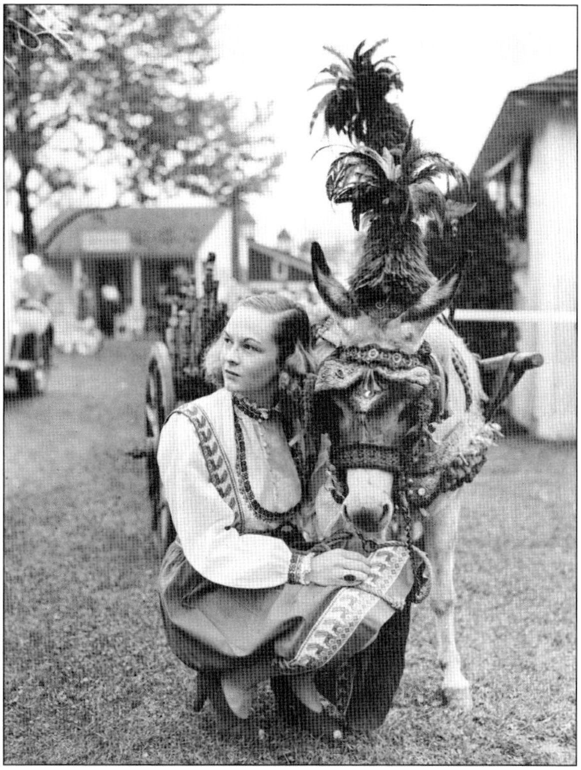

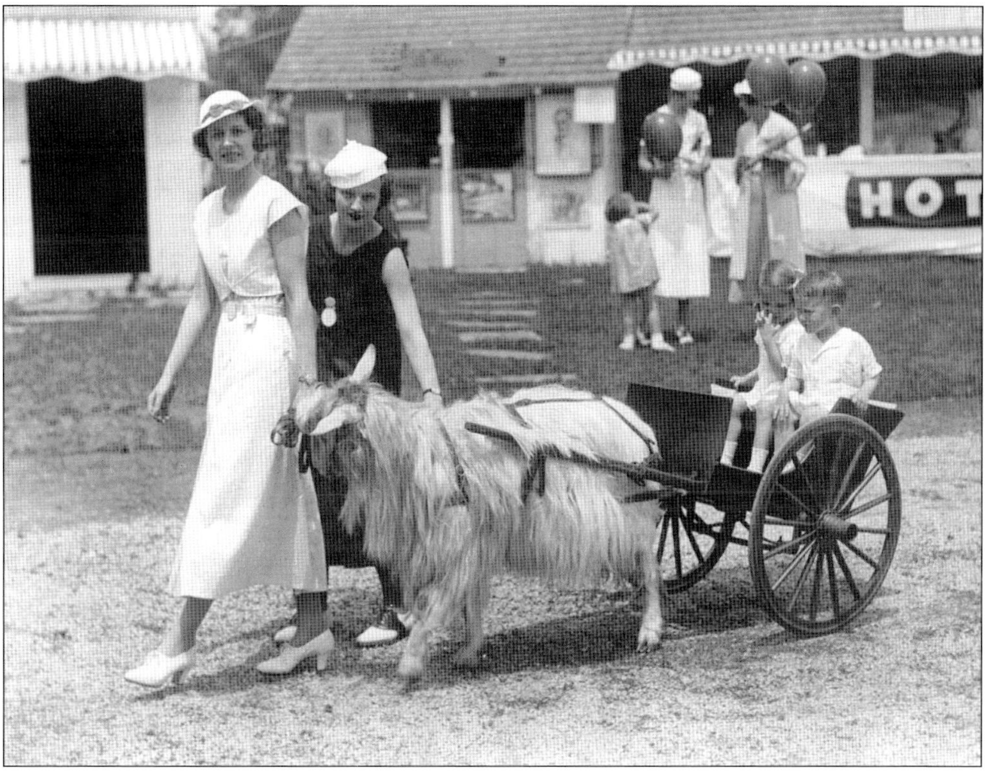

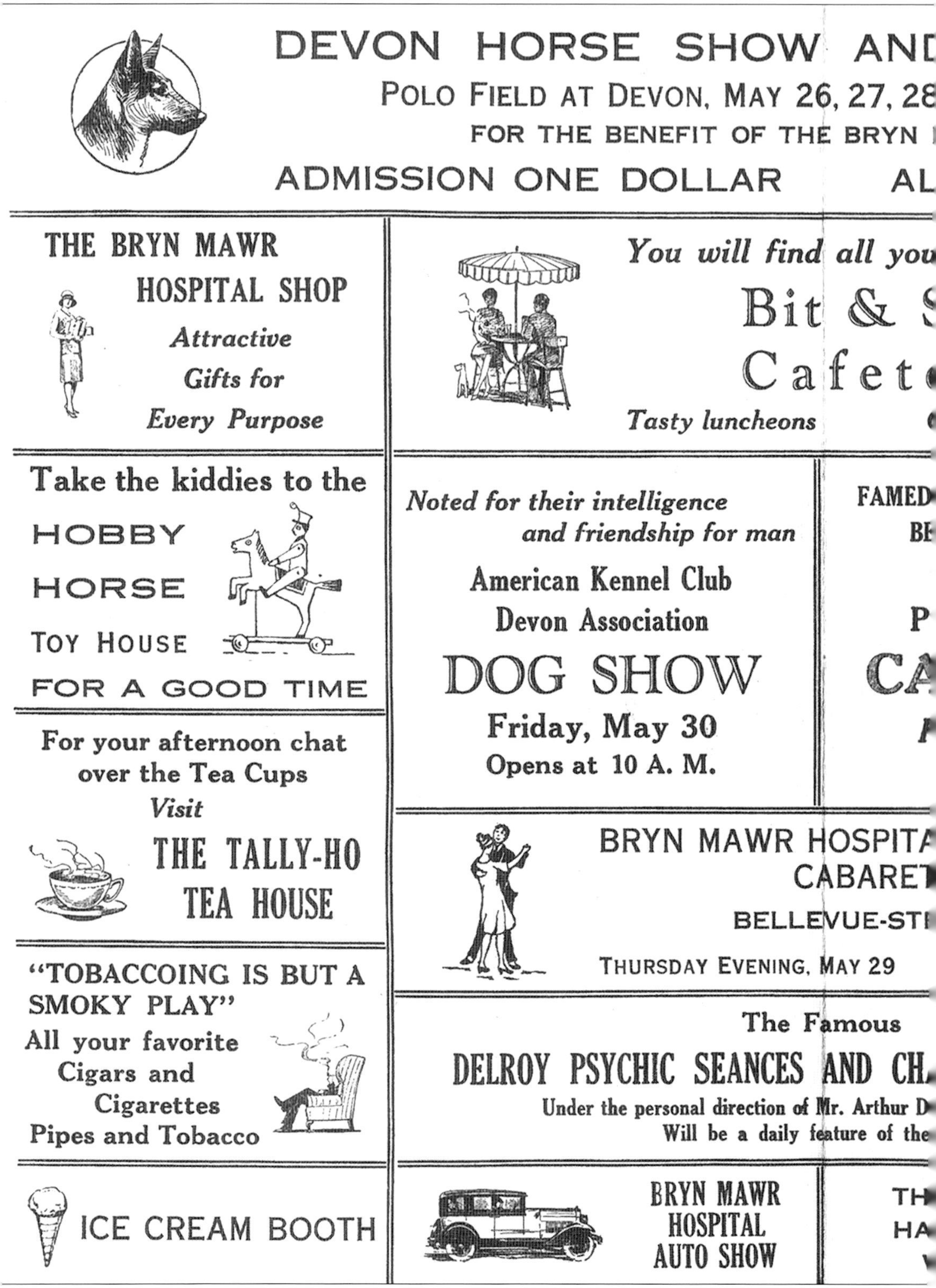

DEVON HORSE SHOW AND

POLO FIELD AT DEVON, MAY 26, 27, 28

FOR THE BENEFIT OF THE BRYN

ADMISSION ONE DOLLAR AL

THE BRYN MAWR
HOSPITAL SHOP
Attractive
Gifts for
Every Purpose

You will find all you
Bit &
Cafet
Tasty luncheons

Take the kiddies to the
HOBBY
HORSE
TOY HOUSE
FOR A GOOD TIME

Noted for their intelligence
and friendship for man
American Kennel Club
Devon Association
DOG SHOW
Friday, May 30
Opens at 10 A. M.

FAMED
BE
P
CA

For your afternoon chat
over the Tea Cups
Visit
THE TALLY-HO
TEA HOUSE

BRYN MAWR HOSPITA
CABARET
BELLEVUE-ST
THURSDAY EVENING, MAY 29

"TOBACCOING IS BUT A
SMOKY PLAY"
All your favorite
Cigars and
Cigarettes
Pipes and Tobacco

The Famous
DELROY PSYCHIC SEANCES AND CH
Under the personal direction of Mr. Arthur D
Will be a daily feature of the

ICE CREAM BOOTH

BRYN MAWR
HOSPITAL
AUTO SHOW

TH
HA

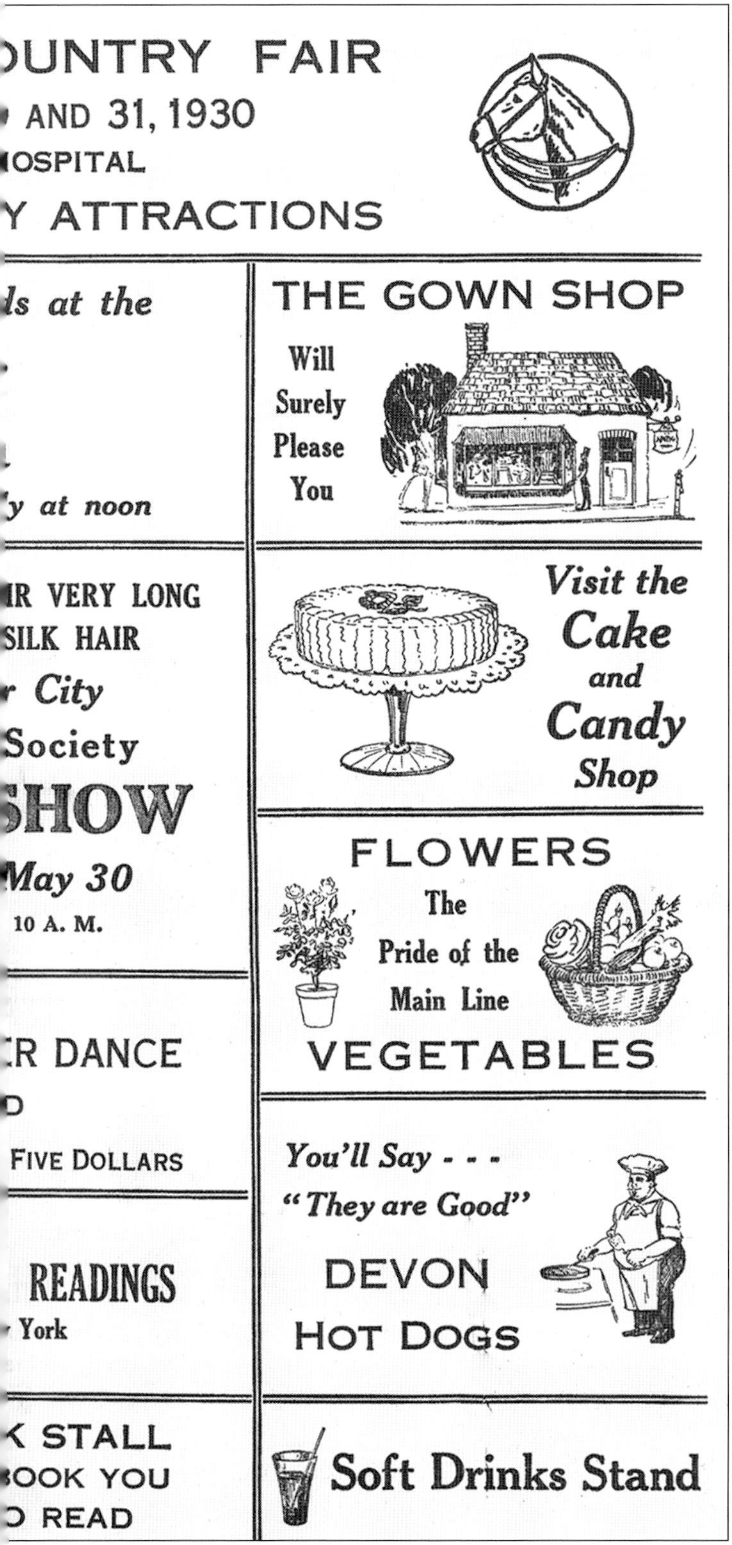

The Devon Country Fair continued to grow as volunteers generated ideas to increase income for the hospital. New booths were built. Volunteers made fudge to sell in the Candy Booth, stitched homemade goods for the Bryn Mawr Hospital Shop, and shopped for gift items for the Hobby House. At the same time, concession booths such as The Gown Shop sprang up on the grounds. Devon discontinued cigarette sales in 1935 to eliminate "a bad element." As the show grew from a three-day event to a six-day one, so did the food booths. While the Ice Cream Booth, Soft Drinks Stand, and Tea House were steeped in Devon tradition, the Hot Dog and Hamburger Booths were introduced and to this day remain staples of the Devon Country Fair.

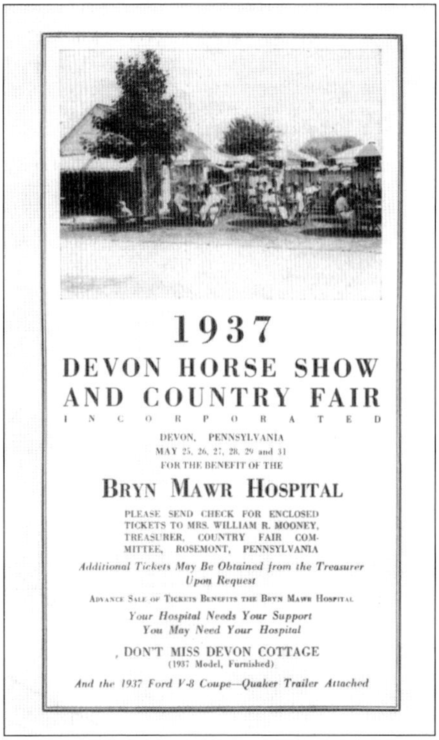

This 1937 advertisement entices spectators to purchase show tickets for the benefit of Bryn Mawr Hospital. Drawings for prizes became quite popular, and a 1937 Ford V-8 coupe with an attached Quaker trailer for family road trips was an item for raffle. The marquee prize was the 1937 Devon Cottage. Isaac H. Clothier Jr. presented a deed to the Devon Country Fair in 1936 for ground adjoining his Radnor estate, Sunnybrook, on which the first Devon Cottage was built.

In this late-1920s photograph, Isaac H. Clothier III (left) and Banning Grange (center) are shown selling chance tickets at the Devon Horse Show and Country Fair to Marion Moll Rollins (right). The grand prize for the raffle that year was a trip to Europe.

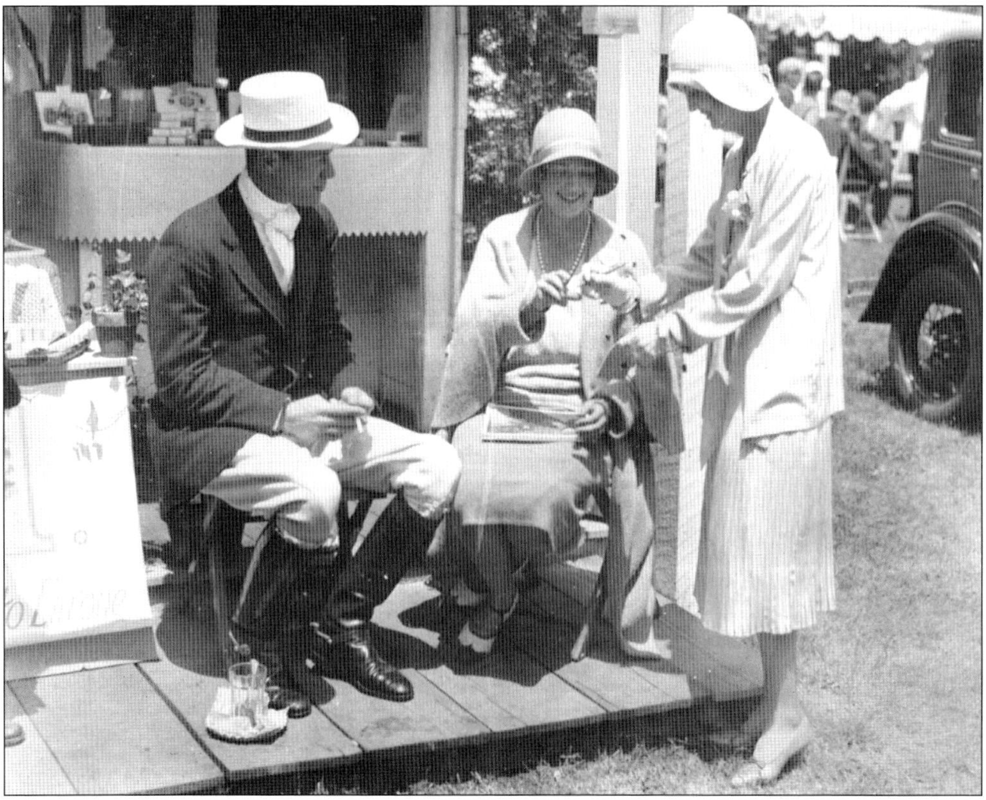

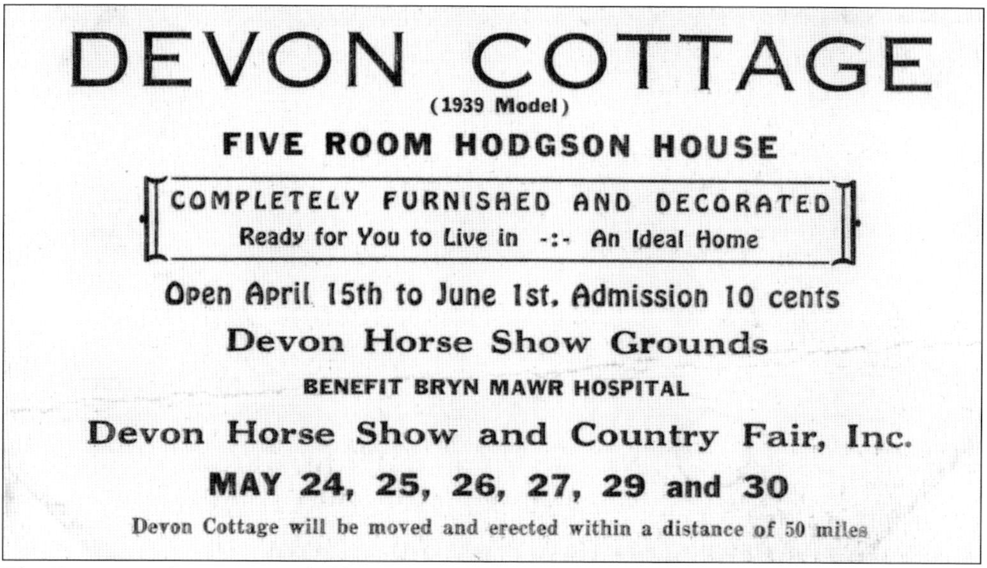

The Devon Derby remains a hallmark of the Devon Country Fair. Although today the Derby features a car donated from local dealerships as the key prize, in years past, the Devon Cottage was the coveted win. The cottage varied in style but was built by Strawbridge and Clothier for the benefit of Bryn Mawr Hospital. Below, Devon Country Fair chair Catherine Clothier Grange and Bryn Mawr Hospital Women's Board member Catherine Warden inspect the Devon Cottage model in 1947. The cottage was shipped to Devon in sections and constructed on the grounds. Decorated by Good Housekeeping Studio, tours were provided during the show. Once a winner was selected, it was moved and erected to a distance within 50 miles of the show. (Below, courtesy of the SCRC, Temple University.)

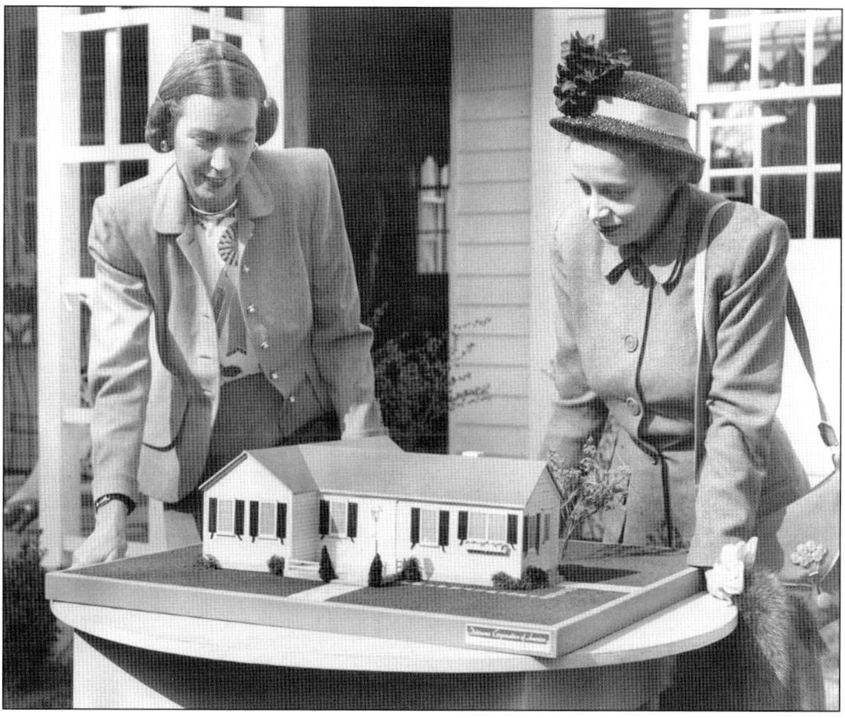

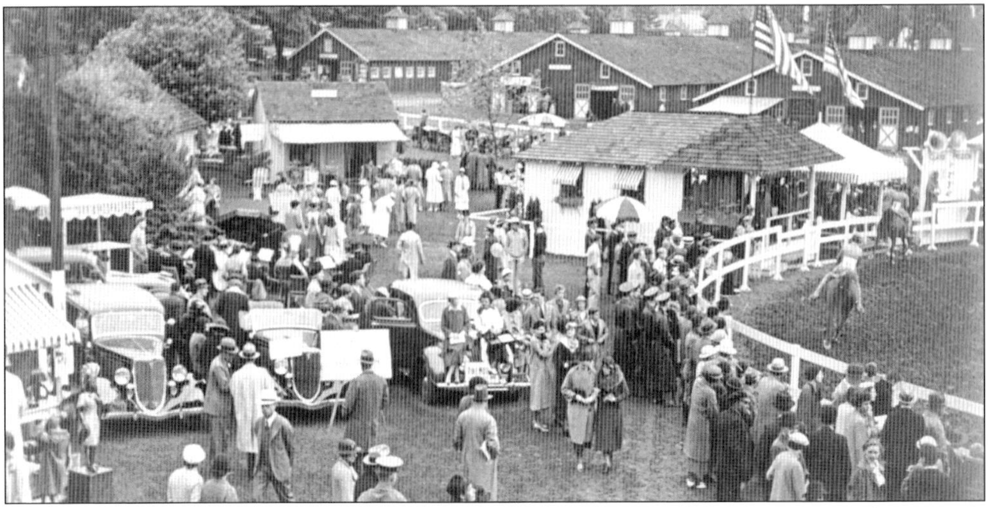

This 1935 panoramic view of the country fair, with spectators ringside to the horse show, is not unlike a scene from Devon today. The Derby prizes no longer feature a house, but luxury cars donated by local dealerships and displayed on the grounds encourage spectators to take a chance, just as they did in 1935. (Courtesy of Suburban & Wayne Times Collection, Radnor Historical Society.)

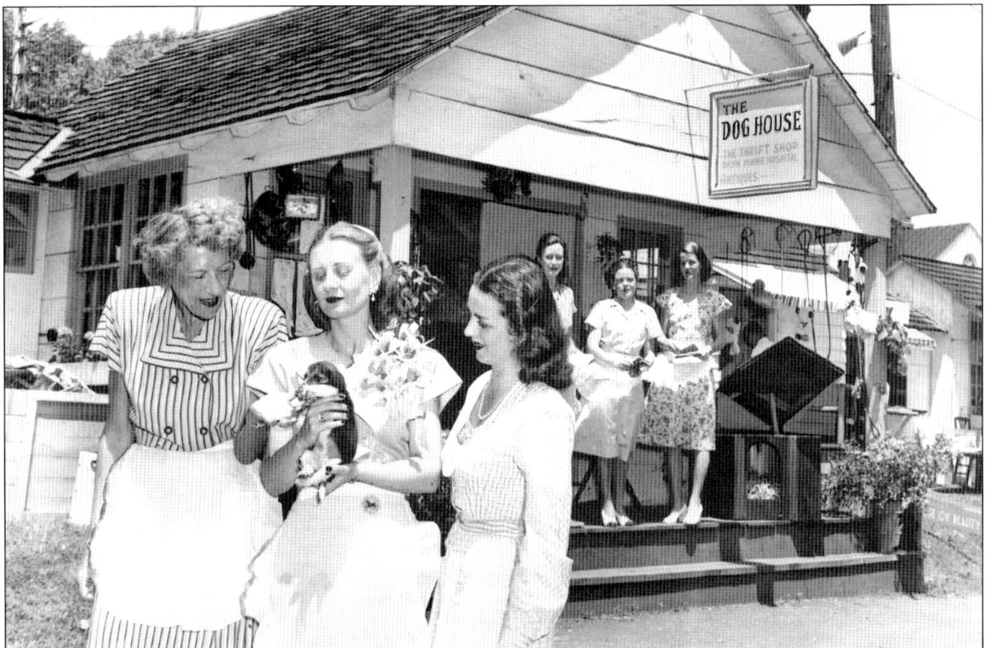

Marjorie Lyden Brownlee, Lillian Graham Snyder, and Emily Rowe Remington hold a puppy to welcome patrons into the Dog House booth at the Devon Country Fair in 1947. Sponsored by the Bryn Mawr Hospital Thrift Shop, the booth featured heirlooms and other collectibles. Antiques booths were popular at the country fair from 1919 until the mid-2000s. Carol Harriman Smith, chair of the New and Old Antique Booth, received a gold wedding ring in the mail sent to the show via special delivery with an anonymous note reading, "You can have it, I don't want it, it meant nothing but misfortune to me." It sold for $1.00. (Courtesy of the SCRC, Temple University.)

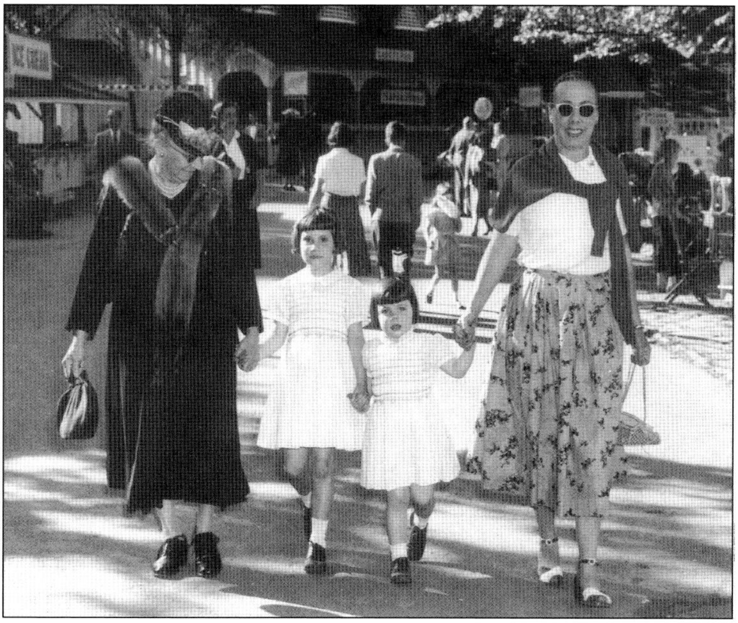

Dorothy Henderson Pinch and her mother take children Robin and Jay through the prominent stretch of the Devon Country Fair featuring the food booths and the Cafeteria. The trees, gazebo, and other structures remain on the grounds today. The Hot Dog Booth now occupies the space of the Ice Cream Booth in this 1940s photograph.

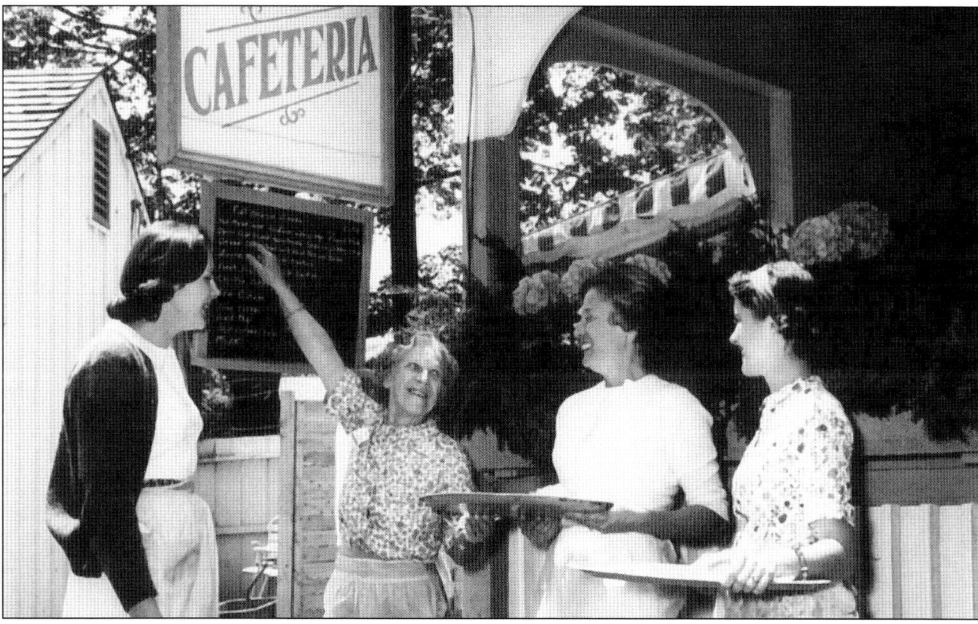

Edith Johnson Croll (second from left), chair of the Cafeteria, reviews the luncheon menu with volunteers, from left to right, Franziska Red, Jane Cooling Heaver, and chair Elinor Brooks Schoettle. After 51 years as a volunteer, Croll's special family mayonnaise was a staple. Her mother was the booth's first chair in 1919. At that time, most of the food was donated, including a planked salmon from the Barclay Hotel in Philadelphia. Chauffeur-driven limousines from local estates would arrive with roasts and fresh produce. Today, the Cafeteria is known as the Garden Café, and it still offers elegant lunches and dinners in the pavilion. With lines out the door on most evenings, the meals are provided by a private caterer, with volunteers assisting in food service. Linen tablecloths and flowers remain the booth's hallmarks, where patrons dine under the pavilion in a wooded grove.

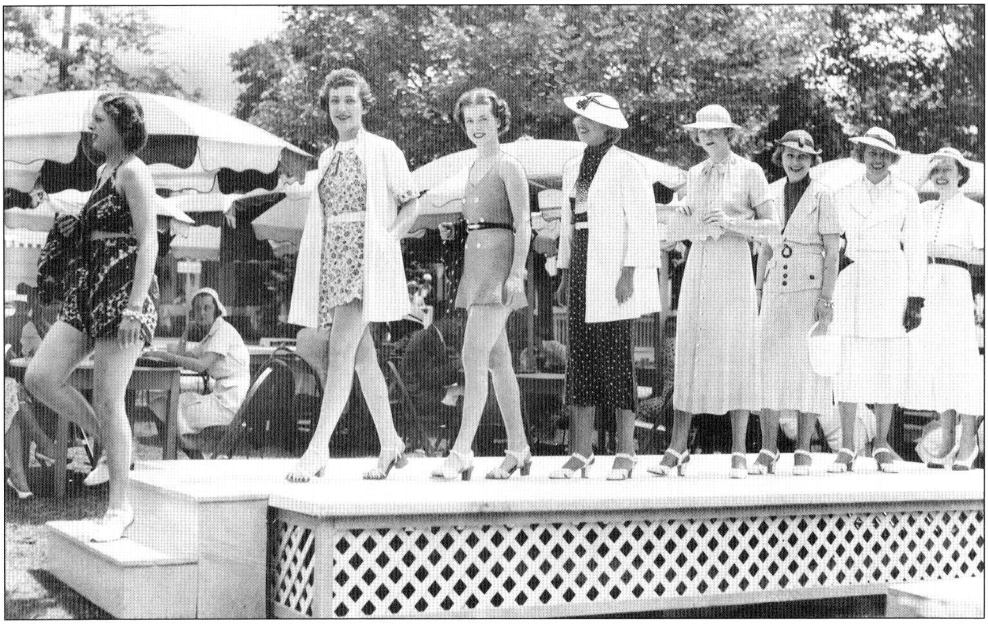

Beginning in the 1930s, fashion shows were a Devon tradition. Young models showed off the latest fashions and mingled with spectators to advertise merchandise. In the late 1950s and early 1960s, booths on the grounds included department stores such as Bonwit Teller, Strawbridge and Clothier, and Saks Fifth Avenue. Bonwit Teller hosted a fashion show daily at 12:30 p.m. Also known as the Showcase of Fashion, Devon volunteers dressed in the latest styles modeled in the Devon Cafeteria pavilion. (Above, courtesy of the SCRC, Temple University.)

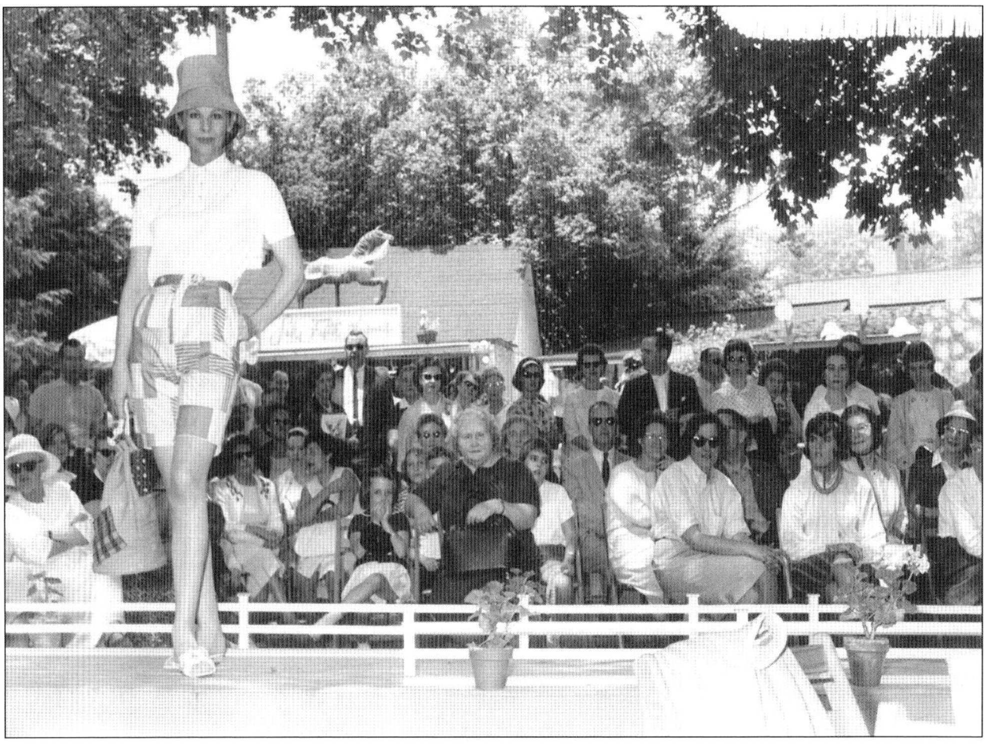

Devon Country Fair
Committees
1955

Mrs. James F. Mitchell, Jr., *Co-Chairman*
Mrs. Karl R. Schoettle, *Co-Chairman*
Mrs. Clarence J. Lewis, Jr., *Secretary*
Mrs. Orus J. Matthews, *Treasurer*

OFFICE
Mrs. Robert G. Wilder, *Executive Secretary*
Bryn Mawr Community Building
9 Bryn Mawr Avenue
Bryn Mawr, Pennsylvania
Telephone: LAwrence 5-0136

EXECUTIVE COMMITTEE

Mrs. Newlin F. Davis, Jr.
Mrs. Everett W. Day
Mrs. Herbert H. Fritz
Mrs. Richard E. Hanson
Mrs. Philip L. Lee
Mrs. Edward B. Myers, Jr.
Mrs. Clarence A. Warden, Jr.

BOARD OF DIRECTORS

Mrs. Roland T. Addis
Mrs. Donald Alexander
Mrs. Walter Annenberg
Mrs. Edward D. Atlee
Mrs. Russell A. Cannon
Mrs. Cummins Catherwood
Mrs. Charles C. G. Chaplin
Mrs. Isaac H. Clothier, Jr.
Mrs. Tristram C. Colket
Mrs. Gribbel Corkran
Mrs. Joseph N. Ewing
Mrs. Howard Fair
Mrs. Romain C. Hassrick
Mrs. William C. Hunneman
Mrs. J. Malcolm Johnston
Mrs. Arthur C. Kaufmann
Mrs. Scott G. Lamb
Mrs. H. Elliott Lambert
Mrs. John Markle, 2nd
Mrs. Samuel McCreery
Mrs. Bingham Milne
Mrs. Sidney W. Milne
Mrs. Charles C., Norris, Jr.
Mrs. Arthur E. Pew, Jr.
Mrs. J. Howard Pew
Mrs. Joseph N. Pew, Jr.
Mrs. William M. Prizer
Mrs. Harry T. Saylor
Mrs. James M. R. Sinkler
Mrs. Joseph N. Snellenberg
Mrs. John A. Stevenson
Mrs. Frederick B. Stimson
Mrs. John B. Thayer
Mrs. William Coxe Wright

COMMITTEE CHAIRMEN

AIDES
CHAIRMAN
Mrs. Charles LeB. Homer, Jr.

CAFETERIA
CO-CHAIRMEN
Mrs. Edwin J. Schoettle, Jr.
Mrs. Warren A. Croll, Jr.
VICE-CHAIRMAN
Mrs. Joseph W. Lippincott, Jr.

CANDY
CO-CHAIRMEN
Mrs. J. Jay Hodupp
Mrs. Joel B. Davis

CONCESSIONS
CHAIRMAN
Mrs. Edward B. Myers, Jr.
VICE-CHAIRMEN
Mrs. Victor L. Drexel
Mrs. A. J. Drexel Paul, Jr.

DEVON DAY AT WOODSIDE PARK
CO-CHAIRMEN
Mrs. C. Egerton Warburton
Mrs. Reeves Wetherill
Mrs. R. Stockton Taylor

DEVON DERBY
HONORARY CHAIRMAN
Mrs. Clarence A. Warden, Jr.
CO-CHAIRMEN
Mrs. William F. Tiernan, Jr.
Mrs. Donald M. Sykes
Mrs. J. Houston Young

DEVON DRESS
CO-CHAIRMEN
Mrs. Francis M. Brooke, Jr.
Mrs. Francis R. Strawbridge, Jr.

DEVON FAIR ON SUBURBAN SQUARE
CHAIRMAN
Mrs. T. L. Emory Eysmans
VICE-CHAIRMAN
Mrs. Harleston R. Wood
FLEA MARKET
Mrs. William Thomas LaRue
FASHION SHOW
Mrs. Albert K. Dannenbaum
Mrs. Richard Fielding
MERCHANT'S DINNER
Mrs. G. Gordon Snyder
TREASURER
Mrs. Russell A. Cannon
WINDOW JUDGES
Mrs. Clarence J. Lewis, Jr.
MYSTERY PACKAGES
Mrs. J. Philip Dunn
Mrs. Shepley E. Evans

GARDEN BOOTH
CO-CHAIRMEN
Mrs. L. Wilfrid Coleman
Mrs. Richard C. Bond
Mrs. Eldridge J. Freeman

GROUNDS
CHAIRMAN
Mrs. W. Scott Smith, Jr.
VICE-CHAIRMAN
Mrs. W. James D. Darling

HOSPITAL SHOP
HONORARY CHAIRMAN
Mrs. Lee Rumsey
CO-CHAIRMEN
Mrs. W. W. Keen Butcher
Mrs. John S. Dixon, Jr.

HOT DOGS
CO-CHAIRMEN
Mrs. Reeves Bunting
Mrs. John F. Spahr

INFORMATION
CHAIRMAN
Mrs. Ernestine C. Dexter

NEEDLEPOINT BENCH
CO-CHAIRMEN
Mrs. Louis H. Palmer
Mrs. Patrick Costello

NYLON PROJECT
CHAIRMAN
Mrs. J. Holcombe Genung

SANDWICHES
CO-CHAIRMEN
Mrs. Osborne R. Roberts
Mrs. Raymond V. Shepherd

SOFT DRINKS AND ICE CREAM
CO-CHAIRMEN
Mrs. George L. Justice, Jr.
Mrs. David E. Williams, 3rd
Mrs. Allan M. Johnson
Mrs. Ralph C. Gifford, Jr.

TEA HOUSE
CO-CHAIRMEN
Mrs. Robert H. Lee
Mrs. Louis H. Allen

TOYS
CHAIRMAN
Mrs. William G. Pierce
VICE-CHAIRMAN
Mrs. George R. Brodie

DIRECTOR OF PUBLICITY
Mrs. Katharine M. David

RADIO AND TELEVISION
CHAIRMAN
Mrs. James F. Warren, Jr.

SATURDAY	MONDAY	TUESDAY	WEDNESDAY	THURSDAY	FRIDAY	SATURDAY
May 28th	May 30th	May 31st	June 1st	June 2nd	June 3rd	June 4th

The Devon Country Fair had 21 booths or committees in 1955. The show ran seven days that year, and there were 1,000 volunteers recorded. The Devon Horse Show and Country Fair donation was nearly $65,000. In social circles at the time, a woman was referred to by her husband's name in formal address. The 1955 Devon Horse Show Program reflected that tradition.

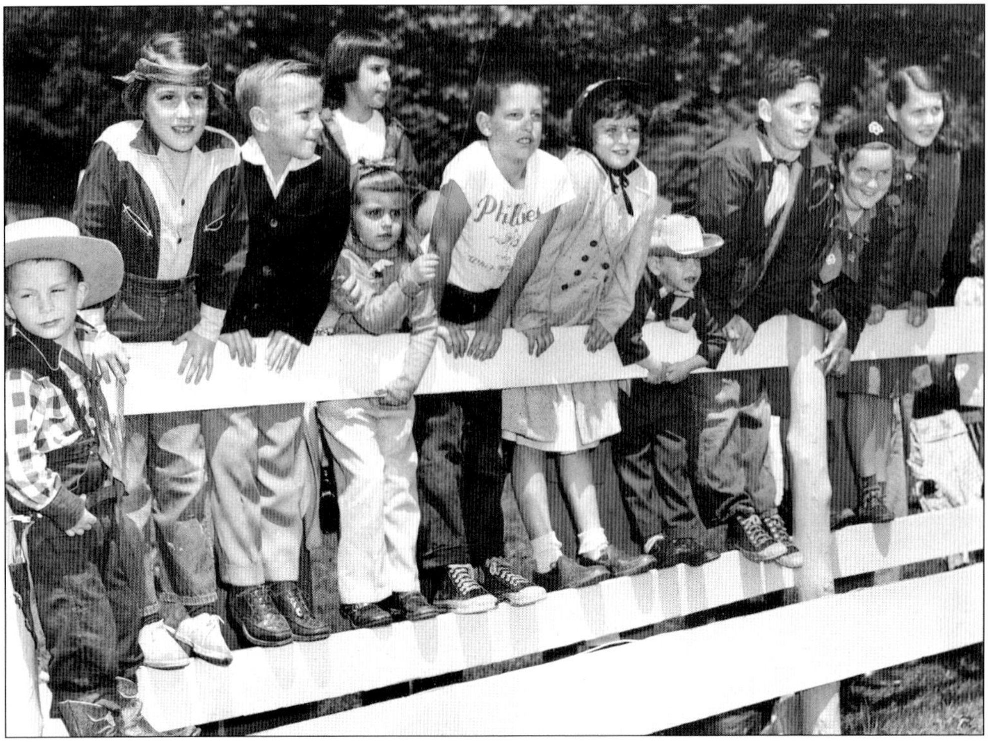

Devon is a magical place for children, whether they are watching the ponies during Junior Weekend or enjoying an afternoon at the Midway. Pictured below, Catherine Mather, Thayer Dixon, and Carla Barringer enjoy the games, rides, and prizes at the Midway, which was introduced to the country fair in the mid-1950s to entice visitors of all ages to the show. With a cone of cotton candy clutched in one hand and a bag of popcorn in the other, the Midway is fun for parents and children alike. Playing the various games or taking a ride on the high-in-the-sky Ferris wheel will keep children of all ages entertained for hours. (Both, courtesy of the SCRC, Temple University.)

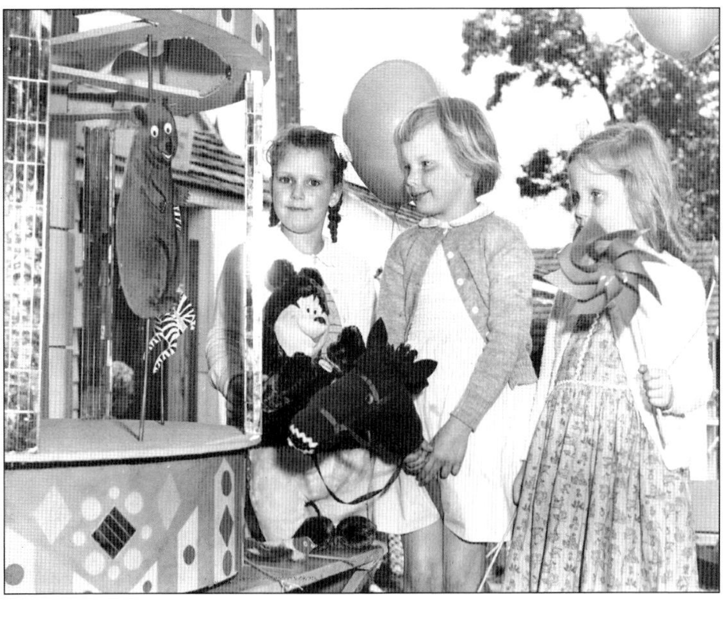

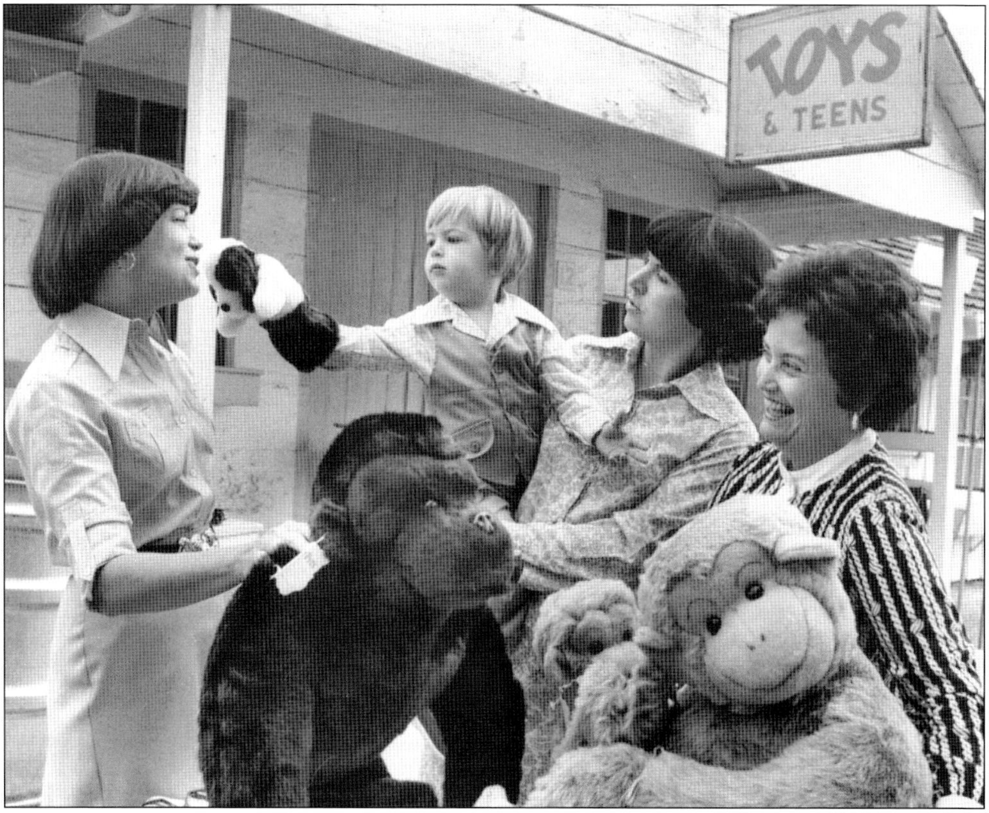

The Toys and Teens booth was a popular place for families. The committee gathered a choice collection of toys and trinkets for children attending the fair. Pictured above, Jeffrey Keller, held by his mother, cochair Cathy Keller (center), entertains cochairs Karen Meyers (left) and Ruth Davin (right) with a hand puppet from the booth in 1977. Pictured at right, Elizabeth Brodie Spence (left) and Frances Lambeth Reynolds (right) sell balloons at the booth in the 1950s. The Toys and Teens booth is no longer at the fair, but the Devon Kids Souvenirs booth now provides toys and gifts for children. (Both, courtesy of the SCRC, Temple University.)

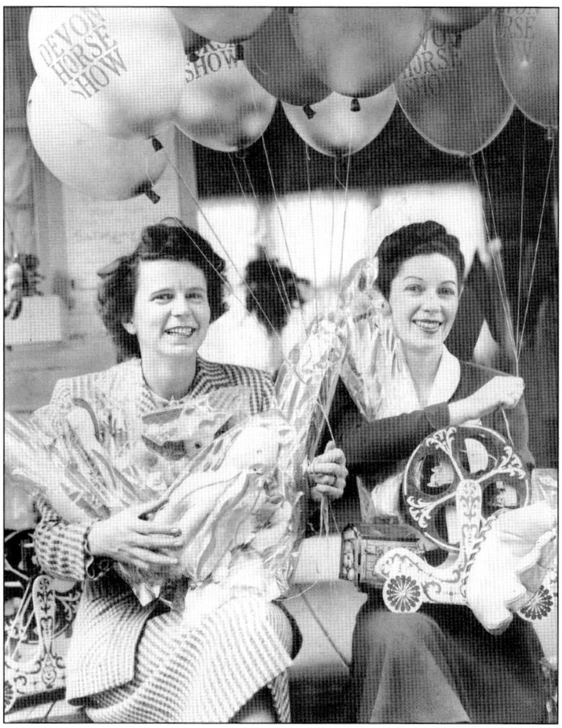

Strictly Off the Record

you are cordially invited to

THE "DEVON-TEEN" DANCE

at the
TV Guide Building
Radnor and Chester Roads
Radnor, Penna.
on
Friday evening, May the Fifteenth

$5 per couple — from 9 P.M. to 11:30 P.M. — $2.50 stag

This includes admission to the Devon Horse Show and Country Fair after 5 P.M.
Saturday, May 23, 1964 ONLY

Tie and Coat requested — Entertainment - Prizes
RSVP by May 11th — Refreshments

Mrs. Walter F. Keenan, Jr. - Mrs. Reeves Bunting, Co-Chairmen
Sponsored by The Devon Hot Dog Committee

The Devon Teen Dance was a new attraction introduced to the Devon Horse Show and Country Fair in 1960, when Warner Bros. movie star and teen idol Tab Hunter was scheduled to visit the show. Below, the Devon teen dance committee meets in 1964 to plan its annual Record Hop. The tickets were sold for $5 per couple or $2.50 stag and included admission to the Devon Horse Show and Country Fair after 5:00 p.m.

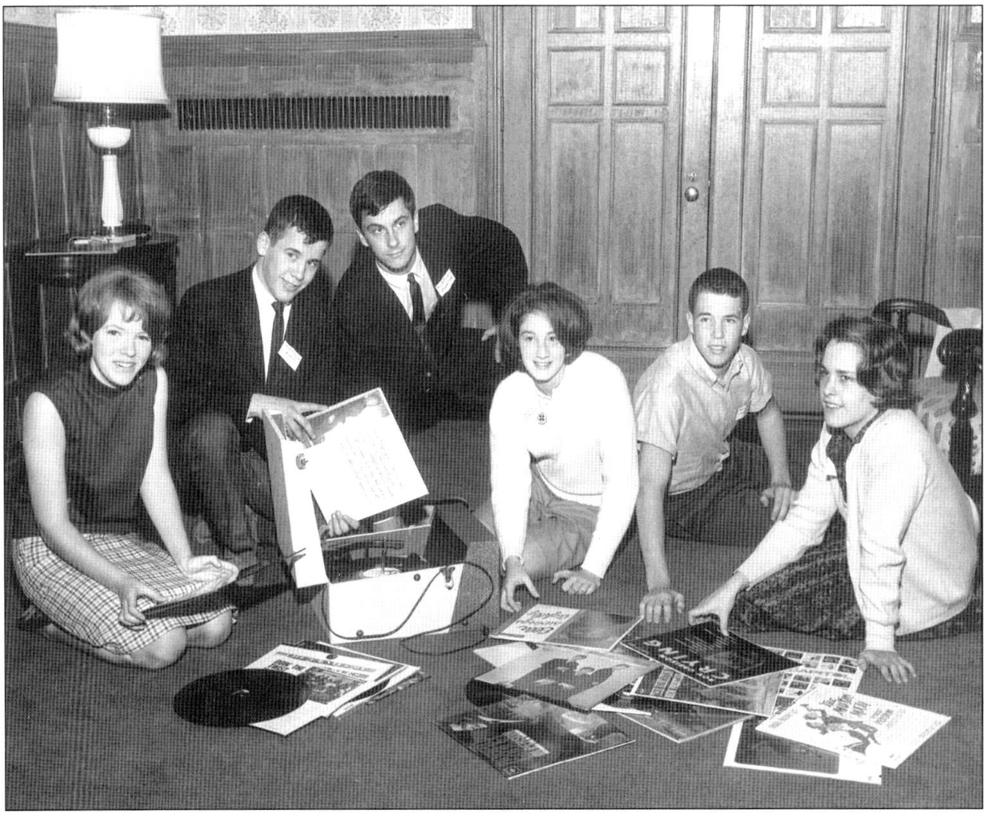

On Devon's 75th anniversary, the Devon Diamond Caper event was held at the Philadelphia jewelry store Bailey, Banks & Biddle. Country fair chairs modeled a $25,000 collection of 20th Century Fox costumes worn by actresses Elizabeth Taylor, Julie Andrews, and Barbara Streisand. In later years, the Devon Country Fair held a pre-event cocktail buffet highlighting an exhibition of porcelain art sculptures and gifts of state to Soviet leader Leonid Brezhnev.

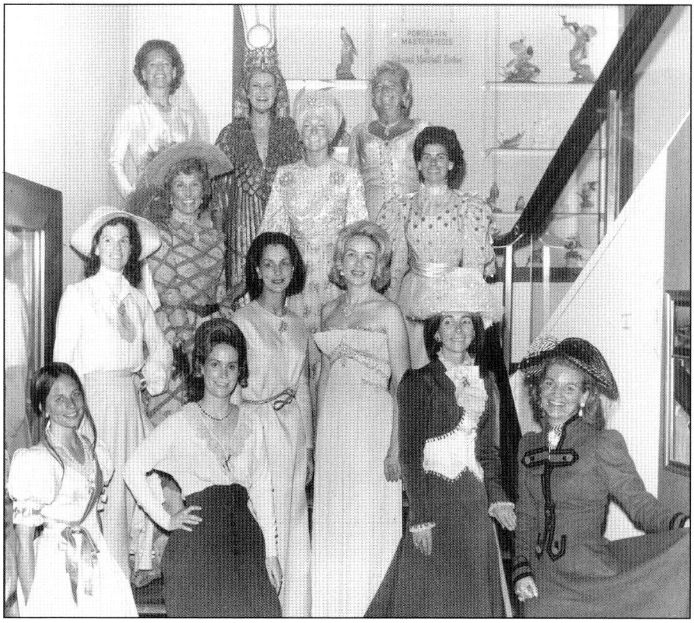

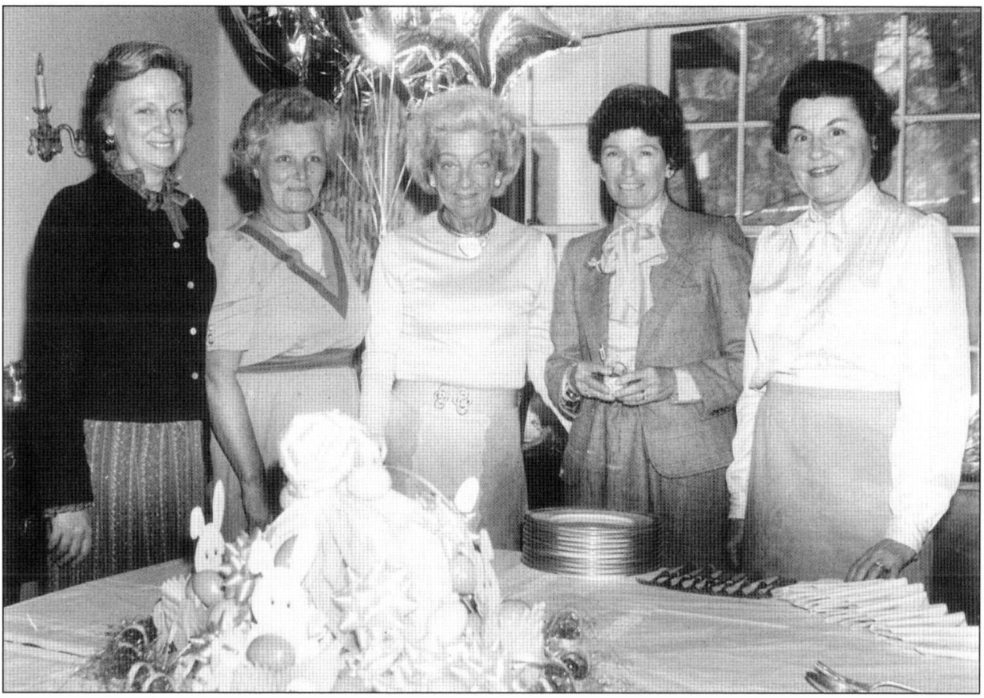

The annual Champagne Devon Derby Tea was a tradition held in January to launch the four-month sales of derby tickets before the show. In addition to a preview of derby prizes, country fair members would model the latest fashions sponsored by department stores and local boutiques. Shown here are, from left to right, Mims Kerr, Nancy Ligget, Priscilla Page, Carol Roberts, and Nancy Lander.

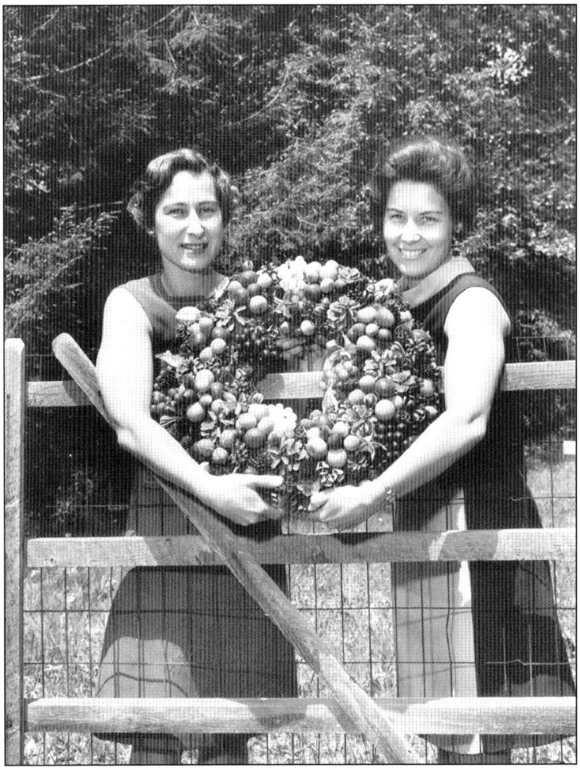

Smiling at the prospect of a bigger and better year at the Devon Horse Show and Country Fair, chairs of the Garden Booth, Virginia Purinton (left) and Ann Marie Hyser (right), pose with a wreath to be sold at the show.

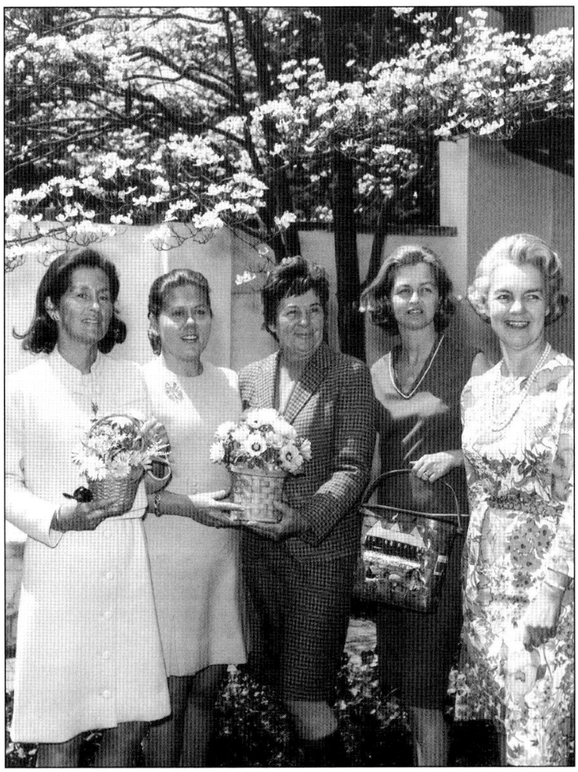

Devon chairs Beth Featherman, Donna Henderson, Phyl Yarnell, and Peggy Borkland pose during a Devon planning meeting. Making plans for the Devon Horse Show and Country Fair is a yearlong volunteer effort.

Crowds gather at the Devon Horse Show in 1963 to purchase tickets at the entrance to the grounds. On opening day, Grand Prix night, and weekend evenings, lines of cars from Lancaster Avenue turn onto Dorset Road to await entry into the show. During the dinner rush, crowds gather outside the Cafeteria and food booths. Lines for the Hamburger, Hot Dog, and Ice Cream Booths and Garden Café still remain today, as spectators enjoy dinner before hurrying to their boxes and seats for the 8:00 start of evening classes.

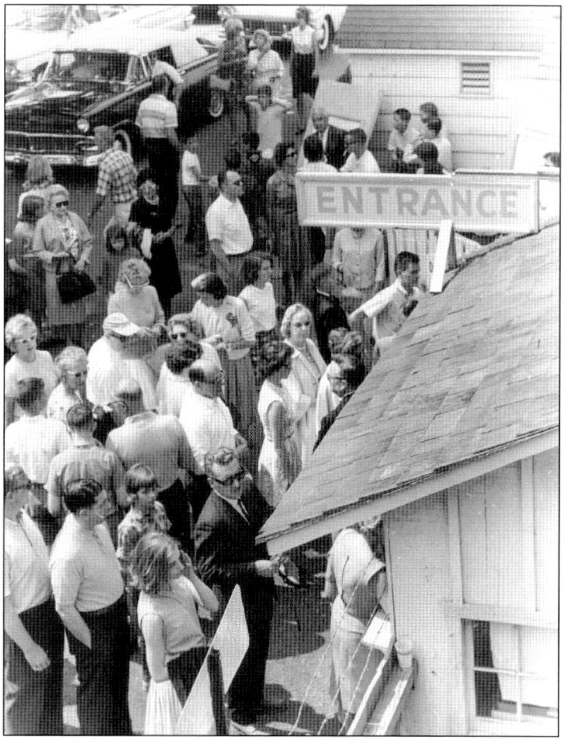

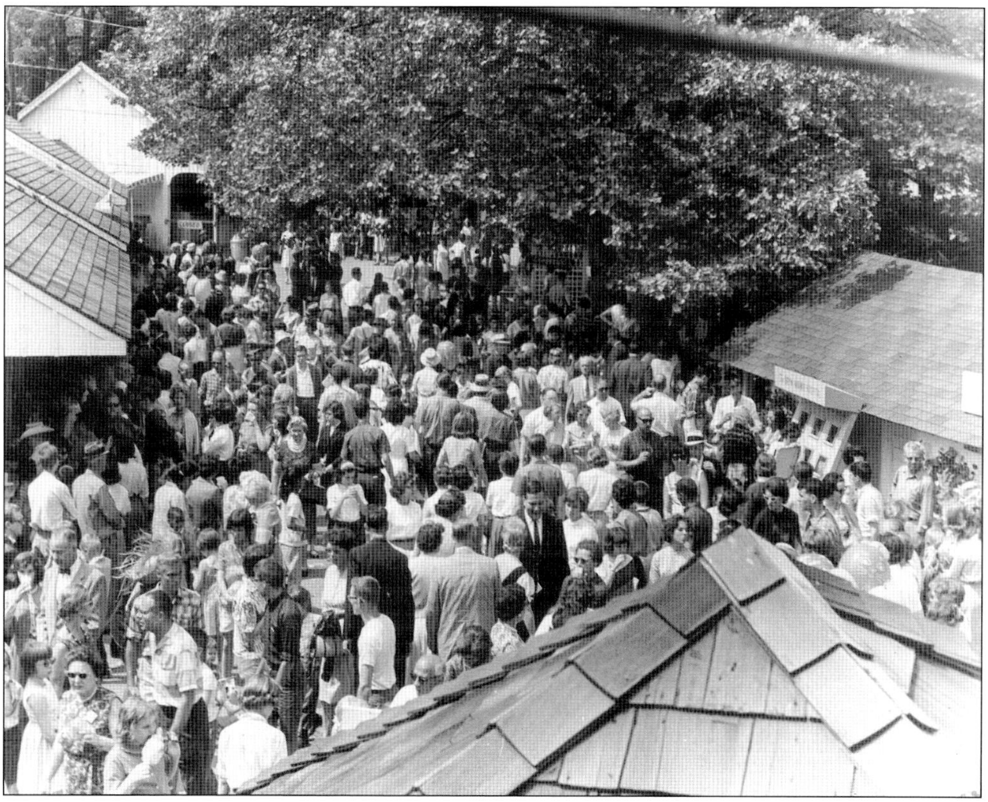

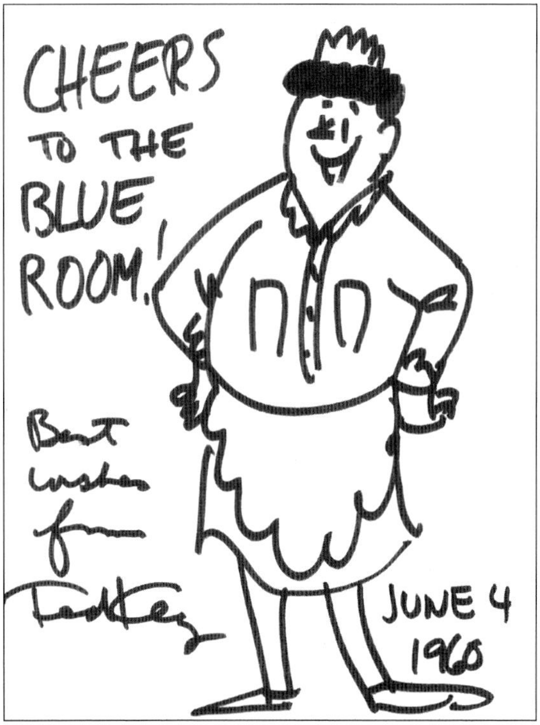

The Blue Room is open to Devon Horse Show and Country Fair chairs, executive committee members, and directors to relax in during the show. Nestled underneath the grandstands, it is a place to connect with fellow volunteers, catch up on the latest show updates, and check to see which country fair booth is beating its numbers from last year in a race to make the largest contribution to Bryn Mawr. A celebrity sighting may happen every now and then. In 1960, Ted Key, the cartoonist best known as the creator of *Hazel*, later a television series, left his mark on the Blue Room, as seen at left. In the image below, Carl Ballantine, who starred as Torpedoman's Mate Lester Gruber in *McHale's Navy*, visits committee members on May 23, 1964.

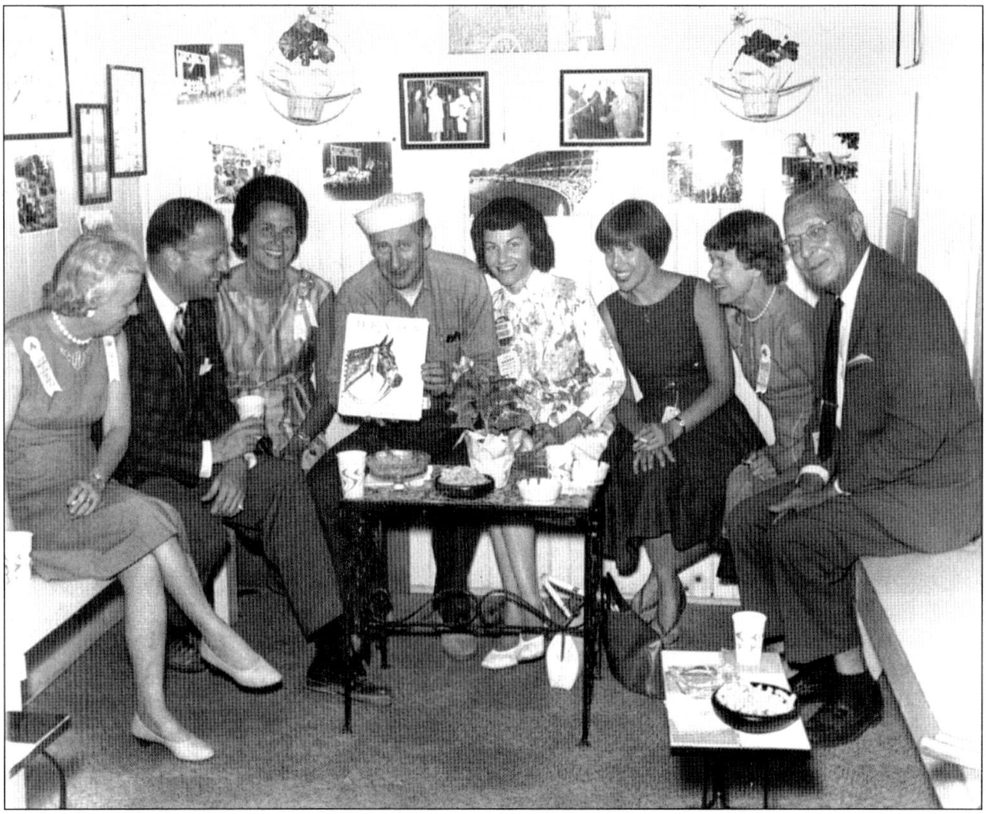

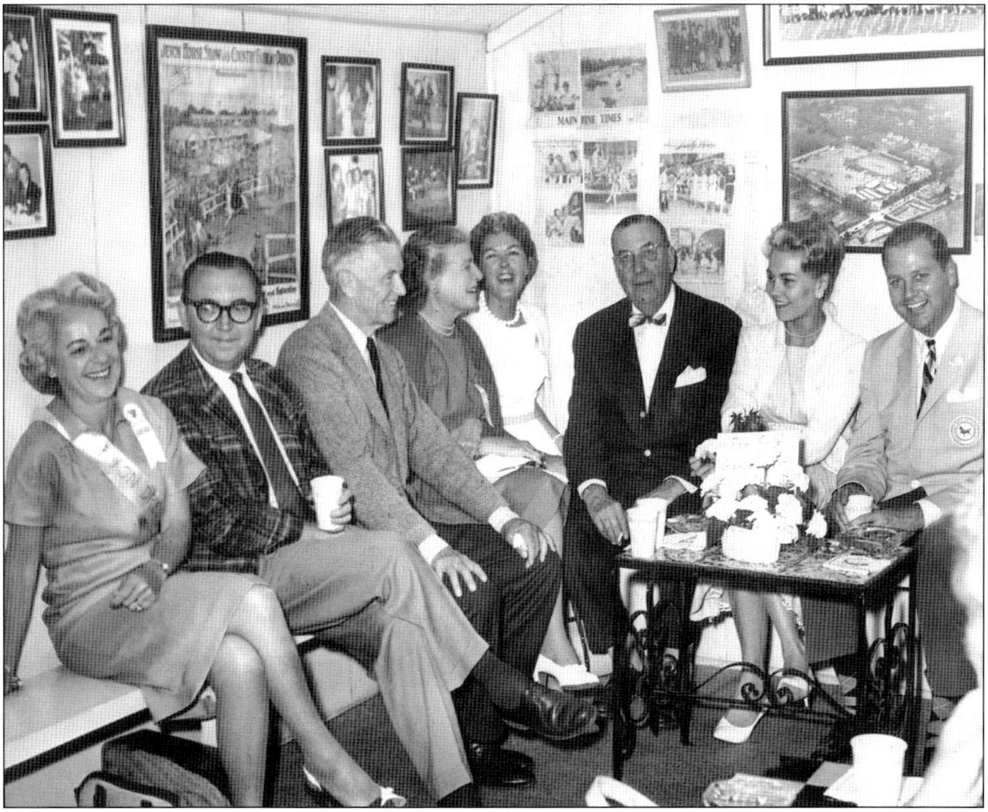

Along the walls of the Blue Room hang archival photographs, artwork, memorabilia, and photographs of Devon legends through the years. In one corner hangs a song written and sung by Devon competitor, philanthropist, chair, and director Helen Hope Montgomery Scott on June 5, 1982, the closing night of the show. Scott has described the chairs of the Devon Country Fair as "thoroughbreds in their own right. . . . They've been absolutely great. I've admired every single one of them."

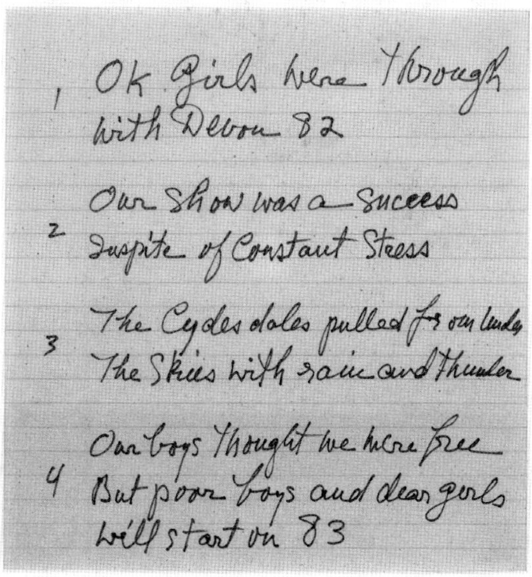

1 Ok Girls were Through
with Devon 82

Our Show was a success
2 Inspite of Constant Stress

The Cydesdales pulled for our lunder
3 The Skies with rain and thunder

Our boys thought we were free
4 But poor boys and dear girls
will start on 83

Hope Montgomery Scott wrote and sang these lyrics in the Blue Room, on closing night of the Devon Horse Show, June 5, 1982

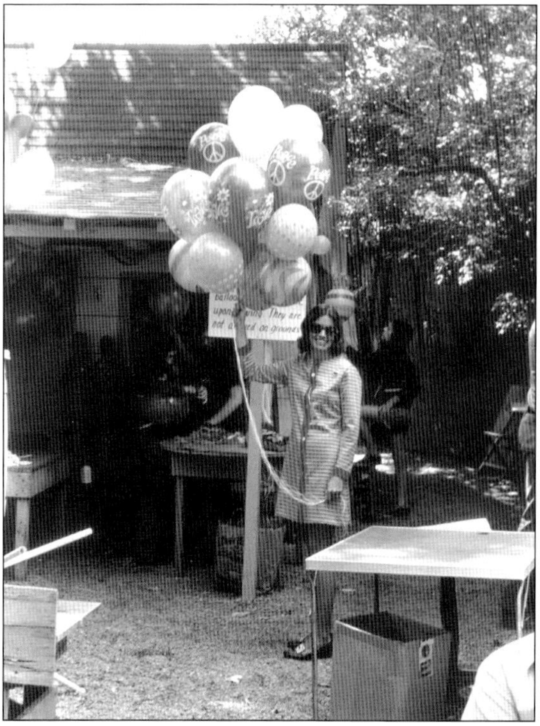

The 1970s brought many changes, but a strong sense of tradition still grounded the Devon Country Fair. Committees were expanded to include more chairs to balance the division of labor, as many had competing professional and family responsibilities. Chairs brought their children to assist them at the show, instilling early on virtues of volunteerism. Selling balloons is chair Karen Meyers, with her daughter Clary lending a hand. Both Meyerses continue to serve as chairs 40 years later.

Judith McNeely Mitchell, her son Andy, and friends Shea Muller, Skip Palmer, Ted Nash, and Brad Newberry watch Junior Weekend classes from her grandstand box seats. Many of the coveted boxes with premier views of the ring have been in families for generations. (Courtesy of the SCRC, Temple University.)

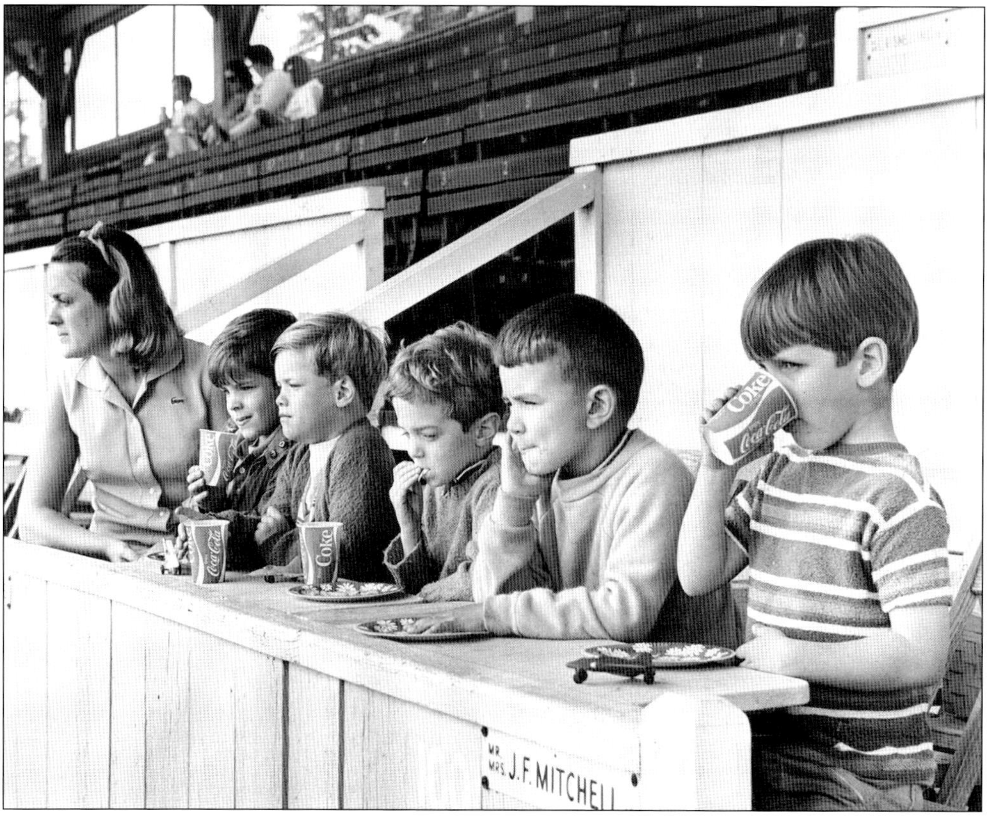

During Junior Weekend in 1969, artist Winnie Rumble creates a portrait of a young horsewoman, Susan Yeabsley. In between classes, young riders stroll through the Midway. (Courtesy of the SCRC, Temple University.)

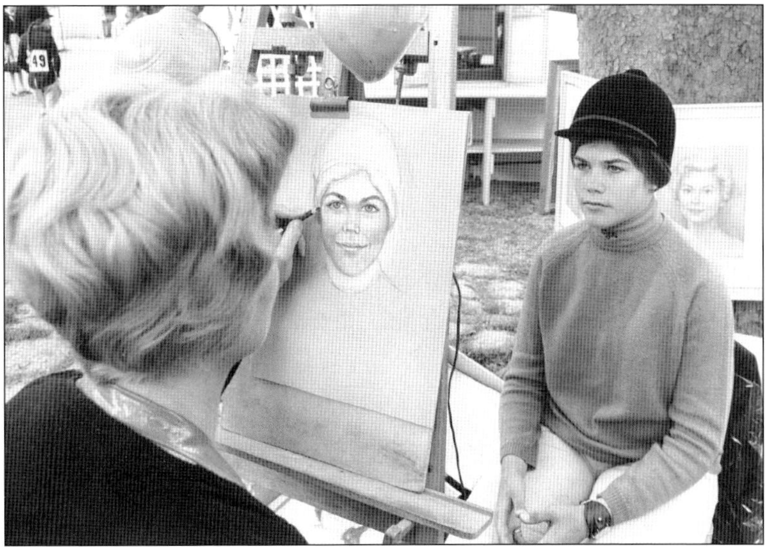

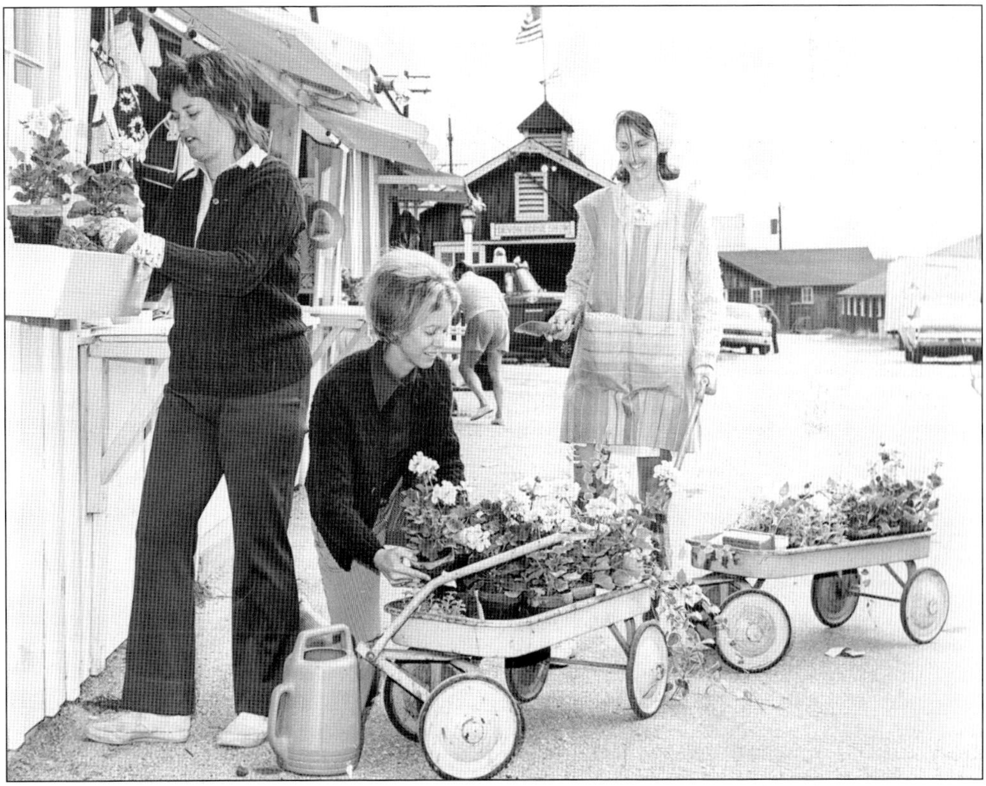

Window box planters are quickly filled with flowers before the start of the show by Anne Girvin, Sue North, and Catherine Mick in 1972. The flowers committee is still "growing" strong today, with plants, shrubs, and the coral pink geraniums sold to buyers on Sunday after the last class of the show. (Courtesy of the SCRC, Temple University.)

THE DEVON COUNTRY FAIR - 1971

Balance November 1st, 1970 . . . . $ 11,401.62

INCOME

African Safari	$ 3,800.00	
Antiques	5,035.71	
Blue Room	32.08	
Cafeteria	8,263.87	
Candy	5,840.69	
Concessions	15,582.72	
Devon Derby	31,167.10	
Devon Diamond Caper	4,025.60	
Devon Duplicate	3,108.80	
Donations	265.75	
Hospital Shop	8,759.69	
Hot Dogs	2,675.69	
Information	71.43	
Interest	6,327.16	
Inventory Credit	877.17	
Midway	19,046.22	
Operation Goldmine	9,181.75	
Paper Pony	2,034.03	
Sandwiches	9,029.15	
Ski Movie	927.89	
Soft Drinks	12,300.89	
Souvenirs	1,893.57	
Tailgate Sale - 1970	4,276.38	
Tea House	5,268.96	
Toys	7,500.00	
Total Income		$167,292.30

DISBURSEMENTS

Flowers	10.84	
Grounds	14,187.00	
Insurance	132.00	
Office Expenses	173.96	
Postage	150.00	
Printing	129.80	
Publicity	3,902.99	
Public Relations	543.73	
Secretarial Services	1,236.00	
Security		
Fire Protection	1,350.00	
Police	3,650.00	
Services of Bank Tellers	560.00	
Social Security	132.27	
Telephone	124.04	
Total Disbursements		$ 26,282.63

GROSS	$178,693.92
EXPENSES	26,282.63
NET PROFIT	$152,411.29
TO BRYN MAWR HOSPITAL	$135,000.00
Bank Balance November 1, 1971	$ 17,411.29

In the 1970s, the Devon Country Fair had 31 separate committees, including the Tea Cart, Cafeteria, Hot Dogs, and Candy. The largest booth income that year was from Devon Derby at $31,167.10, and the overall donation to the hospital that year was $135,000. Today, there are 26 Devon Country Fair committees. In 2019, the Devon Horse Show and Country Fair kicked off its new $2-million pledge to Bryn Mawr Hospital with a donation of $375,000, proceeds from the 2019 show.

In prior years, the committee chair would invite country fair volunteers to the booth. At minimal cost, volunteers would purchase aides' badges, which provided access to the grounds during all days of the show. Today, volunteers may sign up on the show's website and are encouraged to bring friends to join in the fun. They are no longer required to purchase badges, and parking passes are provided.

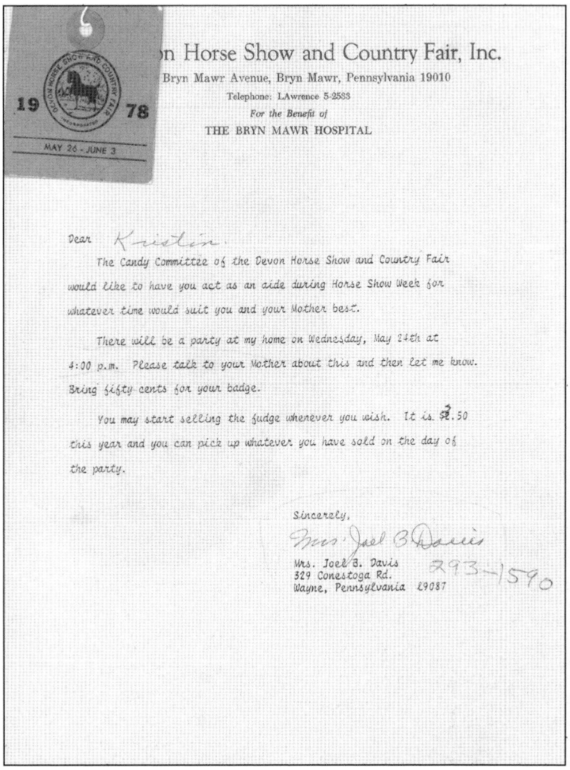

…n Horse Show and Country Fair, Inc.
Bryn Mawr Avenue, Bryn Mawr, Pennsylvania 19010
Telephone: LAwrence 5-2533
For the Benefit of
THE BRYN MAWR HOSPITAL

Dear Kristin.

The Candy Committee of the Devon Horse Show and Country Fair would like to have you act as an aide during Horse Show Week for whatever time would suit you and your Mother best.

There will be a party at my home on Wednesday, May 24th at 4:00 p.m. Please talk to your Mother about this and then let me know. Bring fifty cents for your badge.

You may start selling the fudge whenever you wish. It is $2.50 this year and you can pick up whatever you have sold on the day of the party.

Sincerely,

Mrs. Joel B. Davis

Mrs. Joel B. Davis
329 Conestoga Rd.
Wayne, Pennsylvania 19087 293-1590

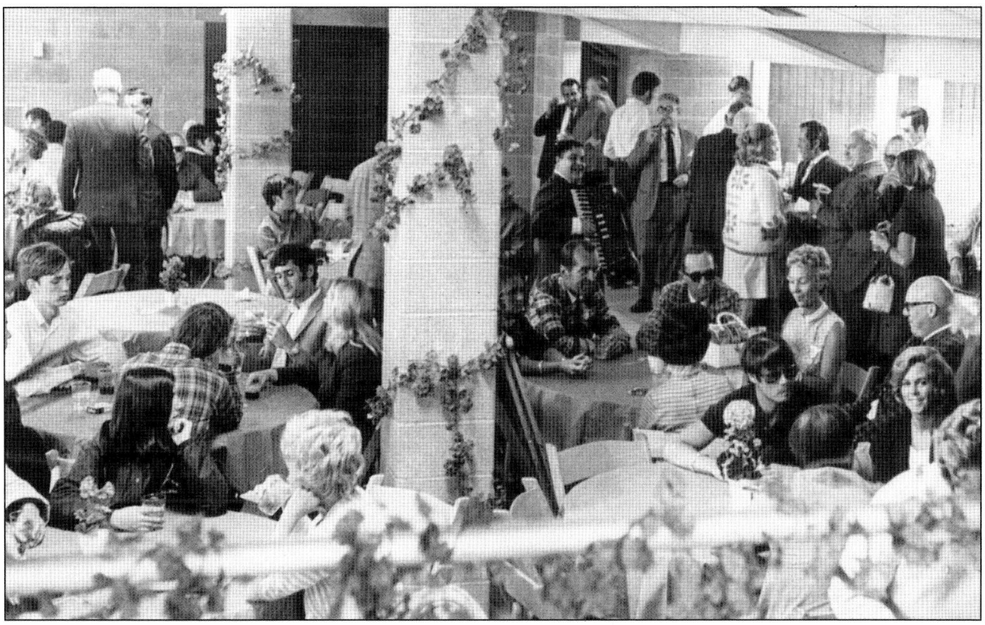

The Hospitality Room, nestled underneath the South Devon Grandstand, hosts horse show and country fair chairmen and executive committee members for various events, programs, and meetings. Here, at its annual press party in 1982, the executive committee welcomes the press and television and radio personalities. Also in this space, Devon Country Fair chairmen gather for meetings and host volunteers at the annual volunteer sign-up party a month before the event.

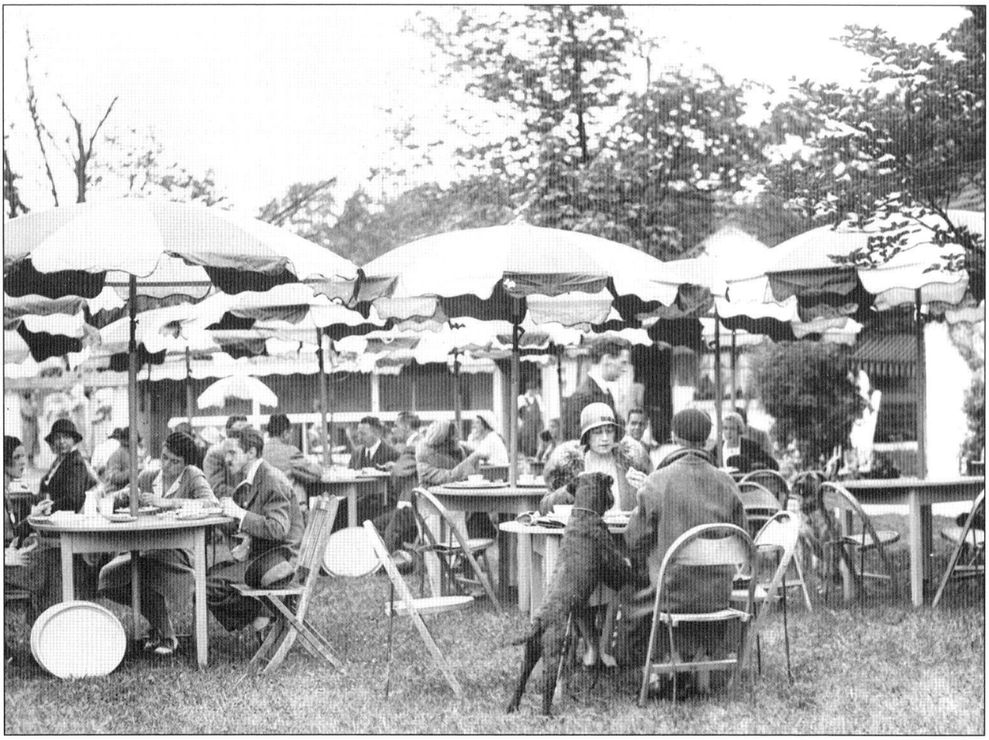

After 125 years, some traditions never change at Devon. Among them are families and friends gathering in the shaded Devon picnic grove under blue-and-white striped umbrellas. Well-behaved dogs on leashes are still welcome on the grounds. (Above, courtesy of The Engraver.)

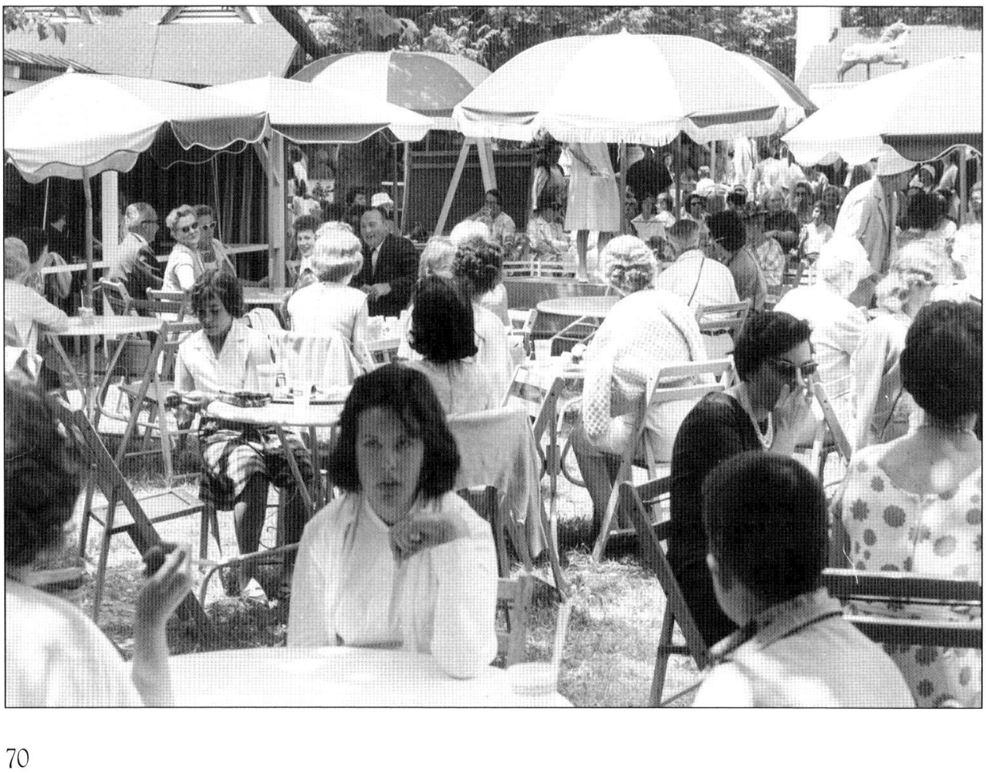

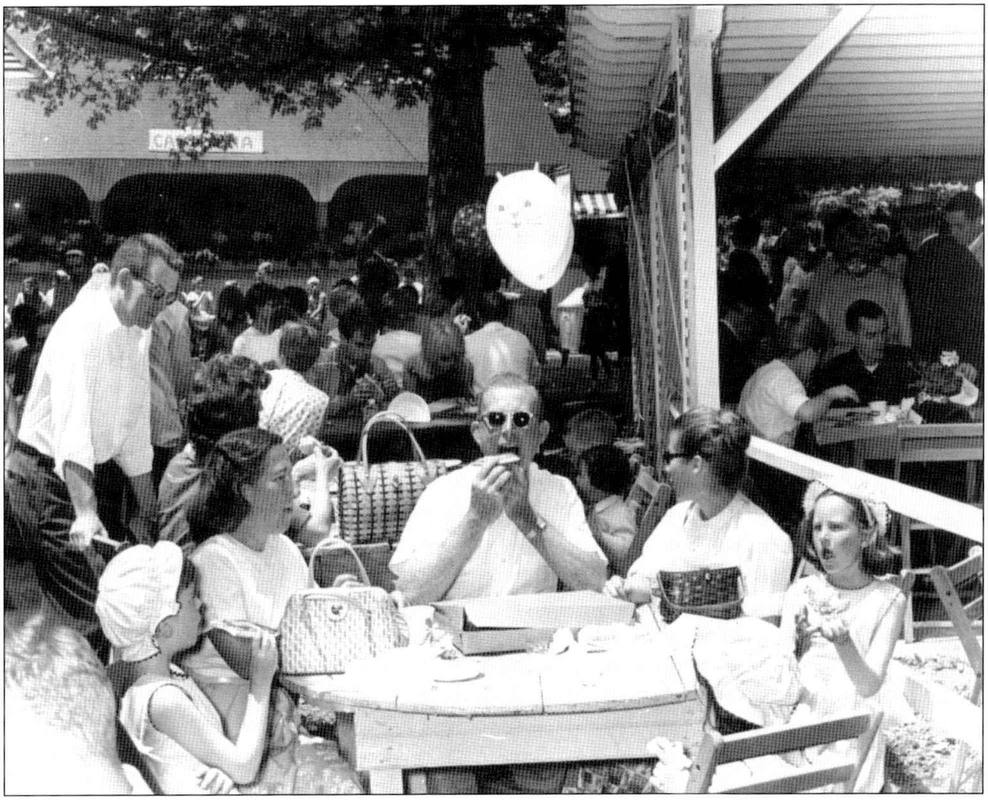

Volunteers no longer make potato salad, chicken salad, or deviled eggs at home to donate to the fair as was the custom in the 1920s. Whether it is a dinner at the Garden Café or a quick burger and fries, Devon meals remain a treat. (Right, courtesy of Brenda Carpenter Photography.)

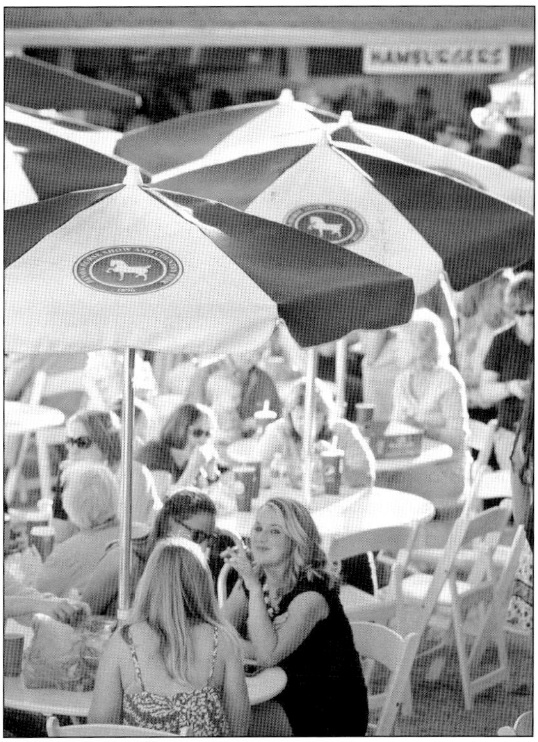

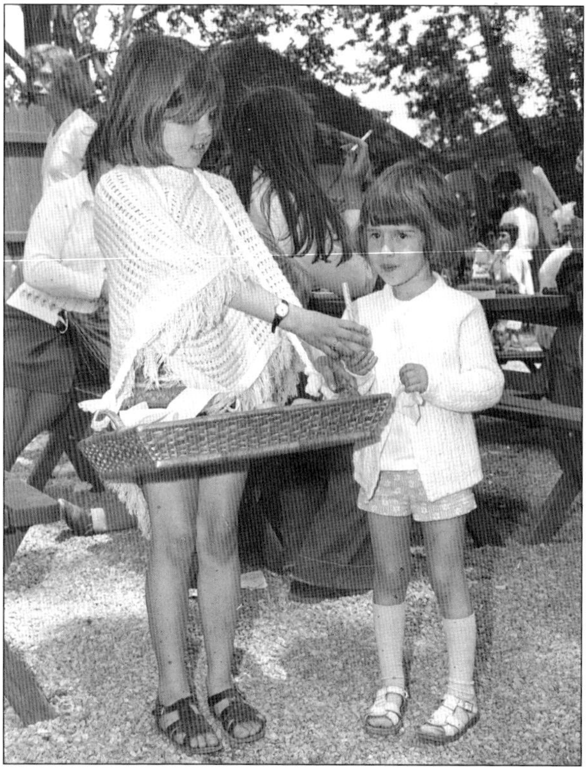

Two perennial Devon favorites are the fudge and lemon sticks, sold in the Candy Booth. The famous Devon Fudge dates back to 1947, when chair Mary Berclay Johnson contributed her family's recipe. Pictured at left, Kathy Lanahan sells a lemon stick to Christine Cannito. Traditionally only those who worked on the candy committee could serve as a candy and lemon stick carrier. A prize was annually awarded to the child who sold the most candy. Pictured below, Rooni the horse, owned by Edward Reeves, shares a lemon stick with Dawn Schwarsman. (Boh, courtesy of the SCRC, Temple University.)

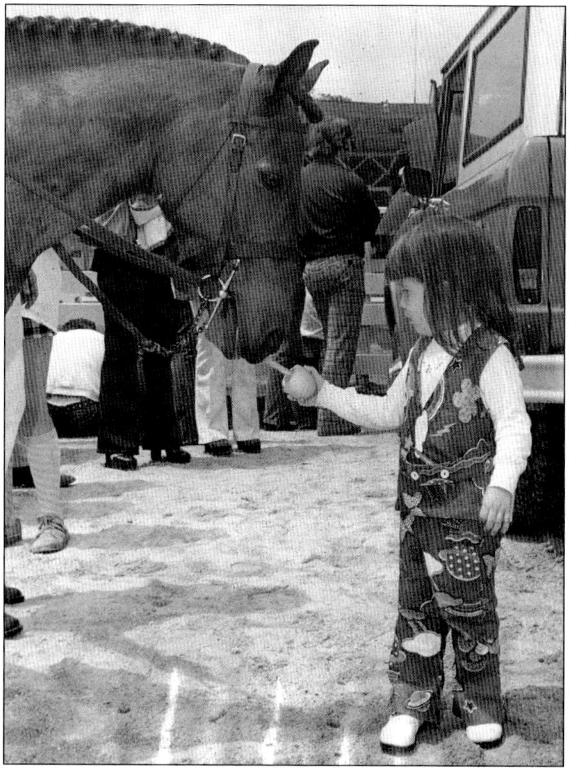

Four

DISCIPLINES AT DEVON

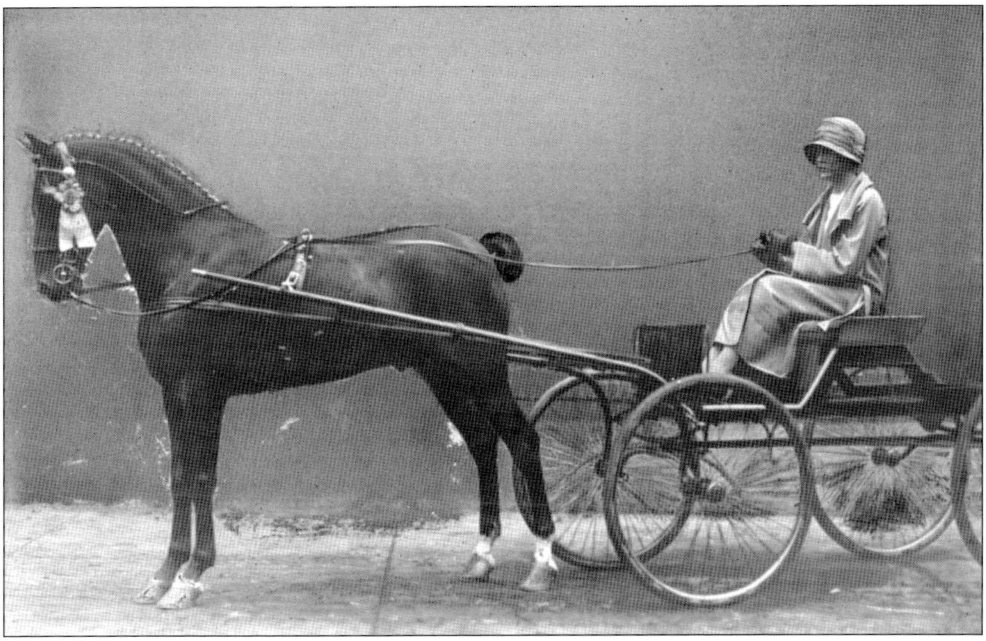

Two of the earliest classes offered at Devon were the Horses in Harness Ladies to Drive class and the Ponies in Harness Not Exceeding 11.2 class. The fine harness classes at Devon featured light refined horses with animated leg action. Philadelphia debutante Alma Wanamaker is shown here driving her fine harness pony Sir Eric. Sir Eric won many blue ribbons due to his excellent movement. Note that his tail has been docked to ensure it does not get caught up in the harness.

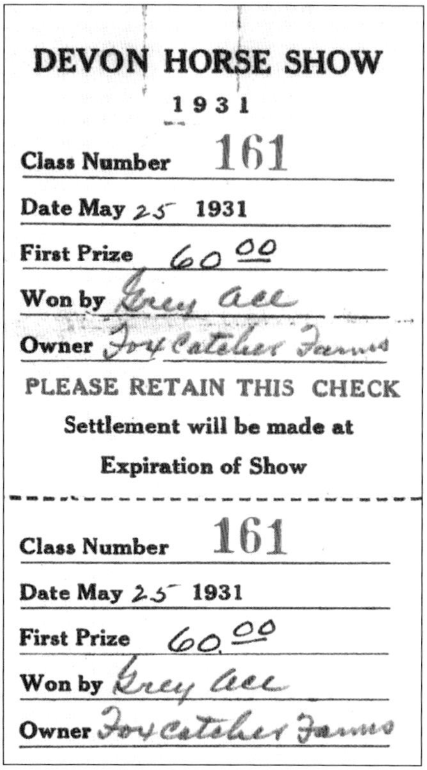

DEVON HORSE SHOW

1931

Class Number 161

Date May 25 **1931**

First Prize 60.00

Won by Grey Ace

Owner Foxcatcher Farms

PLEASE RETAIN THIS CHECK

Settlement will be made at

Expiration of Show

Class Number 161

Date May 25 **1931**

First Prize 60.00

Won by Grey Ace

Owner Foxcatcher Farms

In the 1920s, the du Pont family established Liseter Farms and showed their horses under the *nom de course* Foxcatcher Farms. Located in Newtown Square, Pennsylvania, the farm's ponies dominated Welsh pony events for years. In 1930, Jean Liseter Austin du Pont's horse Gray Ace was champion. He won again in 1931, securing the Deepdale Trophy. This claim ticket entitled du Pont to redeem that trophy as well as her $60 prize.

The first weekend of Devon is known as Junior Weekend, a 125-year-old tradition of events for young equestrians. Junior Weekend serves as a training camp for future champion riders, including potential competitors on junior national teams. Welsh Combination Ponies Class 93 winner Manly Yeoman, ridden by Charles Dresden and owned by Suzanne and Charles Dresden, is shown here. For years, the Welsh ponies occupied the morning classes of Junior Weekend.

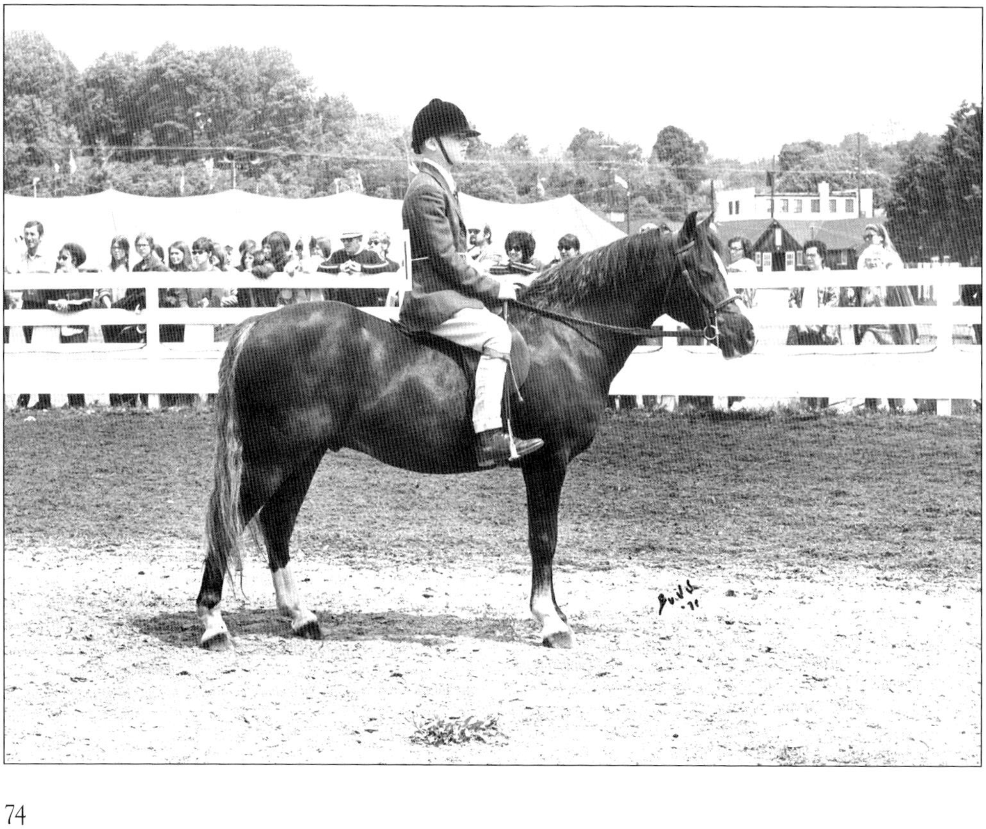

The 1976 Winning Pony Hunt Team, pictured here, included Marion Guyer, Christian Currey, and Holly Butash. During the hunt team competition, three riders compete over a course of fences at the same time. They jump the first seven fences one after another before joining together to jump the last fence side by side.

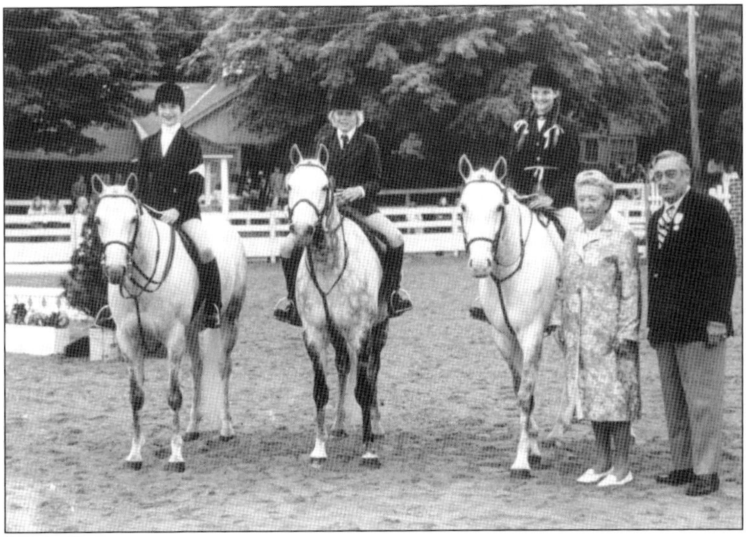

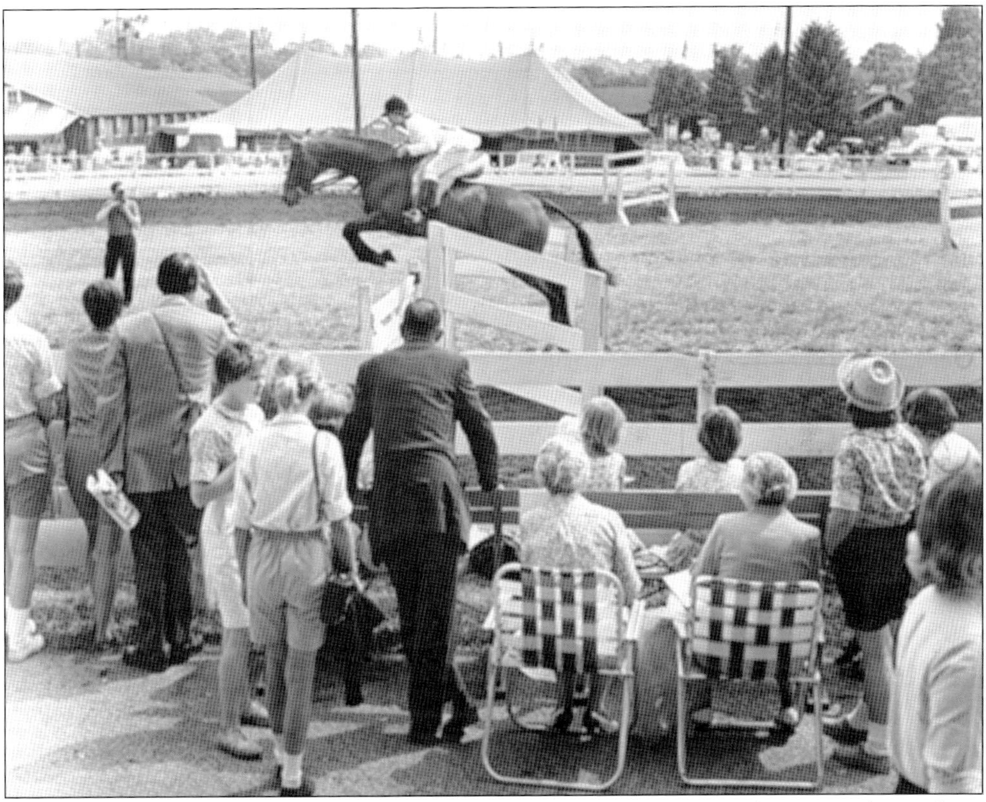

Sixteen-year-old Lynne Morrison expertly leads her pony over a vertical jump in the working hunter competition for young riders during Junior Weekend of the 66th annual Devon Horse Show and Country Fair as spectators watch from the corner of the Dixon Oval. Junior riders may ride horses or ponies. Although only the horse or pony is judged in hunter classes, a good rider makes a difference.

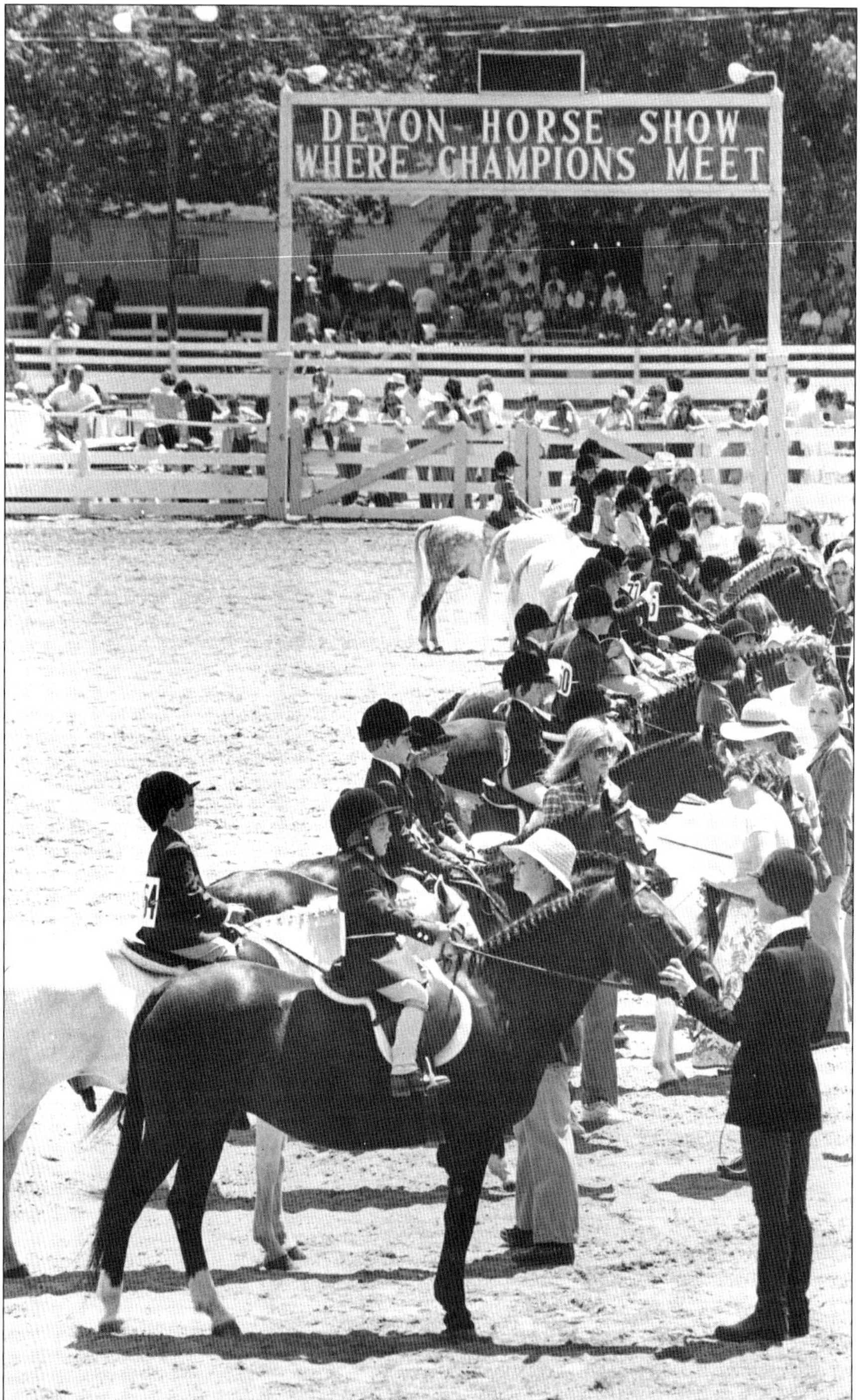

Lead line is a class for children under six years of age. There are two classes of lead line at Devon, three and under and four and five. An adult leads the horse, while the child sits on the horse with reins in hand, although the control of the horse rests with the handler. As shown in this 1981 photograph, there are always many entries.

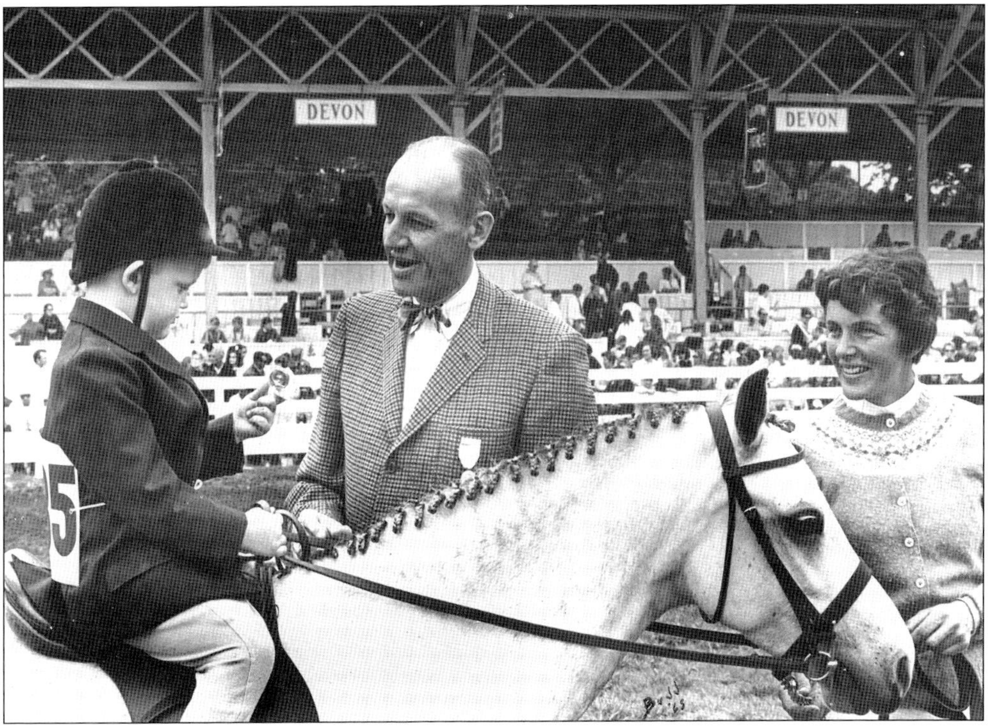

One of the most pleasurable duties as a horse show official is handing out lollipops to lead line participants on the Saturday of Junior Weekend. Children riding in this class are not eligible to compete in any other class. All entries receive a light blue ribbon in addition to a lollipop. In this 1969 photograph, James K. Robinson Jr. (center), chairman of the board, gives a treat to young Jeff Rollins on Trough Hill Dragonette, a Welsh pony led by Joy Hall Cully (right). Pictured below, the tiny riders line up for the crowd.

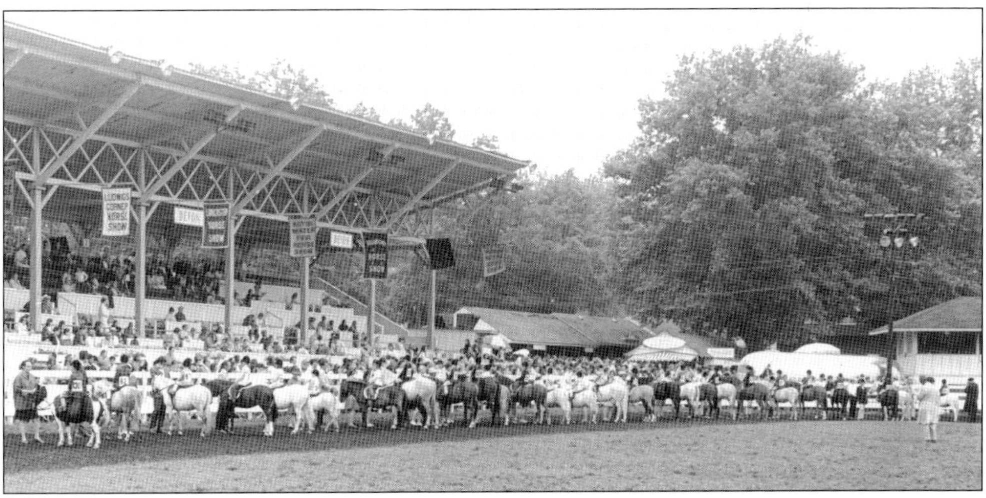

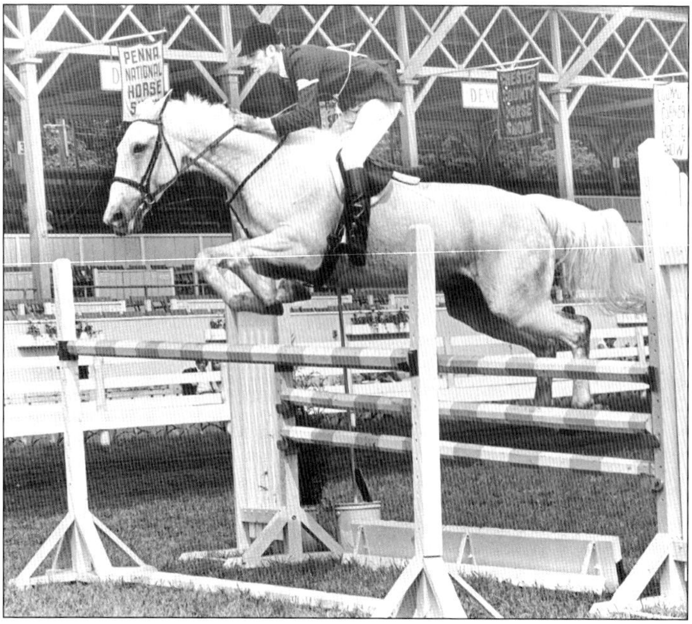

The 1970 Junior Jumper champion, Hombre, owned by Hilltop Stables and ridden by James Hulick, is shown going over a jump. James Hulick also won the American Horse Shows Association (AHSA) Hunter Seat Medal Class and Best Child Rider. Unlike hunter classes, where the horse's turnout is judged, jumper classes are judged based on power and speed. The mane and tail are unbraided, turnout that would be unacceptable for a hunter horse showing at Devon.

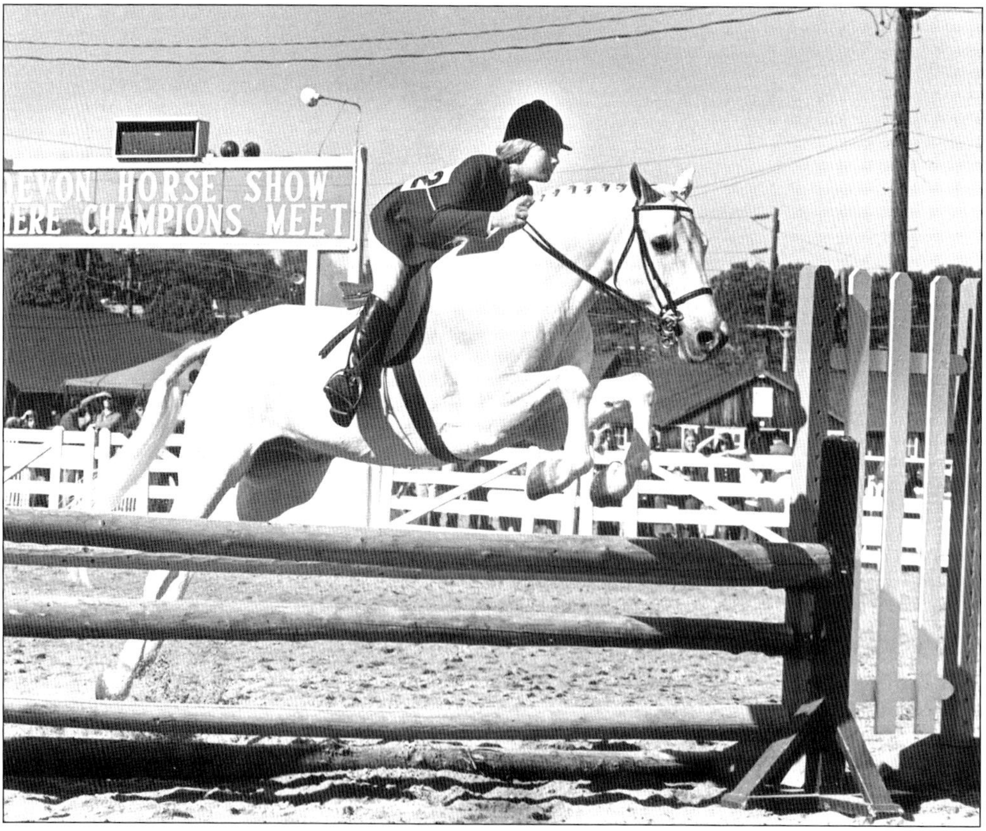

Many classes at Devon are reserved for junior riders like Beverly Huber, shown here winning a class on her mare named Take the Field. Junior riders are 18 years old or younger. Beverly Huber wears a blue armband, indicating that she is eligible for the Best Child Rider on a Horse award.

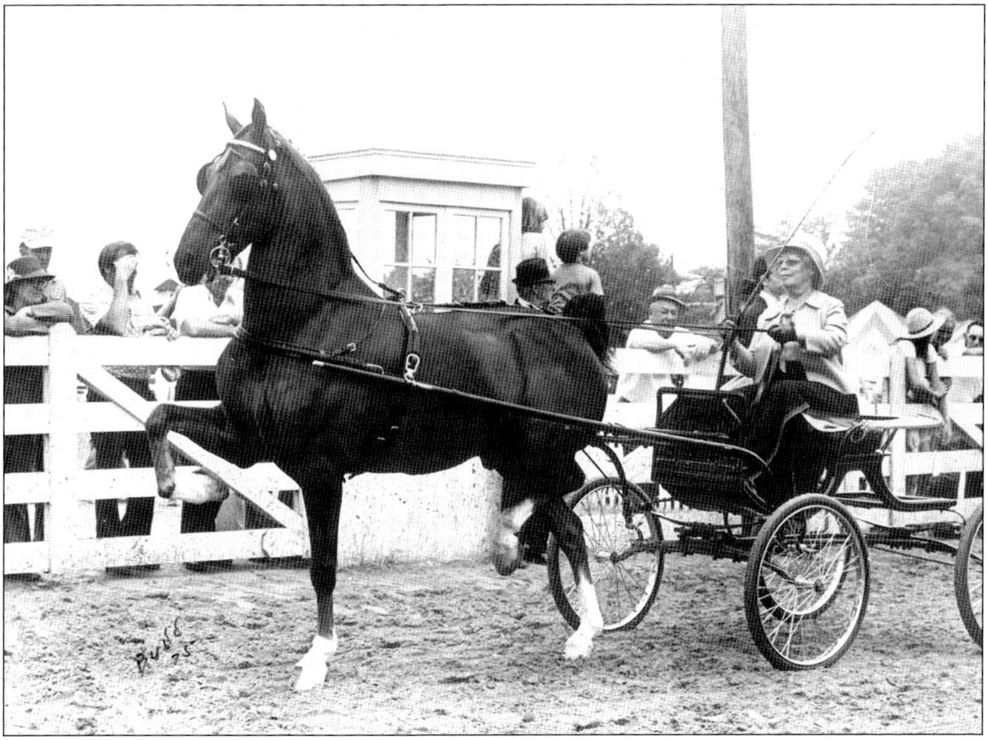

The Hackney horse or pony is known as the "aristocrat of the show ring" due to its amazing athletic ability and presence. The four Hackney pony divisions at Devon are the Hackney pony or cobtail, harness pony, pleasure driving pony, and roadster pony. Pictured here is the 1975 champion Hackney horse Outwood Matire driven by Kathleen Ryan. She began showing Hackneys in 1944 with her husband, Frank Ryan, from their Kilreen Farm outside of Ottawa, Canada.

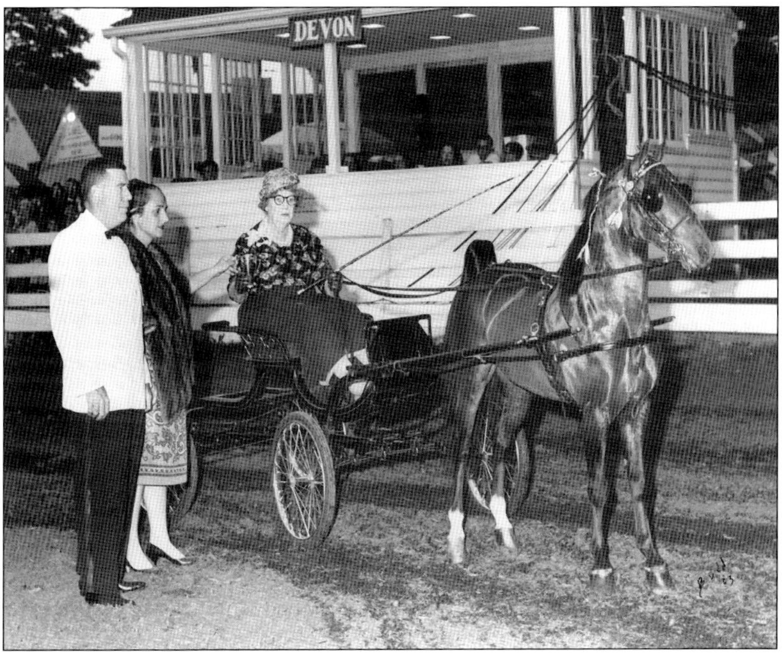

Contrast the size of Outwood Matire with Cassilis Sir Echo, shown here. Hackneys can be either horses or ponies. A Hackney pony may be no taller than 14.1 hands or 57 inches. Taller Hackneys compete as horses. Cassilis Sir Echo, driven by Macy Willets, won the Morris Challenge Trophy for Hackney ponies.

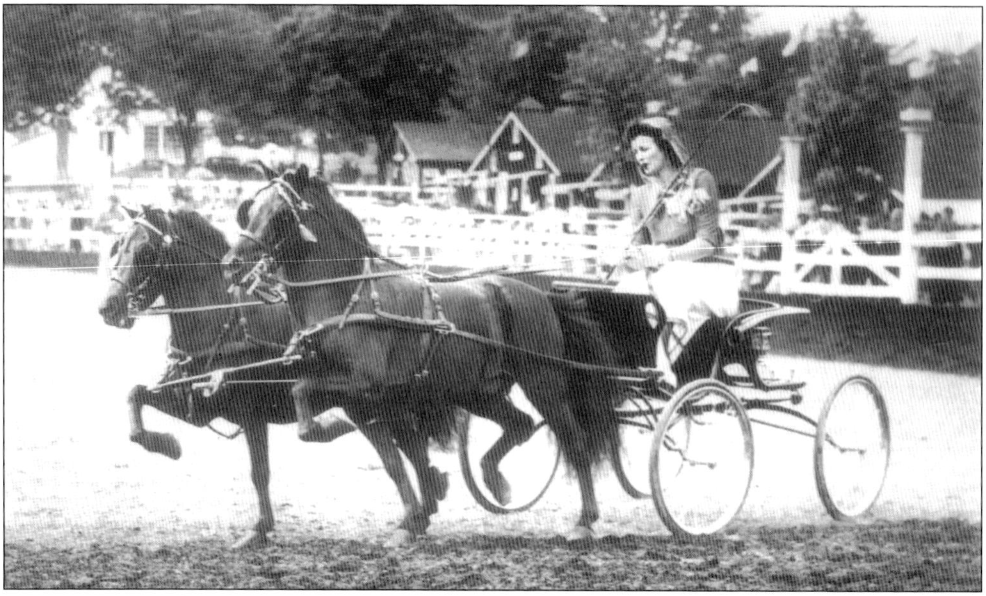

In 1937, Helen Biddle Huggler drives in tandem a pair of black ponies, Venador Larigo and Venola Larigo, owned by Wikoff and Helen Smith's Colebrook Farms in Whitford, Chester County, Pennsylvania. At this time, exhibitors and officials advocated the use of "pneumatic speed wagons, carts or track sulkies" for harness competition, as they were deemed safer and faster on the turns in show rings. Thomas W. Clark, manager of the horse show, opined that "whatever vehicle will enable a high stepping harness horse or pony to make the best performance ought to be deemed 'suitable.' "

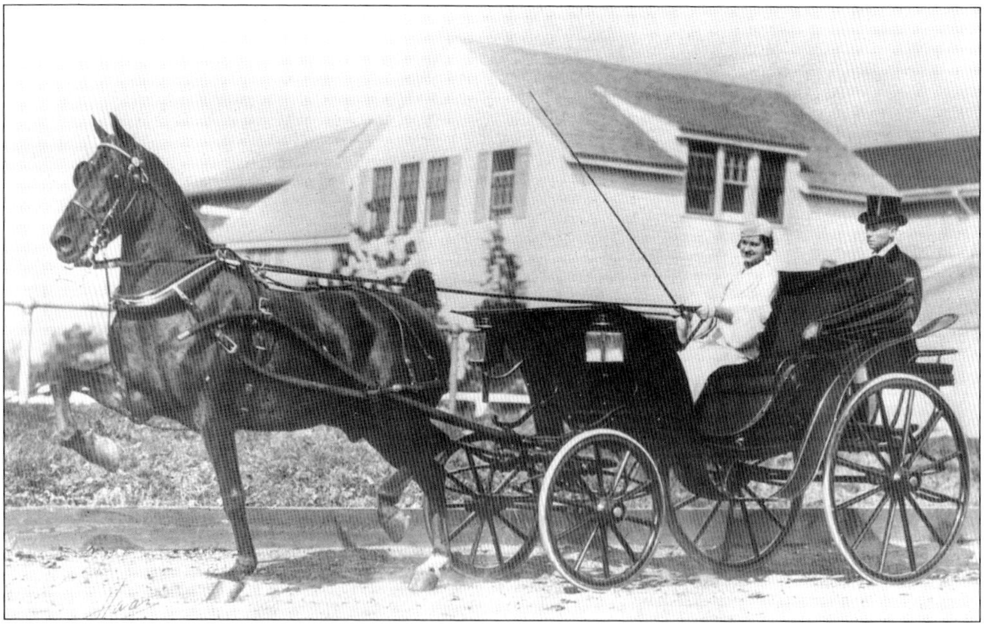

This single-horse carriage is being driven by a woman during the 1920s. Unlike a woman riding a horse, a woman driving a carriage could be dressed in her finest clothes. Coach builders outfitted carriages with women in mind; seats were padded with fine linen, and the interior of the carriage contained storage for toiletries and sundry items.

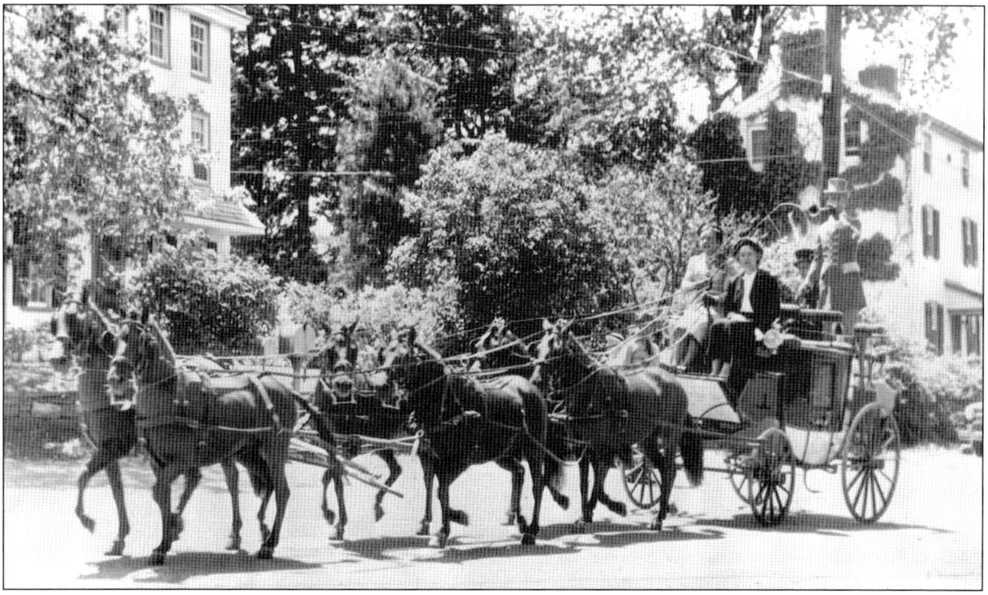

The Devon Pleasure Drive, also known as the Carriage Marathon, is a 4.5-mile trip to the showgrounds through the neighborhoods of Devon. Hank Collins revived the event in 1966 after interest waned in the early 1960s. Spectators gathered at Blackburn Farm on Sugartown Road in Willistown for the noon start. Residents lined the road to watch and wave as exhibitors passed their properties, enjoying picnics on their front lawns. This early photograph shows a six-in-hand carriage. (Courtesy of The Engraver.)

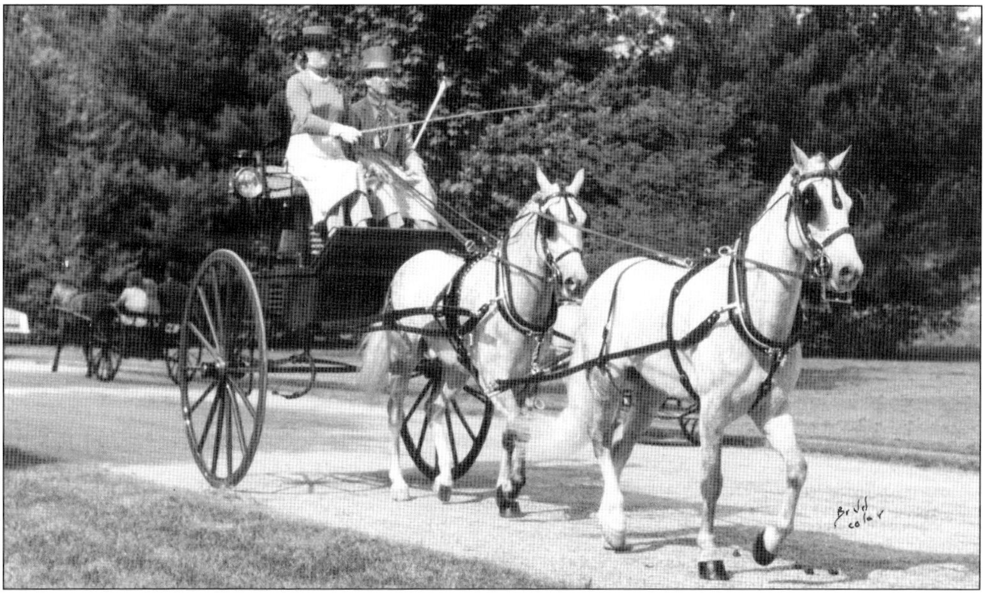

This carriage is driven tandem, with one horse in front of the other. Although this style of driving dates back to the 12th century, it became more popular during the 1800s. The back horse, known as the "wheeler," pulls all the weight. This allows the front horse, known as the "leader," to remain fresher for longer. Note that the driver sits higher in a tandem carriage than in a single-horse carriage. The higher seat allows her to see both her horses. Ailsa Moseley Crawford with her two gray Welsh crossbreds was the 1972 Carriage Marathon champion in a class of 87 starters.

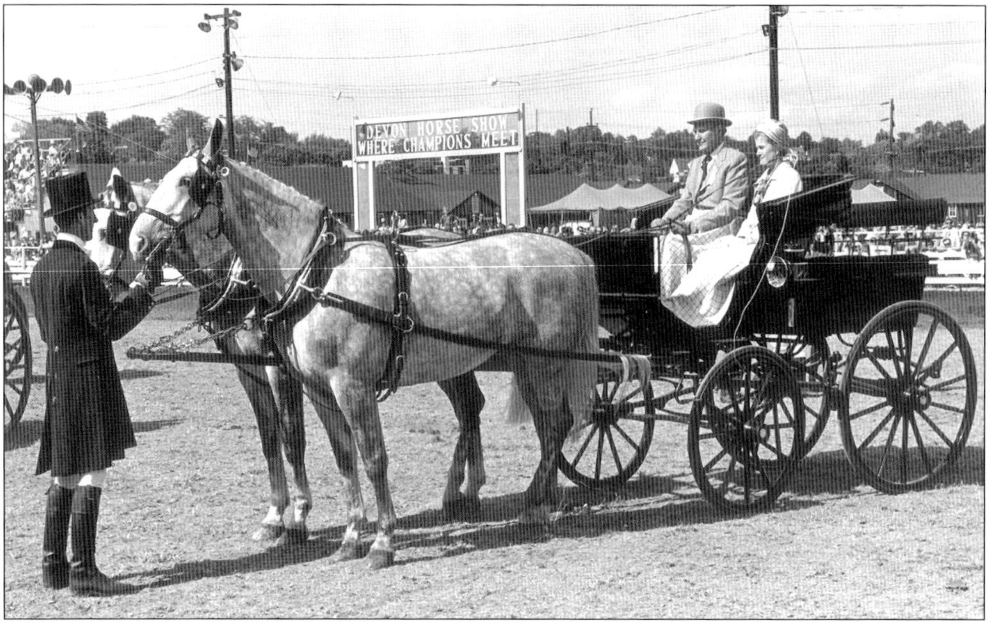

Judging for the Carriage Marathon begins at 12 noon at St. David's Episcopal Church on the first Sunday of the show. The route to the show is 4.5 miles and cannot exceed 40 minutes. When the carriages arrive at the Dixon Oval, they are judged, as shown here. Note how well these horses match each other in terms of size, color, and type. Everything is judged as part of the Carriage Marathon, including the horses, carriage, and driver. The vehicles must be original and restored to new or almost new condition. The harness and clothes worn by the riders and participants must complement the carriage's appearance. Women must wear hats and gloves, and the driver must be covered in a driving apron.

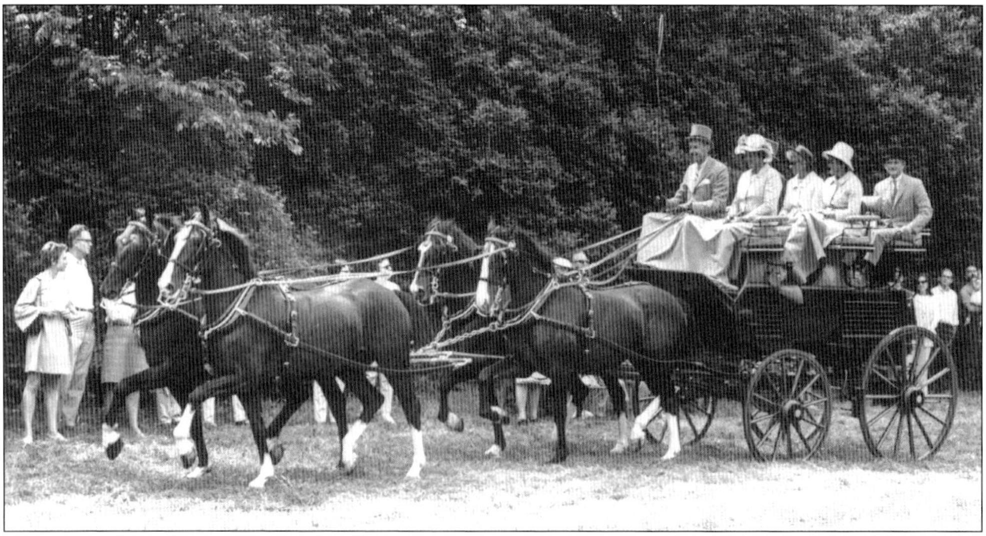

James K. Robinson Jr., chairman of the Devon Horse Show, added the Carriage Marathon and the Four-in-Hand Division to the show's schedule in the early 1950s. For four generations, the Robinson family has shown at Devon in various classes and has made great contributions to the sport and maintaining the tradition of Devon. Here, James and Gay Robinson compete in the Carriage Marathon in the late 1960s with their horses from Crebilly Farm.

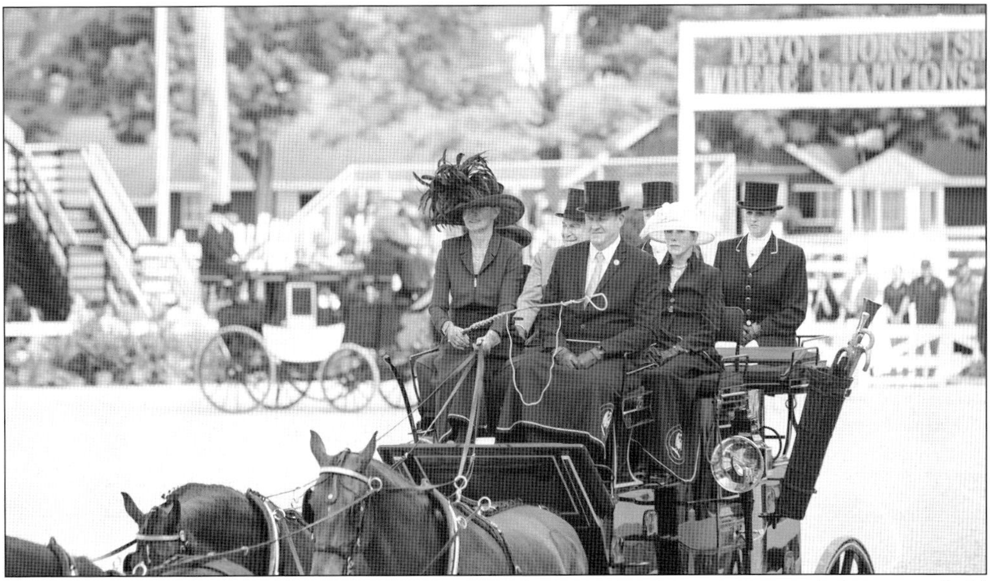

The four-in-hand coaching competitors, so called because the four reins to each horse are held in one hand by the "whip," or driver, are judged as they navigate a course in the ring. The course consists of approximately five to eight markers around which each carriage must navigate. If any markers are knocked down, the competitor earns a penalty. Penalties are converted into seconds and added to the final score. The fastest time is the winner. Although competitors are not judged on their turnout, it is not uncommon to see beautiful clothing and hats like the ones shown on 2018 class winner Misdee Wrigley Miller, pictured here.

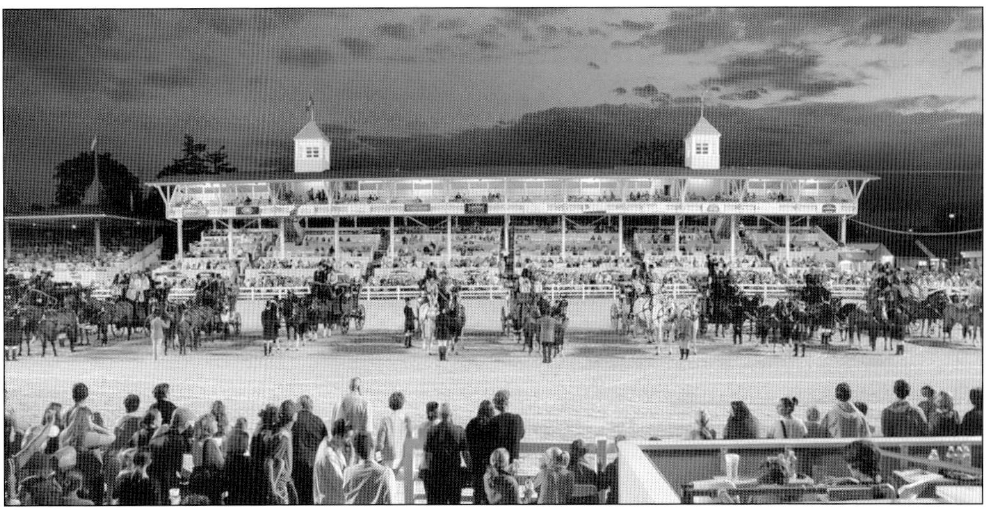

Spectators adore the carriage driving classes because, outside of the Devon Horse Show, many have never seen carriage driving before. Evening classes, like the one shown here, are especially popular. This was the record coaching turnout in 2013.

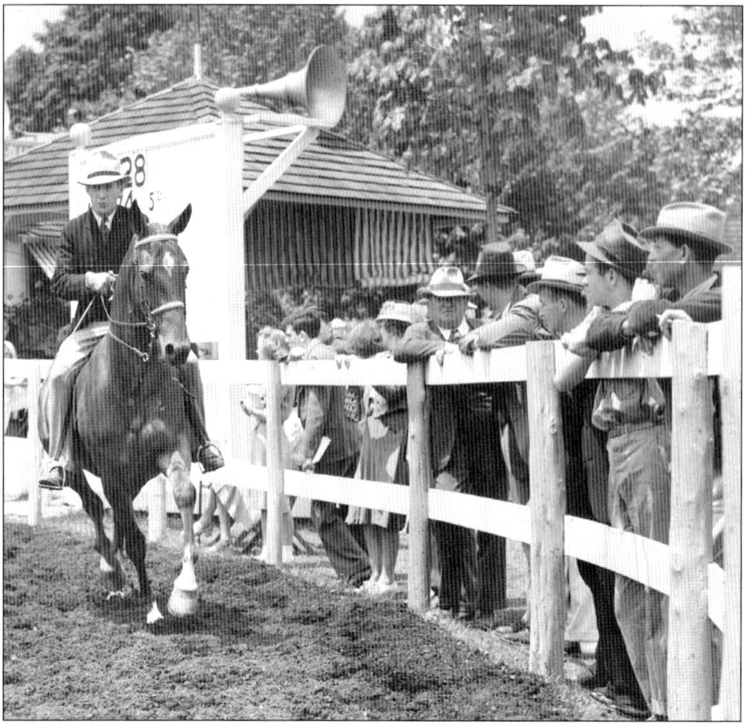

At Devon, the American Saddlebred is exhibited in several different divisions, including five-gaited, three-gaited, fine harness, pleasure, park, and Western. An incredibly versatile breed, the American Saddlebred excels at every division, and it is the only breed that walks, trots, canters, and can be taught to perform two additional gaits, the slow gait and the rack. Shown at right is Judy Cooke aboard the five-gaited winner Commander's Countess. In bicentennial year 1976, the show announced the introduction of an American Saddlebred pleasure horse section. A popular event among Saddlehorse exhibitors, this section remains open to amateur equestrians. (Above, courtesy of the SCRC, Temple University.)

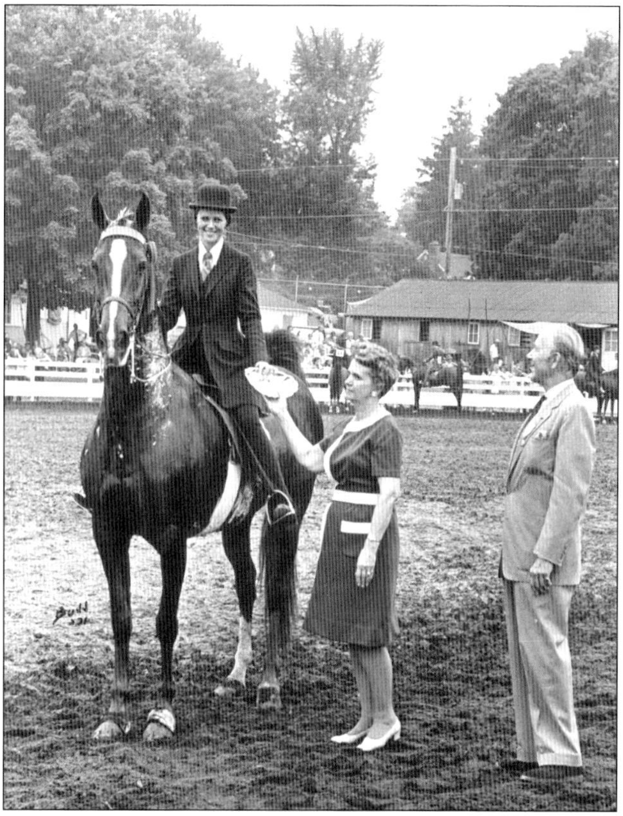

From the 13th to the early 20th century, riding with one's knees together was considered more appropriate for women. Ladies' sidesaddle uses a type of saddle that allows a rider to sit aside, with both of her legs on one side of the horse. In contrast, when sitting astride, the rider has one leg on each side of the horse. Sidesaddle mounts like this attractive appaloosa must be extremely obedient and attentive to the rider's signals or "aids."

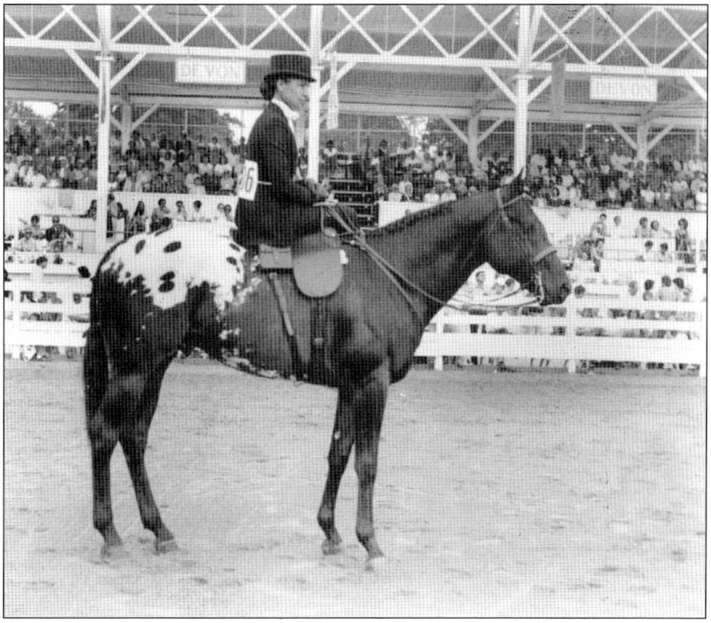

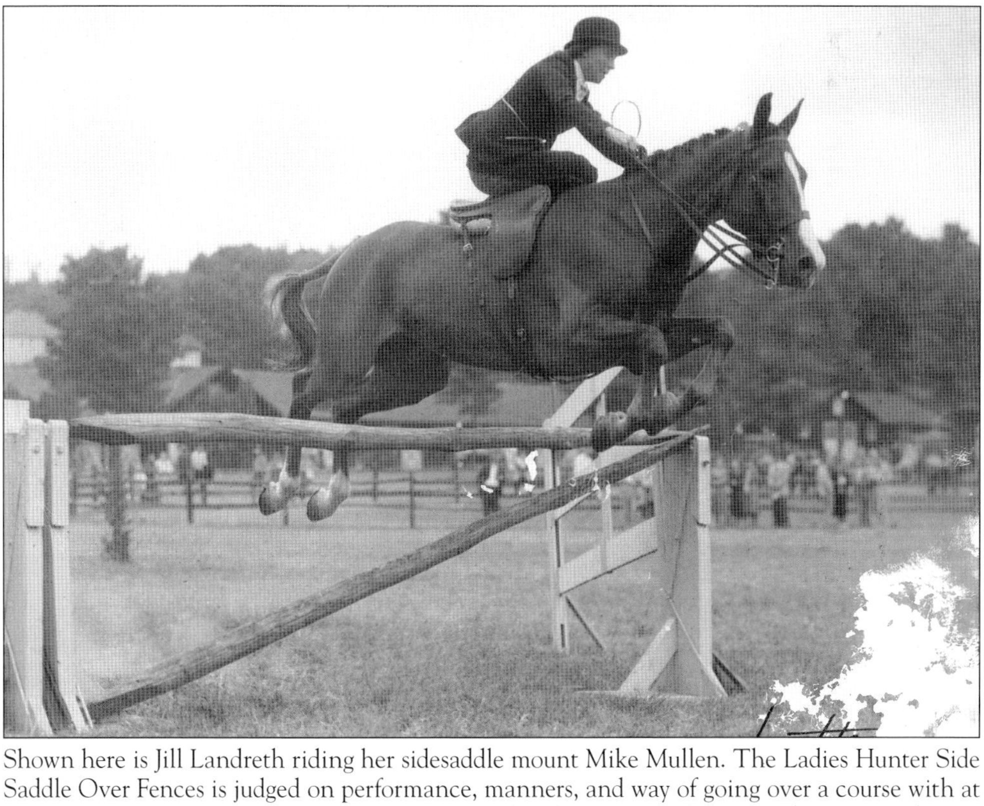

Shown here is Jill Landreth riding her sidesaddle mount Mike Mullen. The Ladies Hunter Side Saddle Over Fences is judged on performance, manners, and way of going over a course with at least eight fences that are three feet in height. The champion and reserve champion titles are awarded to two of the horses who have won the most points in the Ladies Hunter Side Saddle Under Saddle, Side Saddle Hunter Hack, and Side Saddle Over Fence classes. The winner is awarded the True Blue Challenge Trophy.

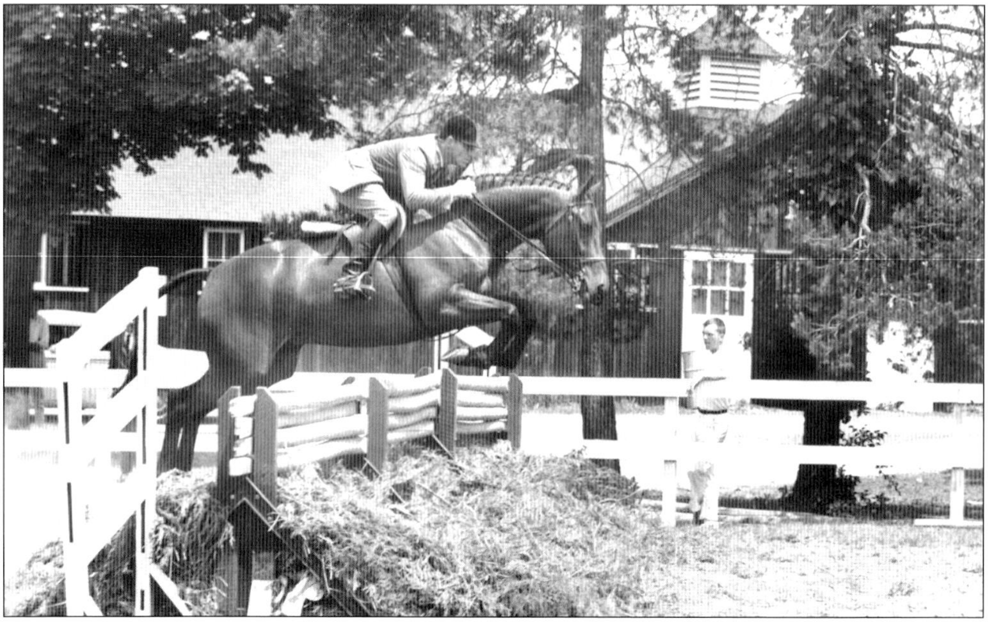

Hunter horses, like the one pictured here, are judged on the horse's movement, presence, manner of going, and jumping ability. The arc the horse's body takes as it goes over a jump is called a "bascule." This horse demonstrates a beautiful bascule, with its front legs high and tight and back naturally round in the air. The rider is in a position known as "two point" or "half seat," freeing the horse's back in the air.

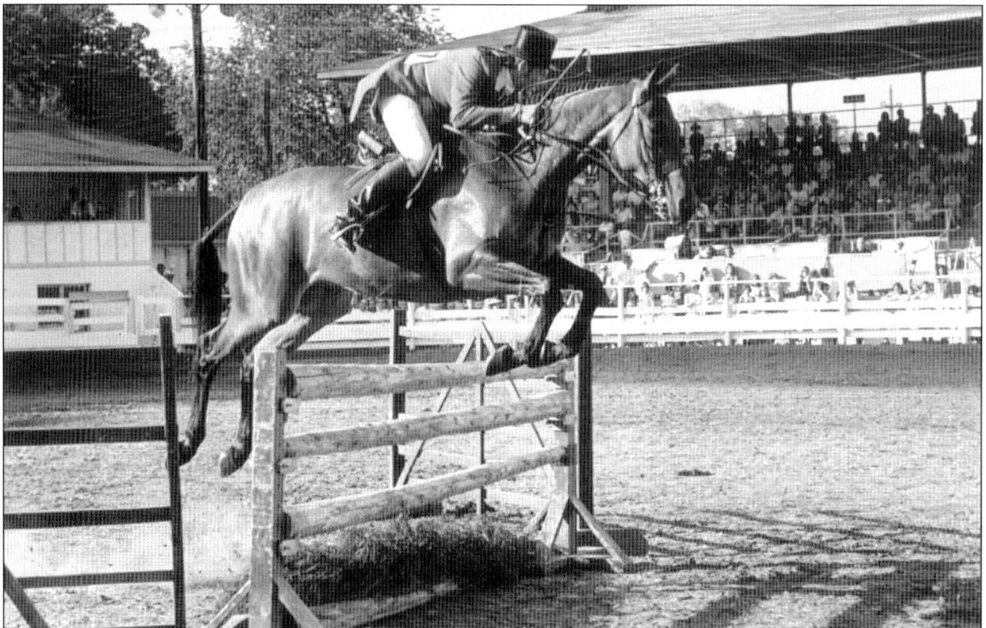

The 1969 class 339 Regular Conformation Hunter champion Spindletop Showdown is shown here going over a jump in the show ring. Born and bred in 1963, the 16.2-hand bay Thoroughbred was owned and ridden by Marvin Van Rapoport. Although this photograph shows the rider in a formal top hat, today riders must wear helmets for safety purposes.

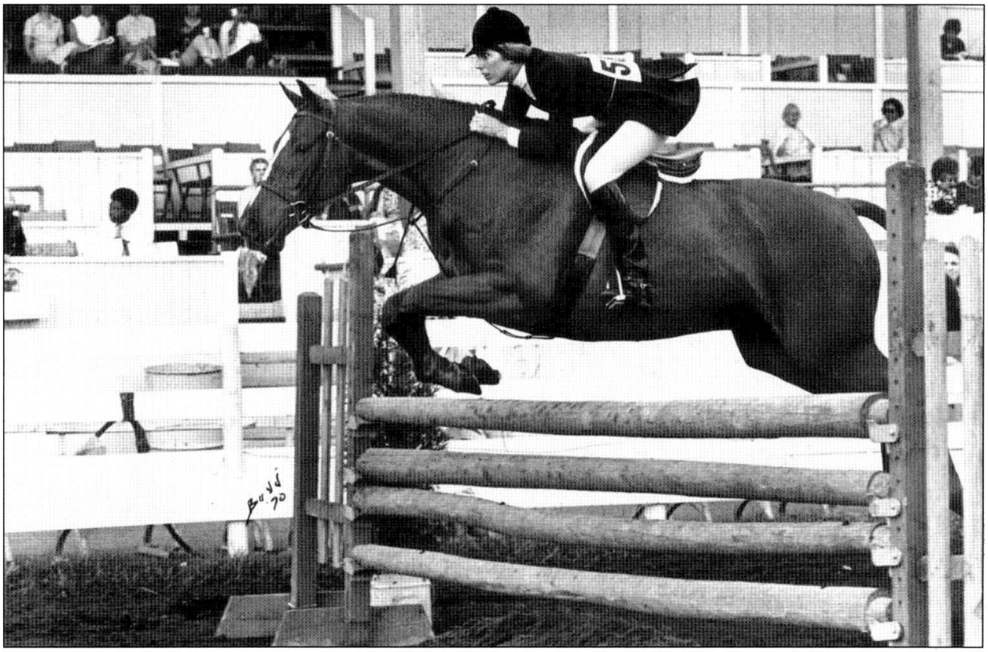

Terry Rudd and Best Chance won the Second Year Green Working Hunter Championship in 1970. The owners were Mr. and Mrs. J. Markley Freed. Although she was only 20 years old at the time, Rudd won first place and the blue ribbon in all three over fences classes on her way to the championship.

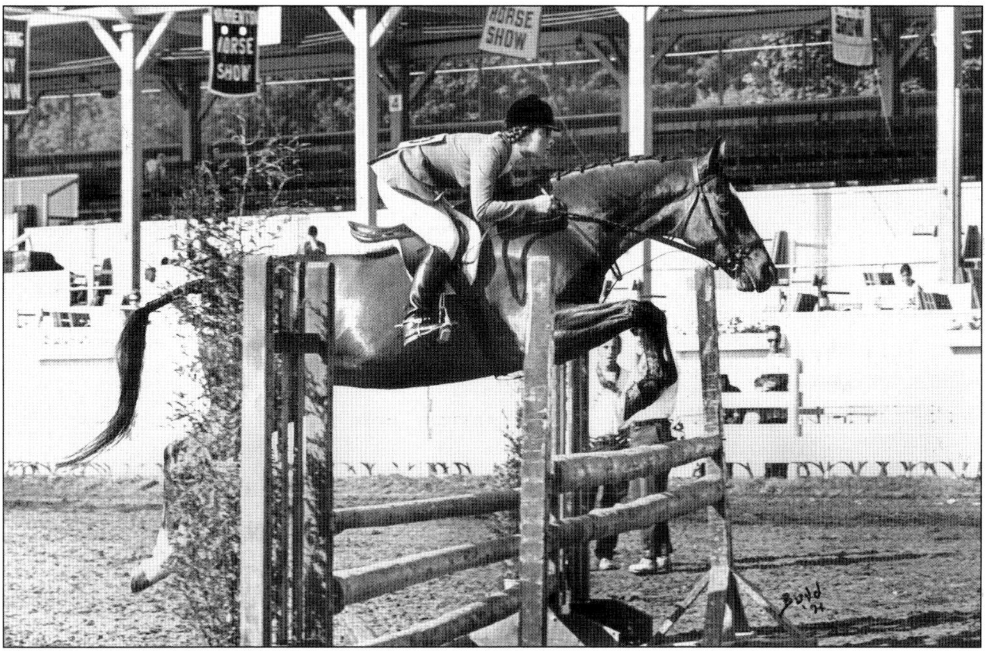

The 1971 Amateur Owner Hunter Championship went to Melody Ryan and her horse Sly Arrival, shown here over fences in class 395. Amateur owner classes give nonprofessionals a chance to compete against other nonprofessionals. Professionals may show in regular working hunter divisions, green hunter classes for novice hunters, and conformation classes.

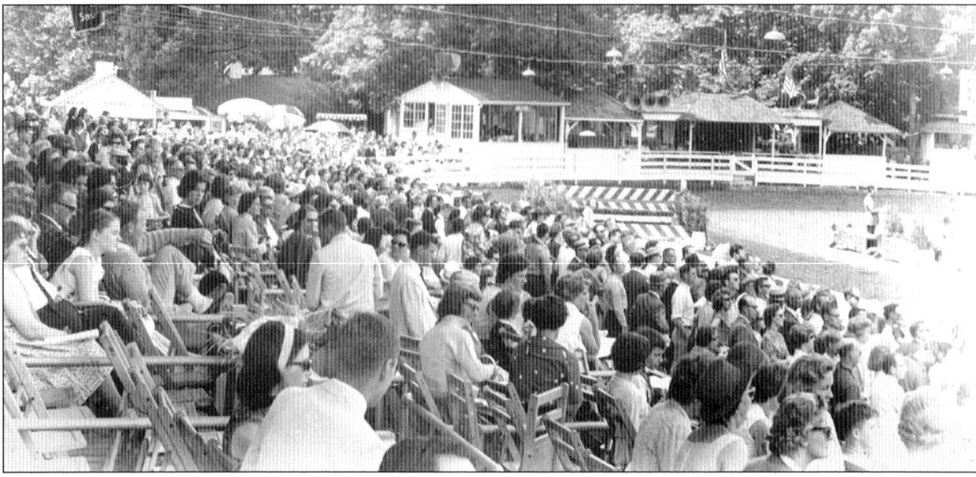

Spectators crowd the stands in 1963 for a jumper class. As the athlete of the show, the jumper's task is to jump, regardless of style or manner. Scoring is objective, based on a point system for faults (knocking down a rail or a refusal) or exceeding the time limit. The winner is the horse with the lowest number of faults. Unlike the jumps in hunter classes, which mimic those in the hunt field, jumper classes feature brightly colored jumps like the one seen here.

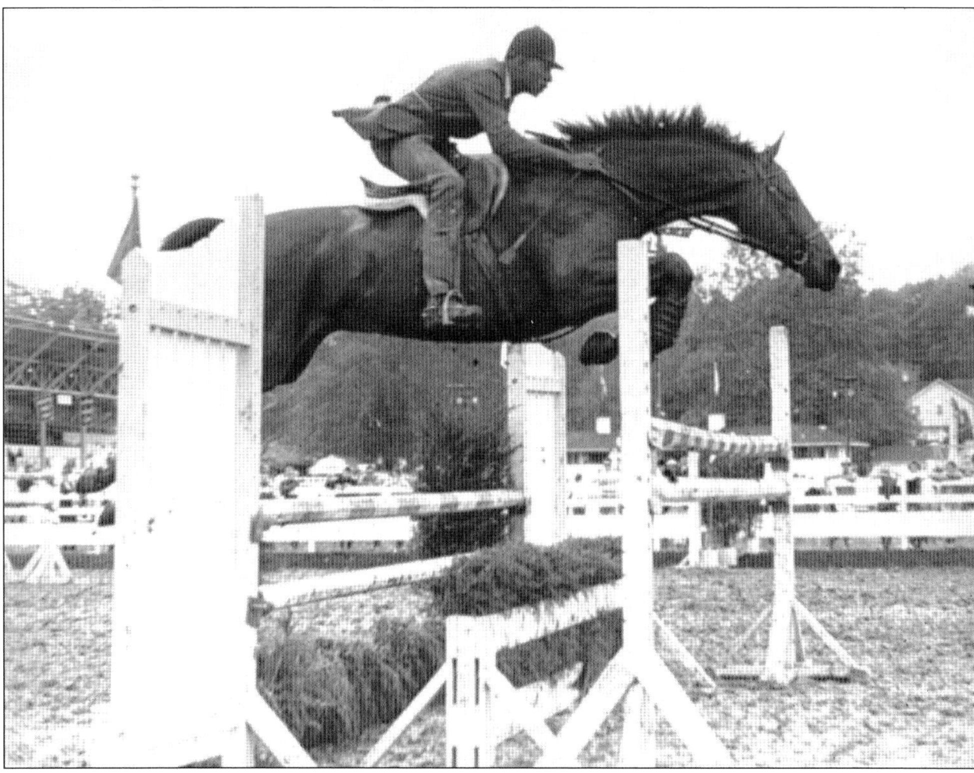

Lyn A. Jones expertly pilots Reenato, formerly a racehorse from Montreal, Quebec, Canada, through the Devon mud in the jumper class in the 1970s. Amateur owner-jumper classes were held for the first time at Devon in 1975. In the ongoing quest to combat the Devon mud, in the early 1970s, the rings and schooling areas were excavated, the draining system extended, and new footing added that sloped to drain off the water. (Courtesy of Lyn A. Jones.)

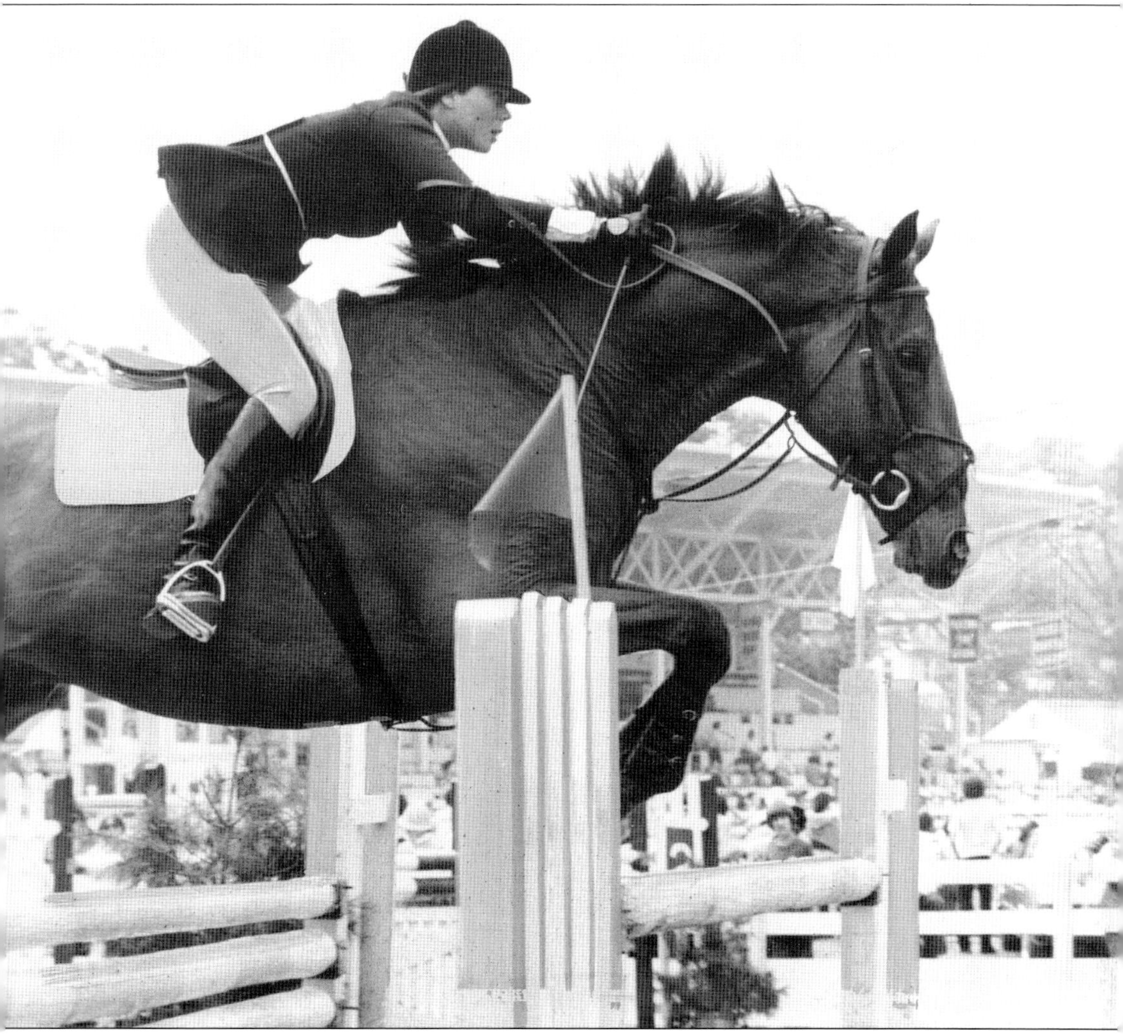

In May 1979, Leslie Burr Howard won the Open Jumper Championship, and she returned to Devon the following year to defend her champion jumper title. Burr won gold at the 1984 Los Angeles Olympic Games and silver at the 1996 Atlanta Olympic Games in team jumping. (Courtesy of the SCRC, Temple University.)

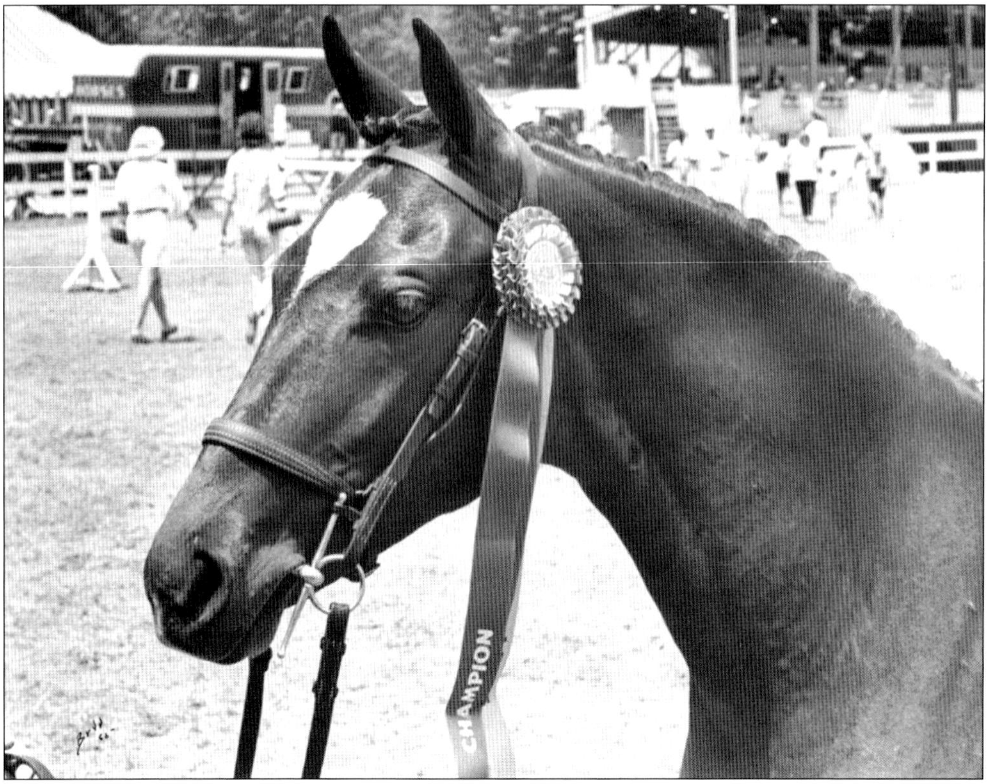

Some horses compete at the Devon Horse Show before they are even old enough to be ridden. Shown here is crossbred filly champion Bonny Reb, owned by Mr. and Mrs. Kenneth Taylor. She was champion of her in-hand class and went on to be a champion under saddle in later years.

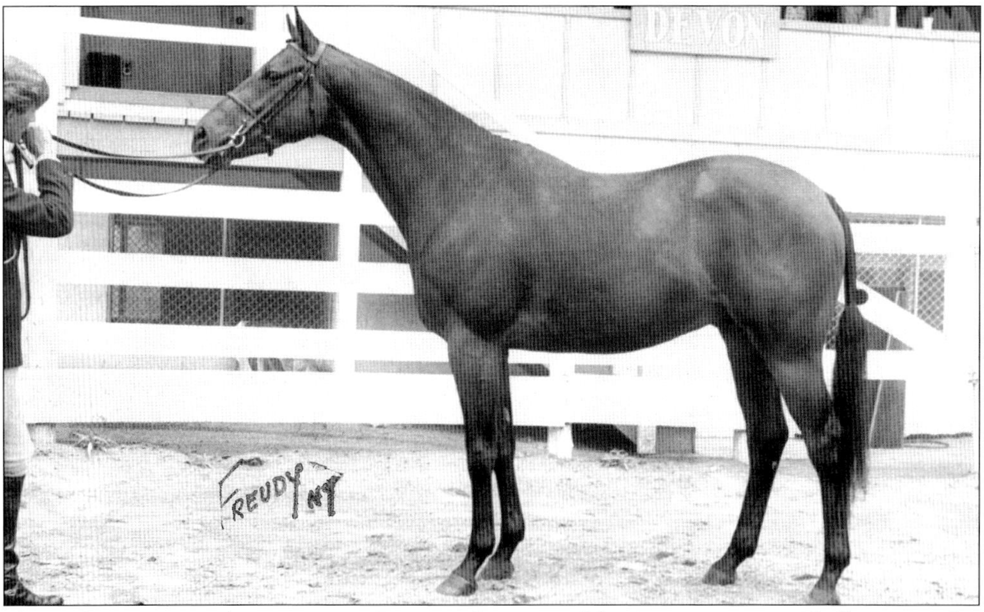

Shown here is Vigor, the Best Young Horse and winner of the Asmont Manor Challenge Trophy. Vigor was owned by Debbie Willson and was exhibited by Rodney Jenkins.

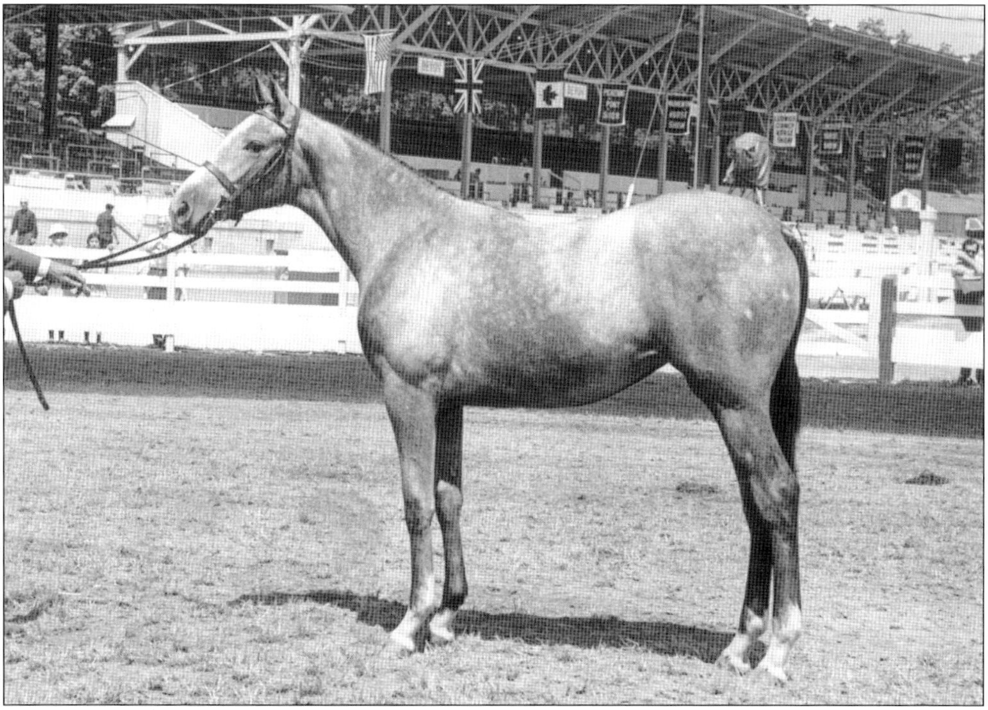

Kimberton Hills Farm's Unnamed Filly By Mighty Monarch won the 1969 Best Pennsylvania Bred Horse class.

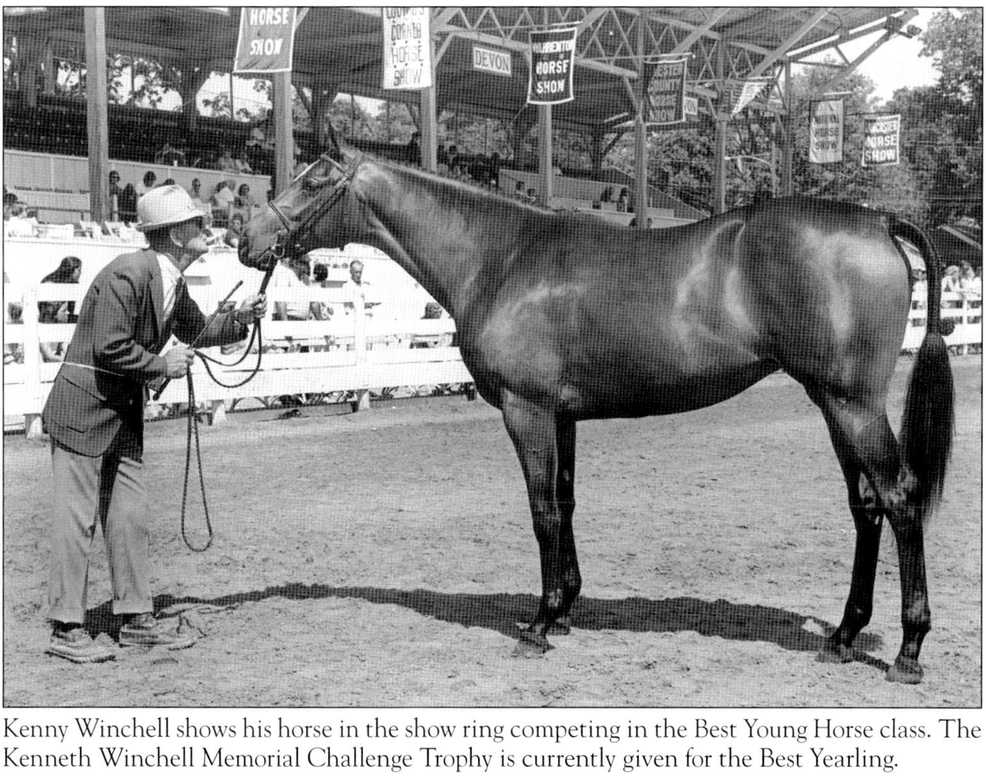

Kenny Winchell shows his horse in the show ring competing in the Best Young Horse class. The Kenneth Winchell Memorial Challenge Trophy is currently given for the Best Yearling.

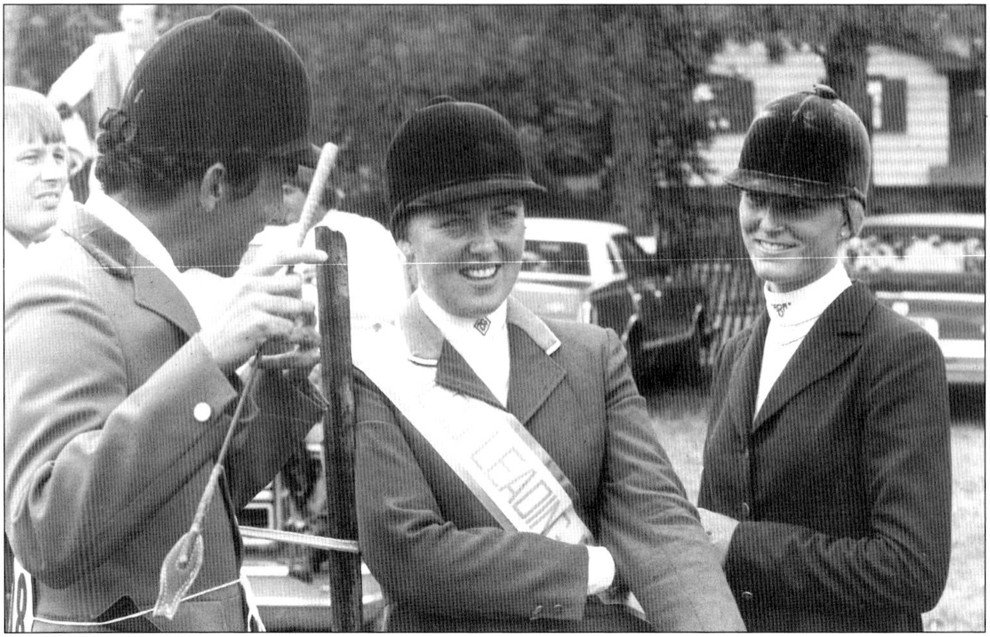

Melanie Smith Taylor and her mount Val De Loire won the first Devon Grand Prix in 1978. Taylor recalled in the *Chronicle of the Horse*, "There's such a feeling of greatness when you walk into that ring, and the crowd, it's just thundering, and they're just right there on the rail practically. . . . It was very, very special to win there." Smith went on to win the gold medal at the 1984 Summer Olympic Games in Los Angeles for team jumping.

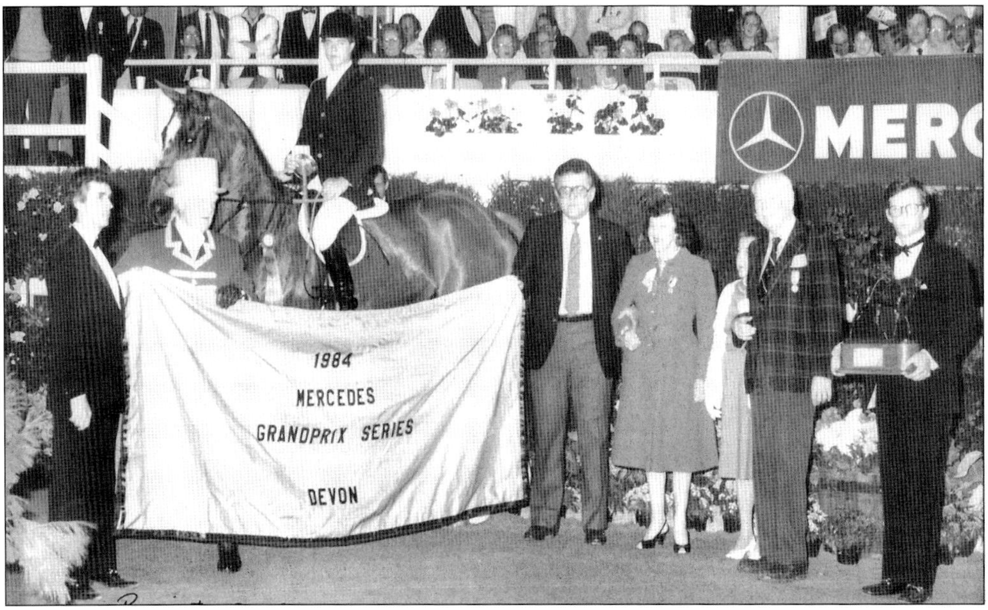

The Devon Grand Prix upgraded the level of competition in the jumper division. A $10,000 purse was offered in 1978, and today it is $250,000. The Grand Prix served as a United States Equestrian Team (USET) Pan American Games selection site in 1979, a World Equestrian Games selection trial in 1990, an Olympic trial in 1992, and an Olympic observation trial in 2012. Pictured above, Donald Cheska and Eadenvale took the 1984 Mercedes Grand Prix.

Five

Trophies and Traditions

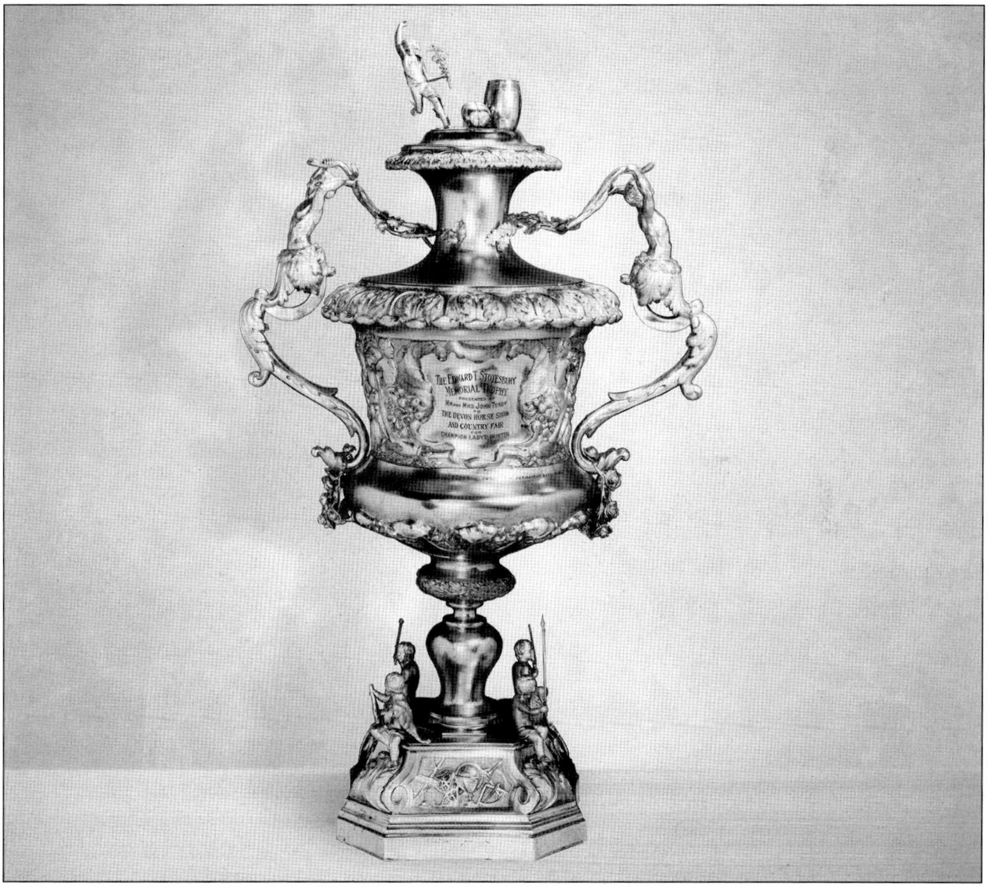

The Devon Horse Show trophy collection includes some trophies that are almost as old as Devon itself. The oldest and most ornate of the Devon trophies is the 1902 Edward T. Stotesbury Perpetual Trophy, awarded to the Best Child Rider on a Horse. This historically significant trophy was purchased and donated to Devon by Dr. Betsee Parker.

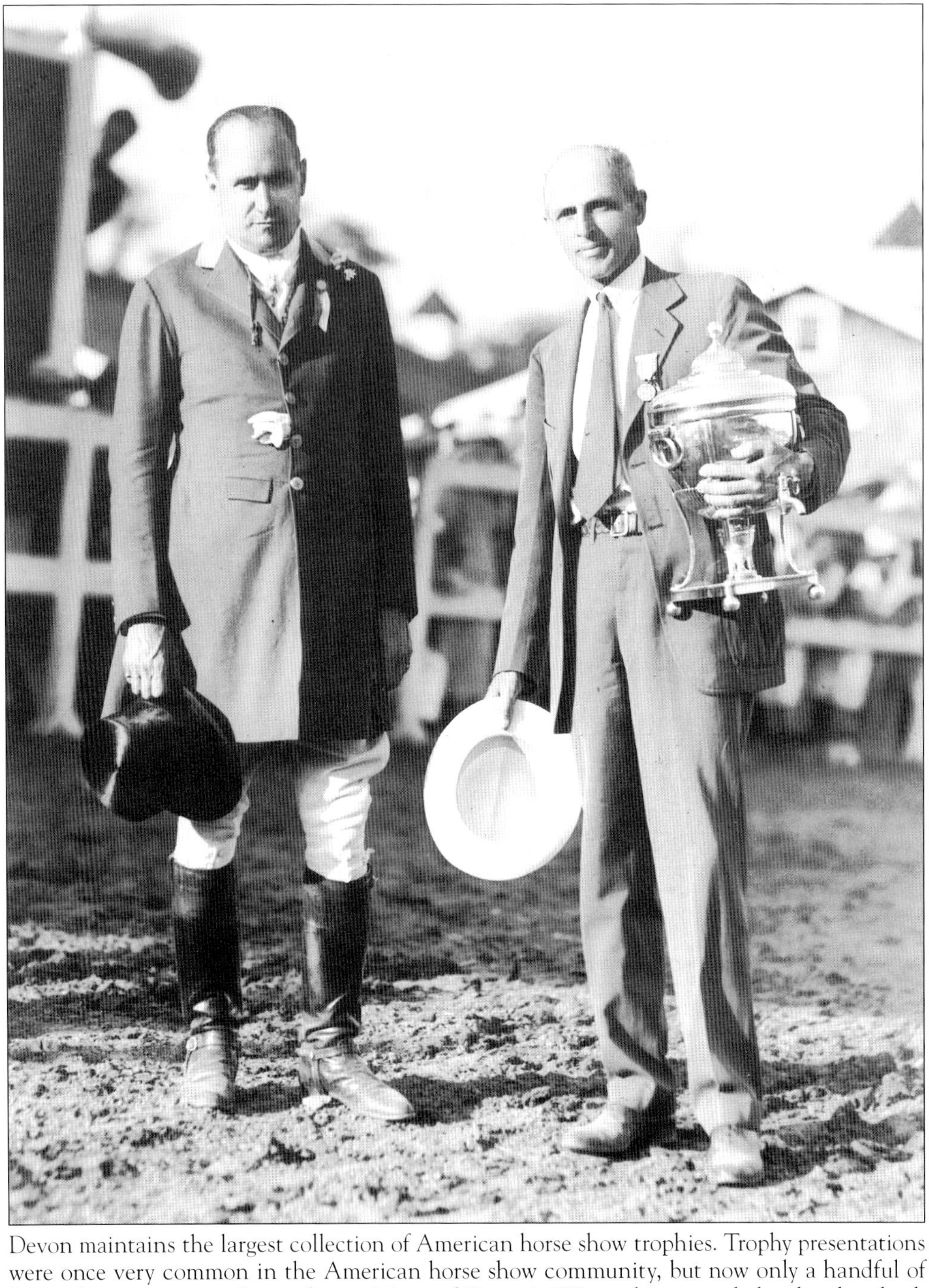

Devon maintains the largest collection of American horse show trophies. Trophy presentations were once very common in the American horse show community, but now only a handful of horse shows maintain the tradition. Many of Devon's 183 trophies awarded today date back over 100 years. In this early photograph, the George S. Hasbrouk Jr. Memorial Trophy for the High Performance Working Hunter class is presented to Isaac H. Clothier Jr. This trophy is still presented today for the $2,500 High Performance Hunter class.

At the 1931 show, 13-year-old R. Peter Richards won the Palmer Trophy riding Dilwyne Farms' Old Guard. Many trophies are awarded permanently to an entry that wins the same class multiple times. Dilwyne Farms gained permanent possession of the cup with its 1931 win. Richards later became a marine lieutenant and was lost in battle in 1942 at the Battle of Guadalcanal during World War II.

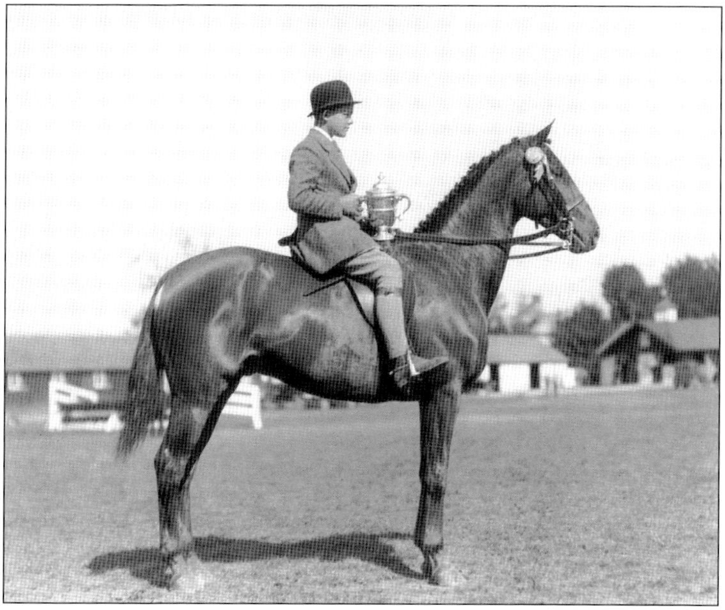

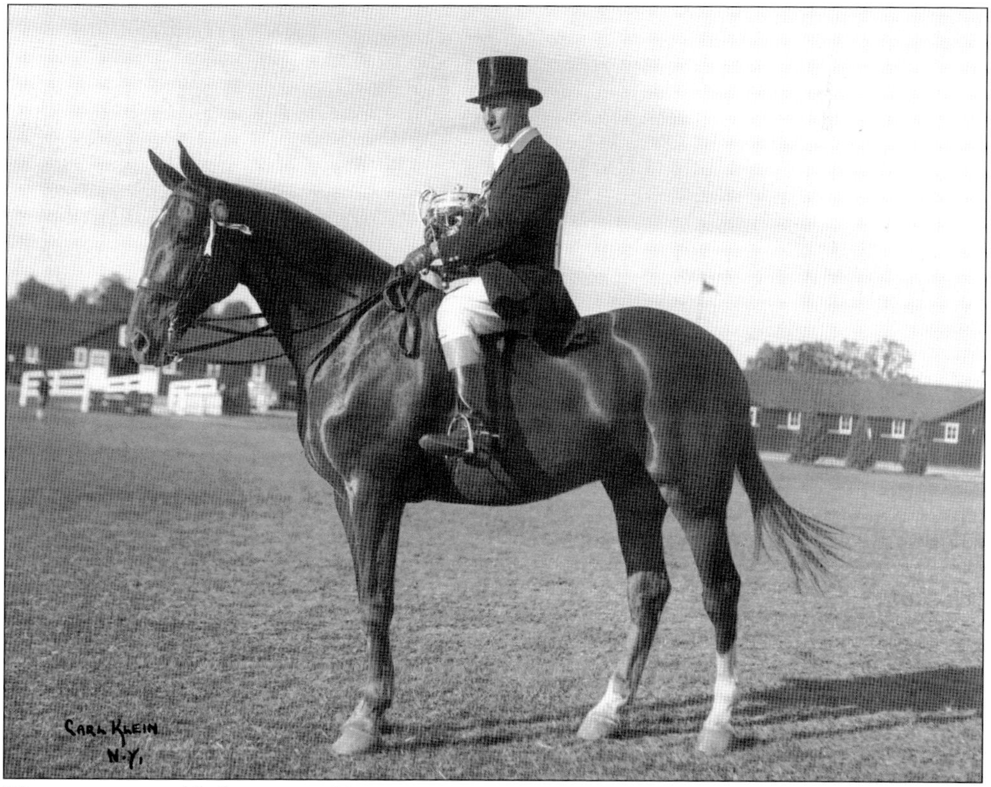

This nine-year-old chestnut gelding, Iron Man, captured the Clarence H. Geist Challenge Trophy for the Corinthian Class Hunters at the Devon Horse Show on May 28, 1936. Shown by Maj. Clifford Sifton, this was the third straight win for Iron Man, rendering him in permanent possession and retiring the trophy. A new trophy was named and unveiled after he retired the Geist Challenge Trophy.

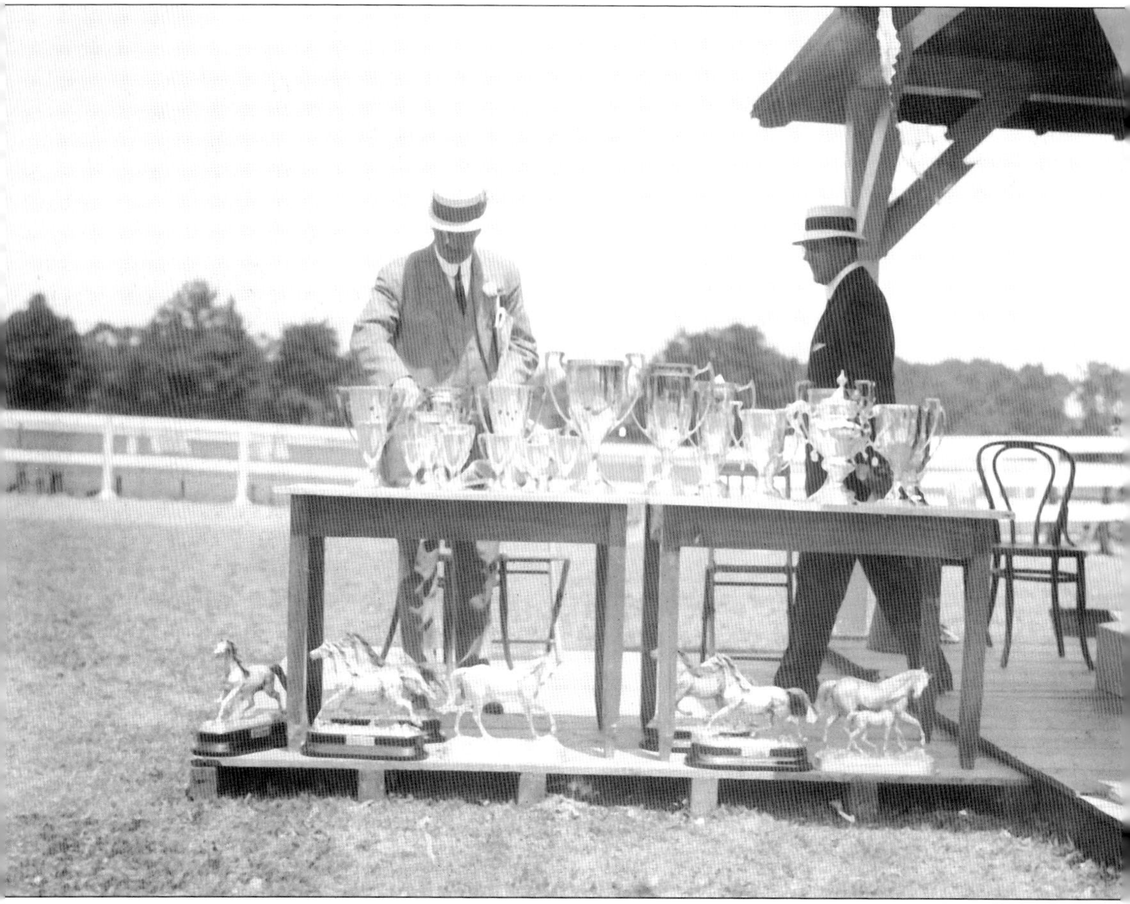

The 1920 Devon Horse Show was held from May 26 to 31, with a fifth day added to accommodate the nationwide entries from New England, New York, Kentucky, and the West for 157 classes. As the classes increased, so did the expansion of Devon's trophies. In this photograph, the array of pitchers, urns, and cups that are the diverse hallmarks of Devon's trophy collection are displayed. Bronze trophies, like the ones on the lower shelf in this photograph, are still presented today for classes including yearling, colt/gelding, and Thoroughbred. Perpetual trophies stay in a show's collection indefinitely, while challenge trophies may be retired. The qualifications for retiring a trophy vary, but the award must be won three times by either the horse and owner, or the same owner, for permanent possession.

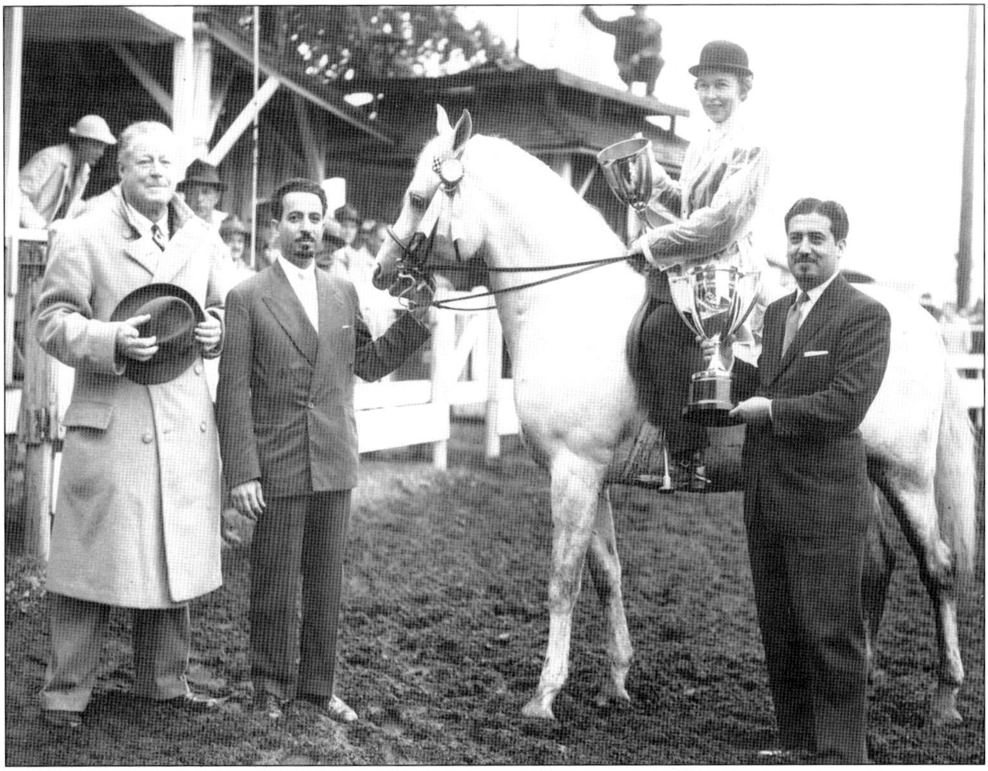

Throughout the years, trophy presentation protocol has remained consistent, as seen in these 1956 (above) and 1989 (below) photographs. The Trophy Committee maintains the Devon Horse Show's presentation traditions. Members of the Trophy Committee do not present trophies; their roles are to escort the trophy presenter, who is either the donor of the trophy or the sponsor of the class for which the trophy is being presented. If neither is available, a female volunteer will present the trophy on behalf of the donor. Every trophy presented at Devon should include a female presenter. Pictured below, Betty Moran (left) and Hope Montgomery Scott (right) are the female presenters in the Dixon Oval.

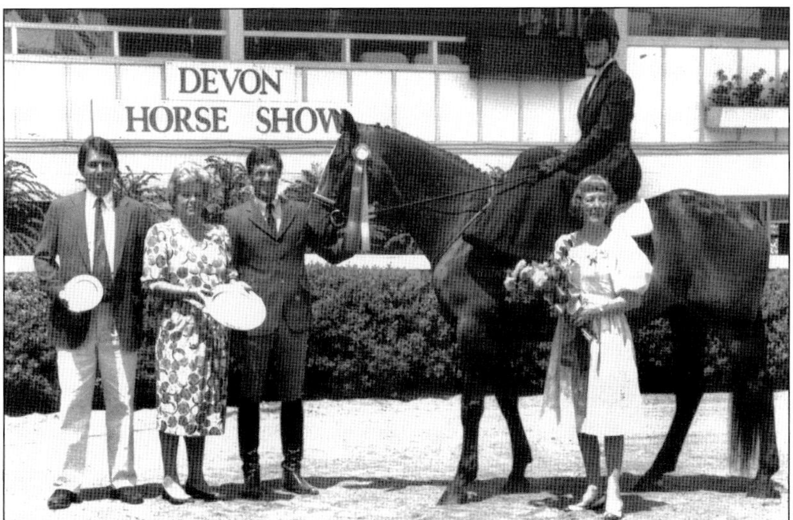

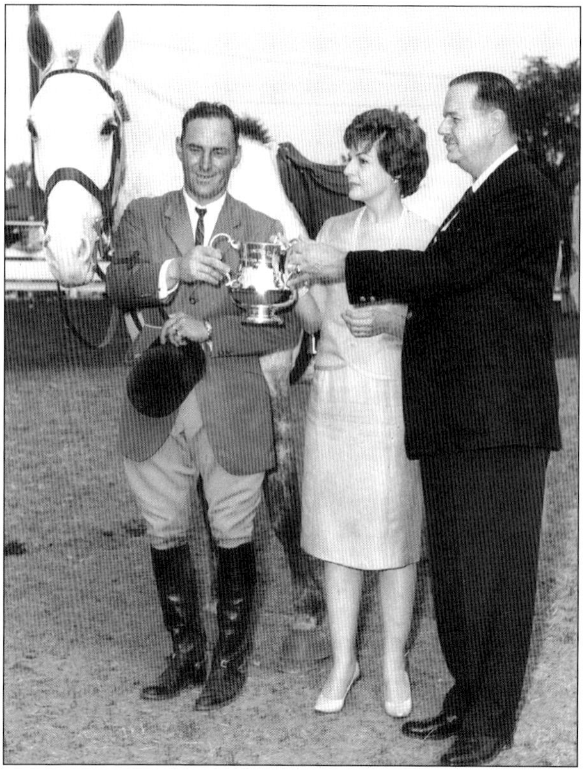

American Canadian actress and singer Dorothy Collins (center) and US senator Hugh Scott (right) present a trophy to David Kelley (left) in the 1960s. David Kelley, record holder for hunter jumper wins at the National Horse Show, showed Harry de Leyer's Snowman while de Leyer was hospitalized. Snowman was inducted into the Show Jumping Hall of Fame in 1992.

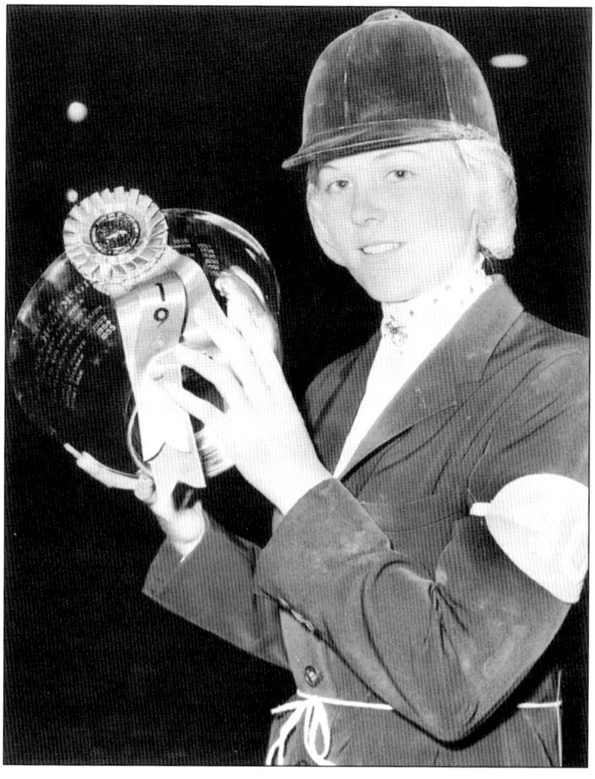

One of the highlights of Junior Weekend is the announcement of Best Child Rider, a competitor under 18 years of age. Here is the 1963 trophy winner for the Best Child Rider. This trophy, once won three times, is given permanent possession.

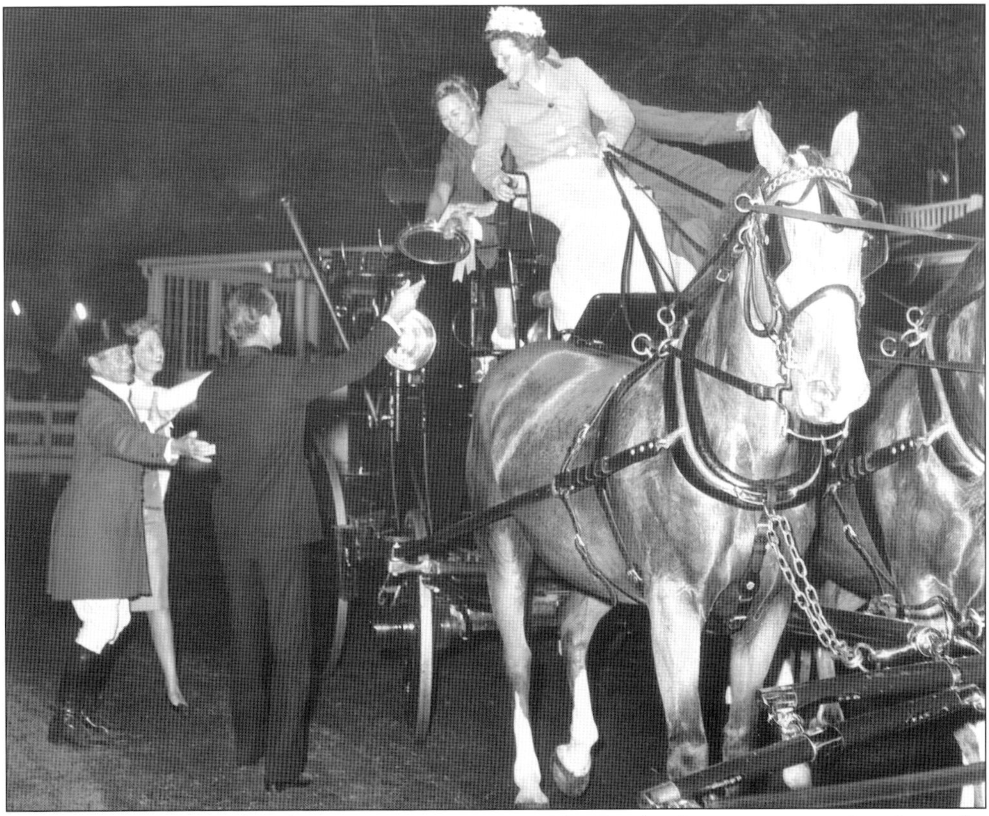

Shown here is the award of the 1963 Carriage Winner. The Trophy Committee provides a keepsake trophy for every class winner, and for classes without trophies, these keepsakes are silver bread and butter plates affixed with Devon's logo. All winners of classes with trophies receive a trophy winner plate made out of pewter.

Photographed here is the award of the 1963 Hackney class. At Devon, male Trophy Committee escorts will always offer a female presenter their left arm. This continues a tradition that originates from medieval times, when men escorted women around town and through the fields.

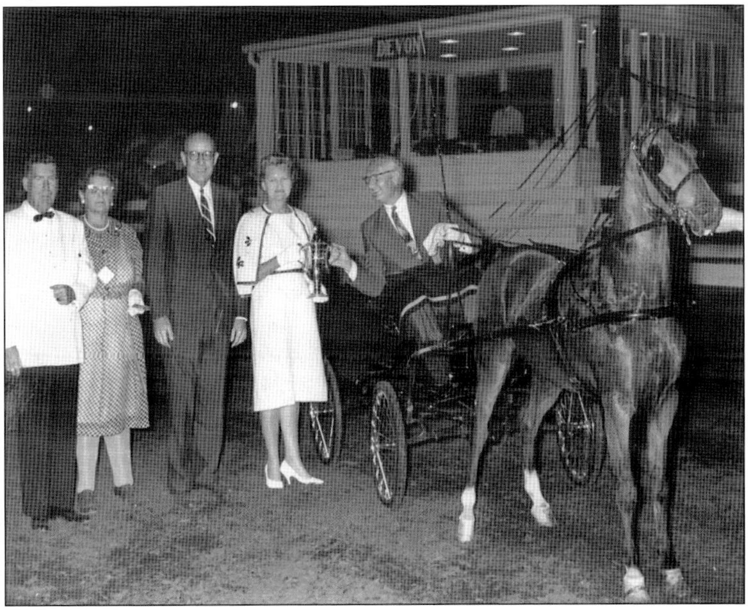

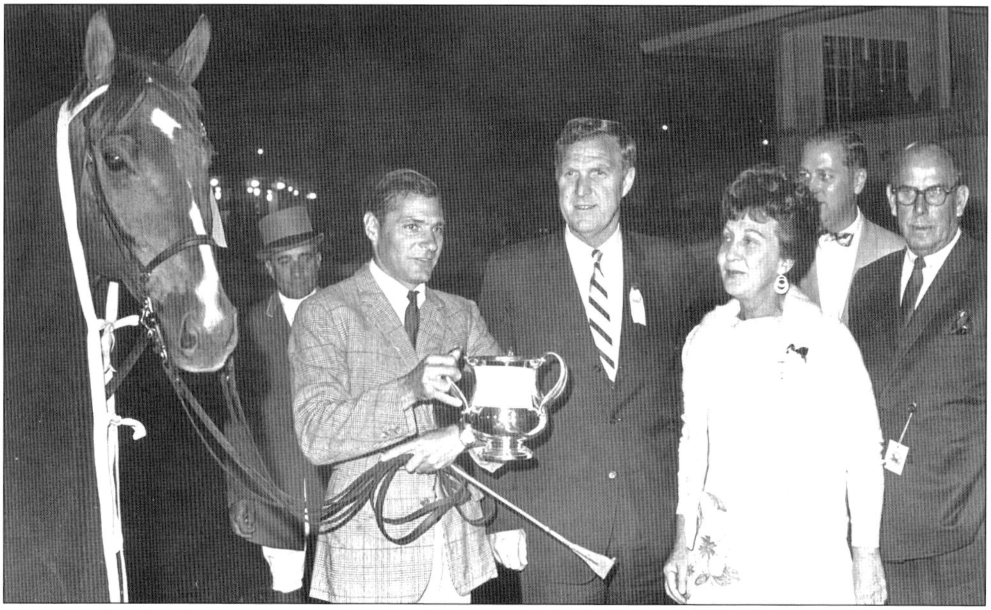

In 1968, Frank Chapot won the Green Jumper Stake on Sandcatcher. Frank Chapot competed in six consecutive Olympic Games, from 1956 to 1976. He won two silver medals in team show jumping, one at the 1960 Rome Olympics and the other at the 1972 Munich Olympics. He was inducted into the US Show Jumping Hall of Fame in 1994. His daughters Laura Chapot and Wendy Chapot Nunn still show at Devon today.

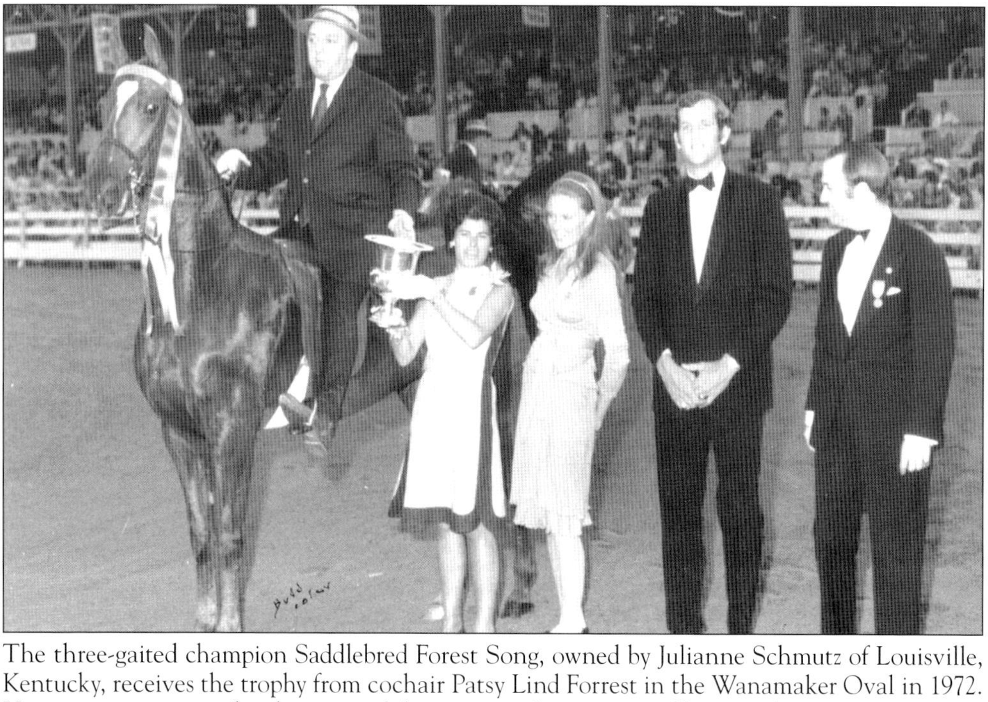

The three-gaited champion Saddlebred Forest Song, owned by Julianne Schmutz of Louisville, Kentucky, receives the trophy from cochair Patsy Lind Forrest in the Wanamaker Oval in 1972. Horses competing in the three-gaited division are the epitome of beauty, elegance, refinement, and expression. They perform in a precise manner and are judged on the animated walk, park trot, and canter.

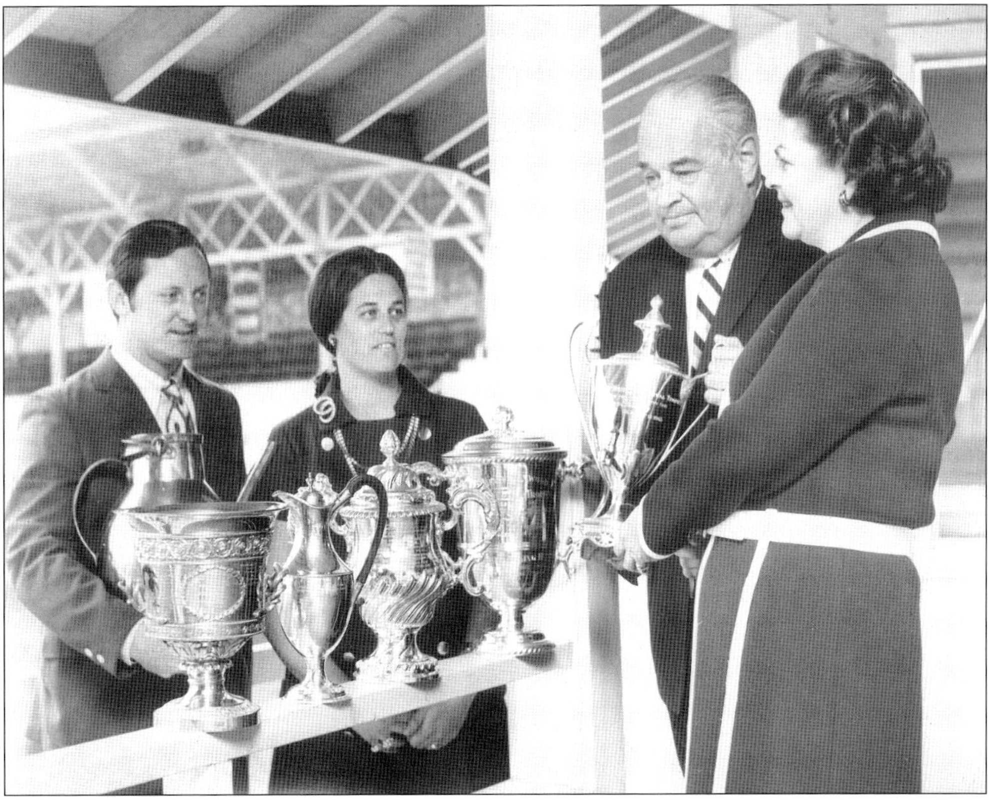

In this late-1960s photograph, John and Anne Girvin and her parents, Charles Egerton and Bunny Warburton, prepare the Devon trophies in the Committee Stand for presentation in the ring. Shown as part of this elaborate and ornate collection are the Vaughn Hackney Trophy and the Mrs. J. Mary Willitz Perpetual Trophy. Charles Egerton Warburton served as chair of the Trophy Committee for years. His father, Barclay Warburton, was a judge in Devon's first show in 1896.

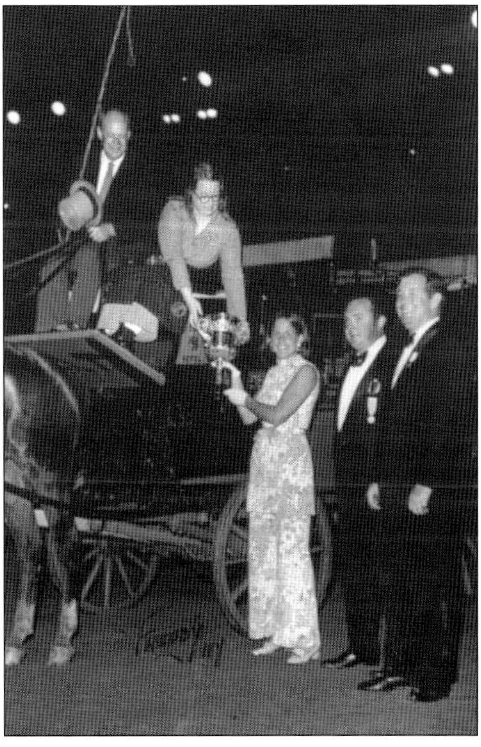

Hawthorne Melody Farm, with Philip Hornung as the whip, won the 1975 class 156 champion for the four-in-hand competition. The trophy being presented is the Mr. and Mrs. Thomas Foster Bright Perpetual Trophy.

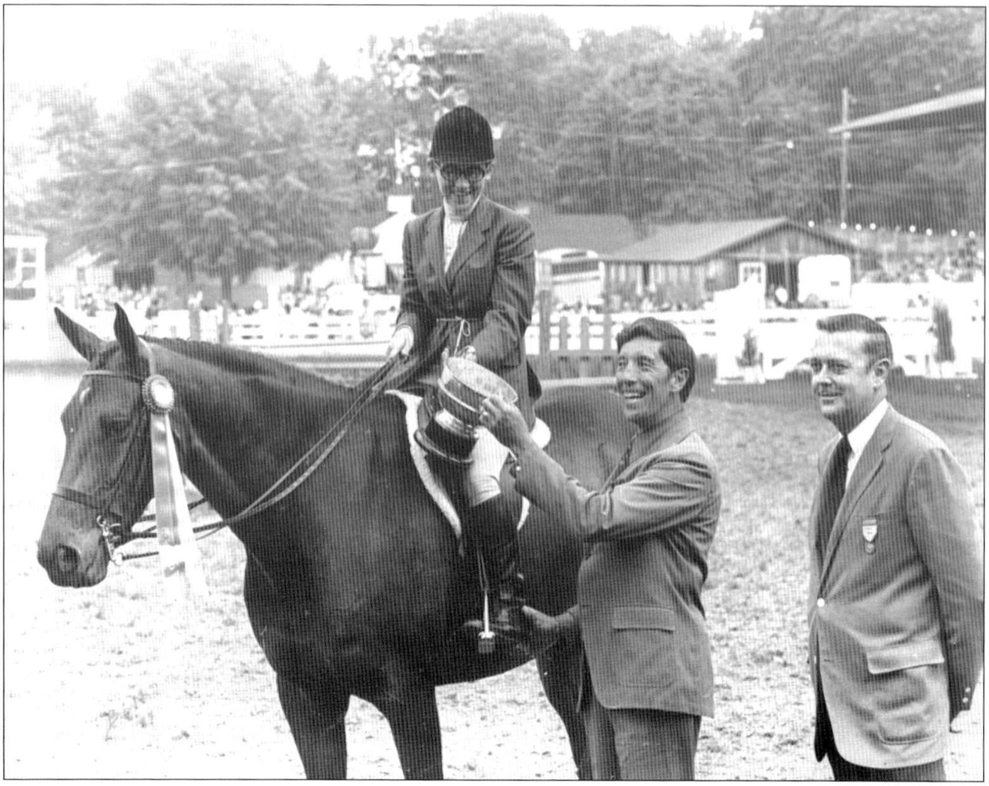

Michelle McEvoy, owner and rider of Amabette, was the champion of the 1970 Large Junior Hunter division. She is pictured here receiving the Cedar Lodge Challenge Trophy, presented by Victor Hugo-Vidal. In 1971, Hugo-Vidal was named as the AHSA Horseman of the Year. He trained a large number of students who retired the Hunt Team Trophies at both the National Horse Show and the Devon Horse Show.

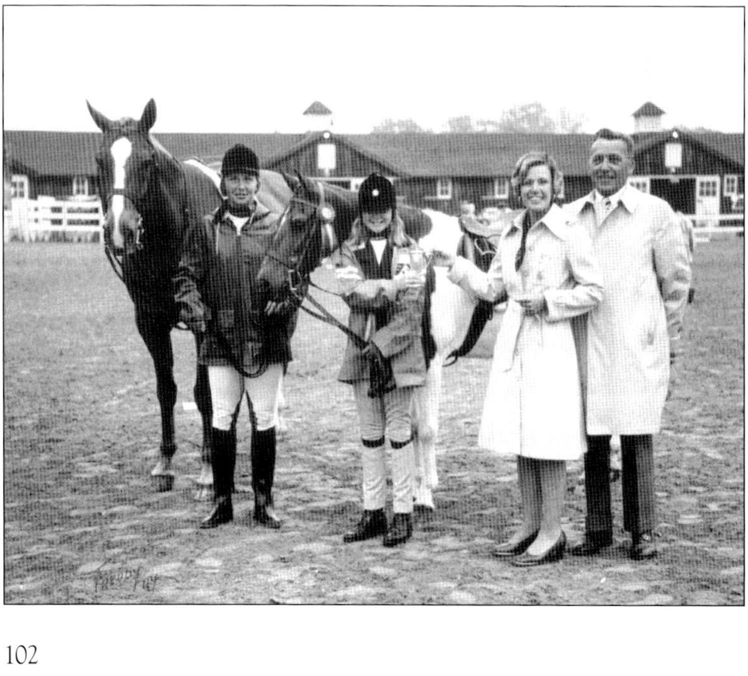

Devon's Rose Tree Cup is presented to the Walsh family by Sue Richards, escorted by Max Moran, in 1976. The Rose Tree Cup, given to the Devon Horse Show by the Rose Tree Fox Hunting Club of Delaware County, Pennsylvania, is now retired.

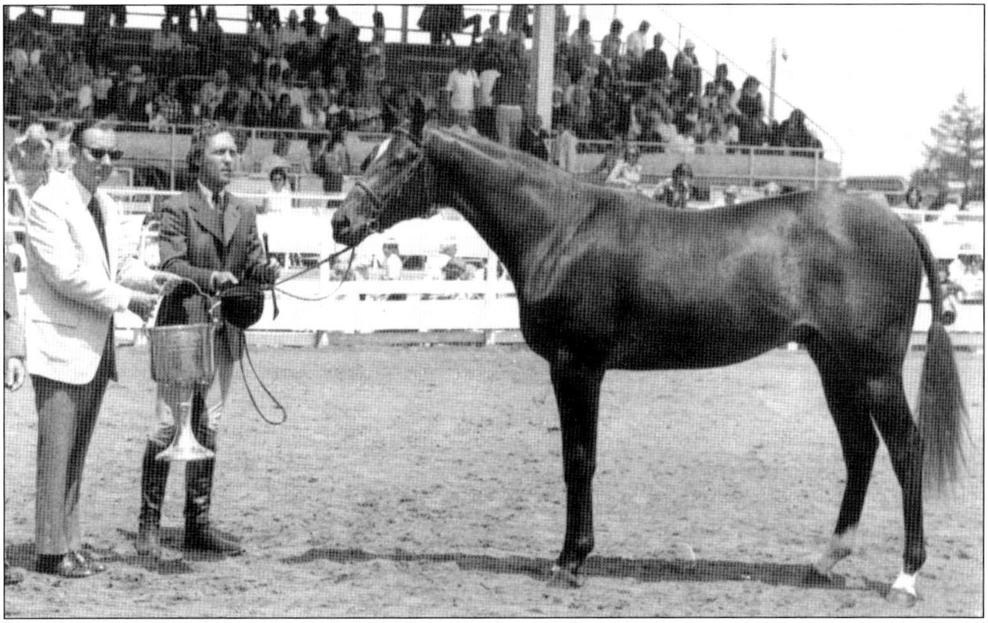

In 1976, J. Arthur "Bucky" Reynolds II showed Rocky Racoon to a victory for the Best Young Horse. The trophy presented in this photograph is retired. Reynolds was selected for the National Show Hunter Hall of Fame and honored at the 2017 Devon Horse Show and Country Fair. He was a leading figure and frequent champion on the nation's hunter jumper circuit, officiating at every major horse show in the United States.

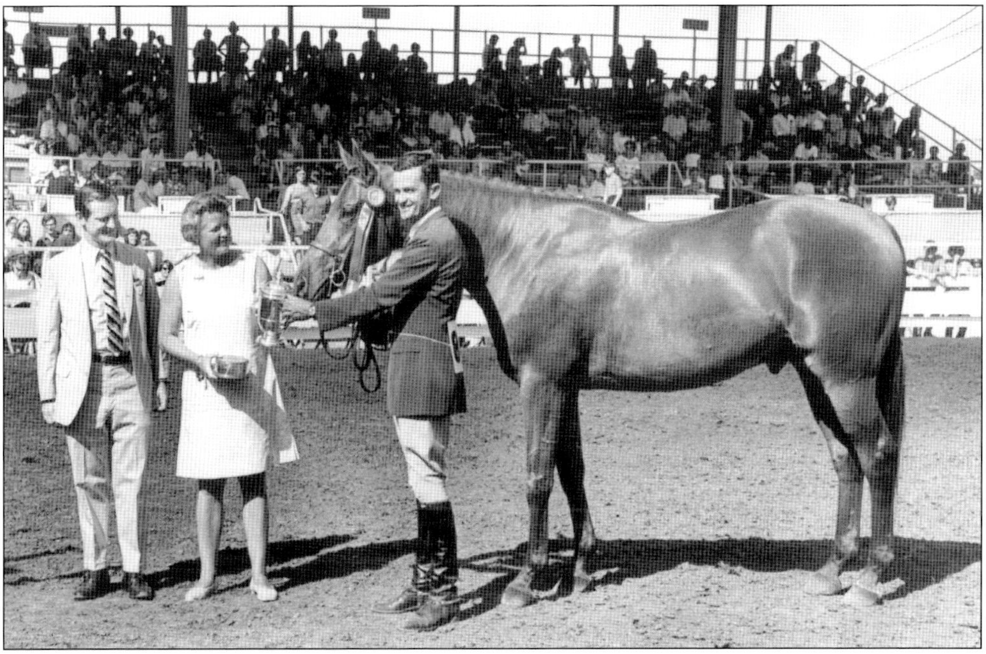

Chestnut Thoroughbred Old Dominion, owned by Mr. and Mrs. A.E. Cunningham and shown by Gene Cunningham, won hunter class 329 in 1973. Old Dominion was later shown by Katie Monahan Prudent, and they were champions throughout the East Coast in the conformation hunter division.

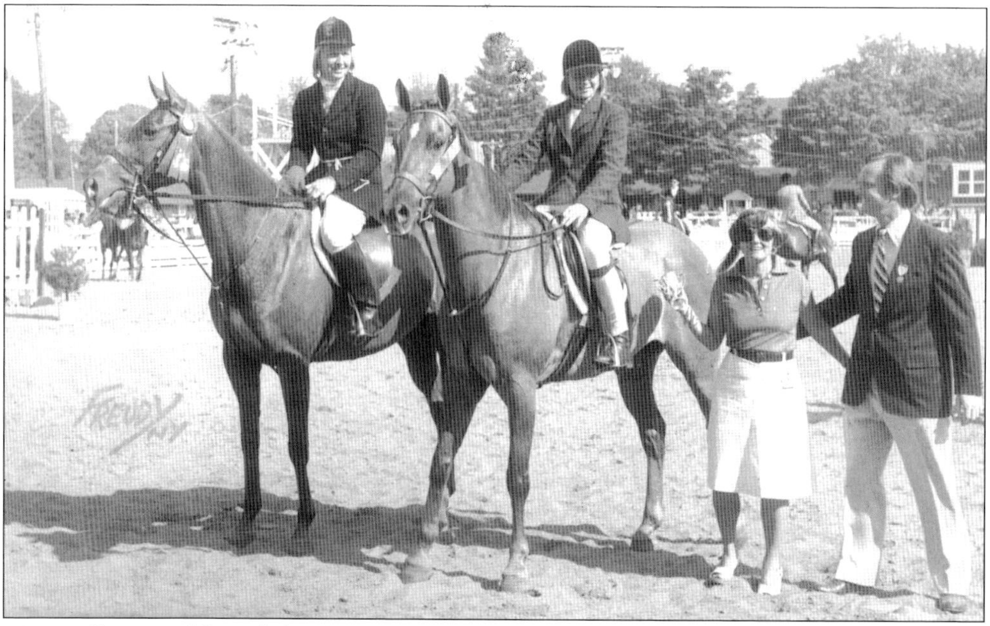

Mrs. William Walsh and daughter Mary win the 1977 Parent and Child class. The class is a hunter class ridden by a parent-and-child team over jumps not to exceed three feet. Each horse or pony is limited to one team. The family class is another event where immediate family members show horses and/or ponies under saddle at a walk, trot, or canter. Classes are judged on manners, performance, and suitability.

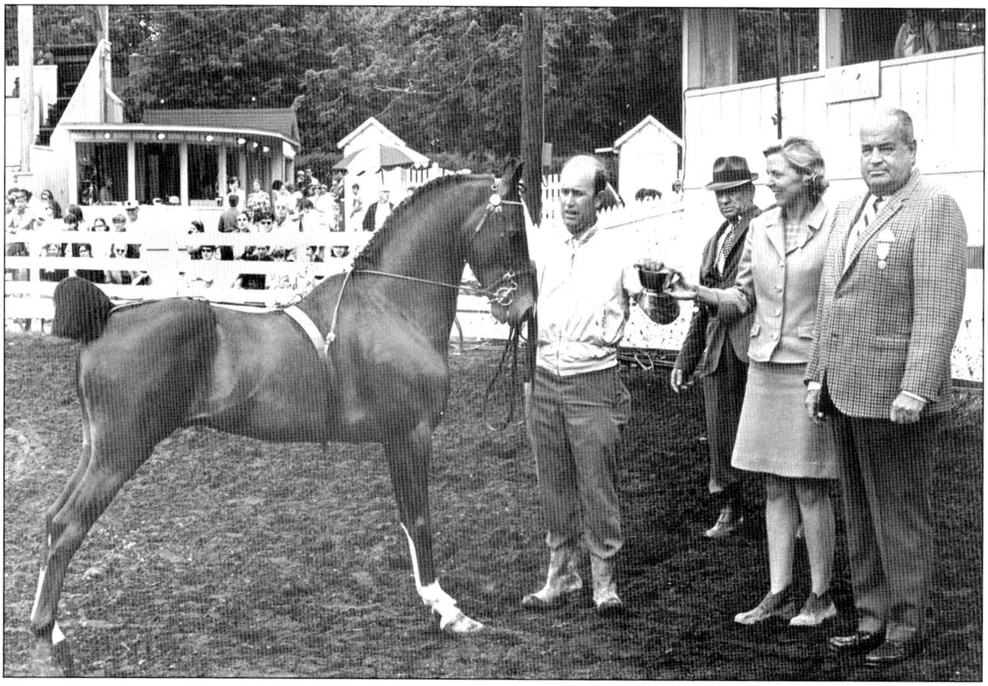

Here, David LaSalle receives the class 123 trophy from Isabel Robson in the Devon show ring. In 2017, the Northeast Hackney Association donated the David LaSalle Perpetual Trophy to the winning team in his honor.

Shown here is Ken McAfee and Blast of Bourbon, a three-gaited Saddlebred. Bunny Meister is shown as the Trophy Committee escort.

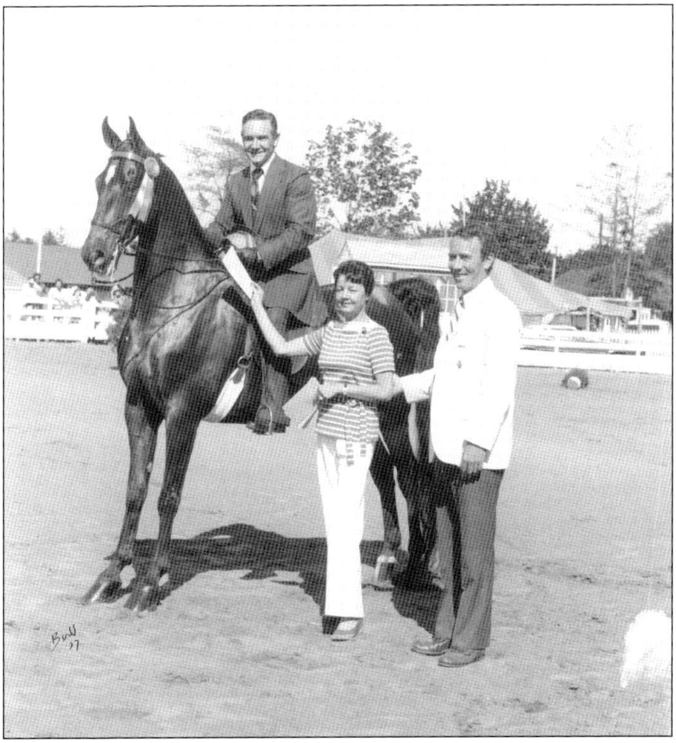

A role of the Trophy Committee is to uphold and perform the Devon Horse Show's trophy presentation traditions. There are specific rules governing the trophy presentation process, including the sequence of who descends the stairs into the ring, where to stand, how to hold the trophy being presented, and when and how to exit the ring.

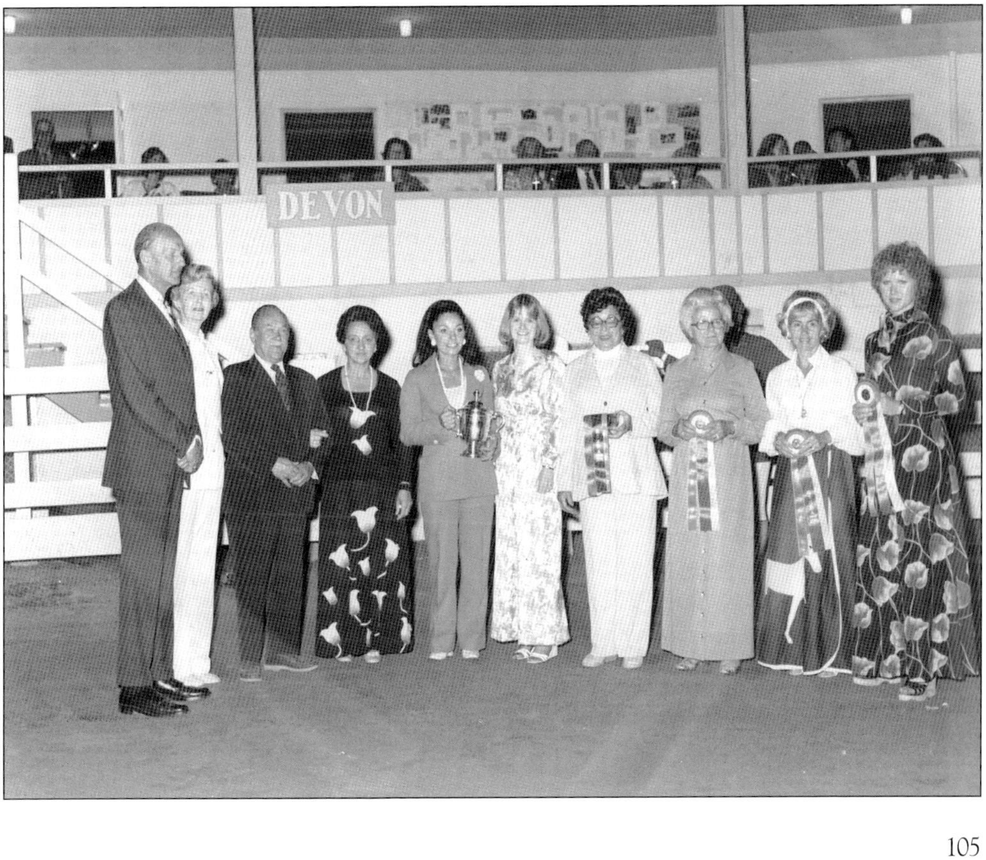

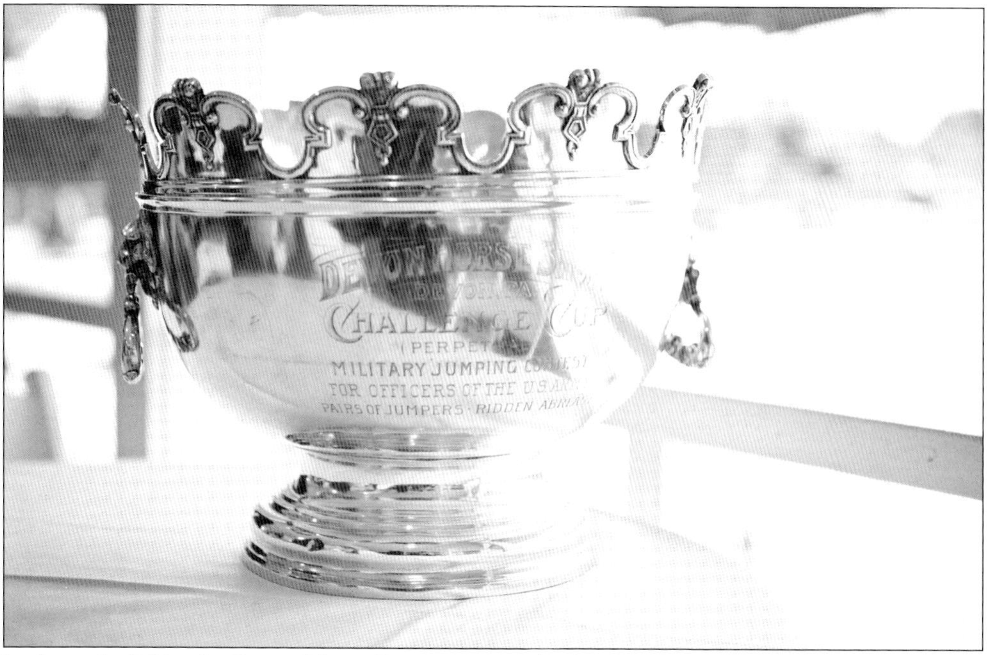

In the early 1900s, the Devon Horse Show recognized military riders with special classes restricted to active cavalry. The Devon Military Jumping Contest Challenge Cup, seen above, was the top prize for a class open exclusively to officers of the US Army. To win this class, two riders had to compete over fences, riding side by side on a pair of horses. In 1916, Capt. George S. Gibbs and Capt. William Mitchell won the Devon Military Jumping Contest Challenge Cup. The trophy has been a family heirloom, kept in the Gibbs family for over 100 years. Captain Gibbs's grandson donated the trophy back to Devon in a special ceremony in 2017. Pictured below are, from left to right, Wayne Grafton, chairman of the show; Rosalyn Gibbs; David Gibbs; and Eric Corkhill, Trophy Committee. (Both, courtesy of Brenda Carpenter Photography.)

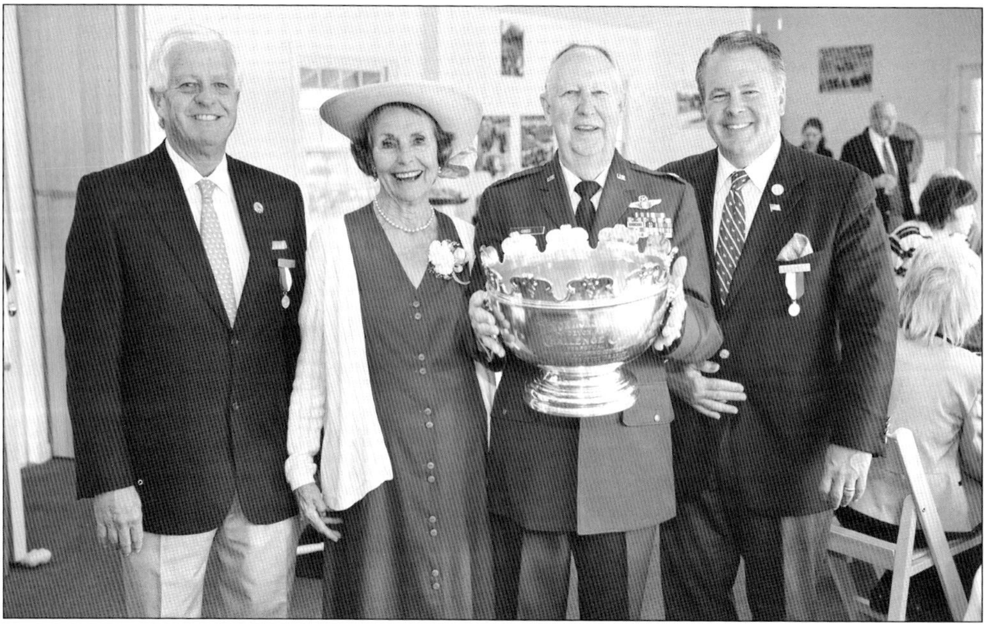

Six

Devon Legends and Celebrations

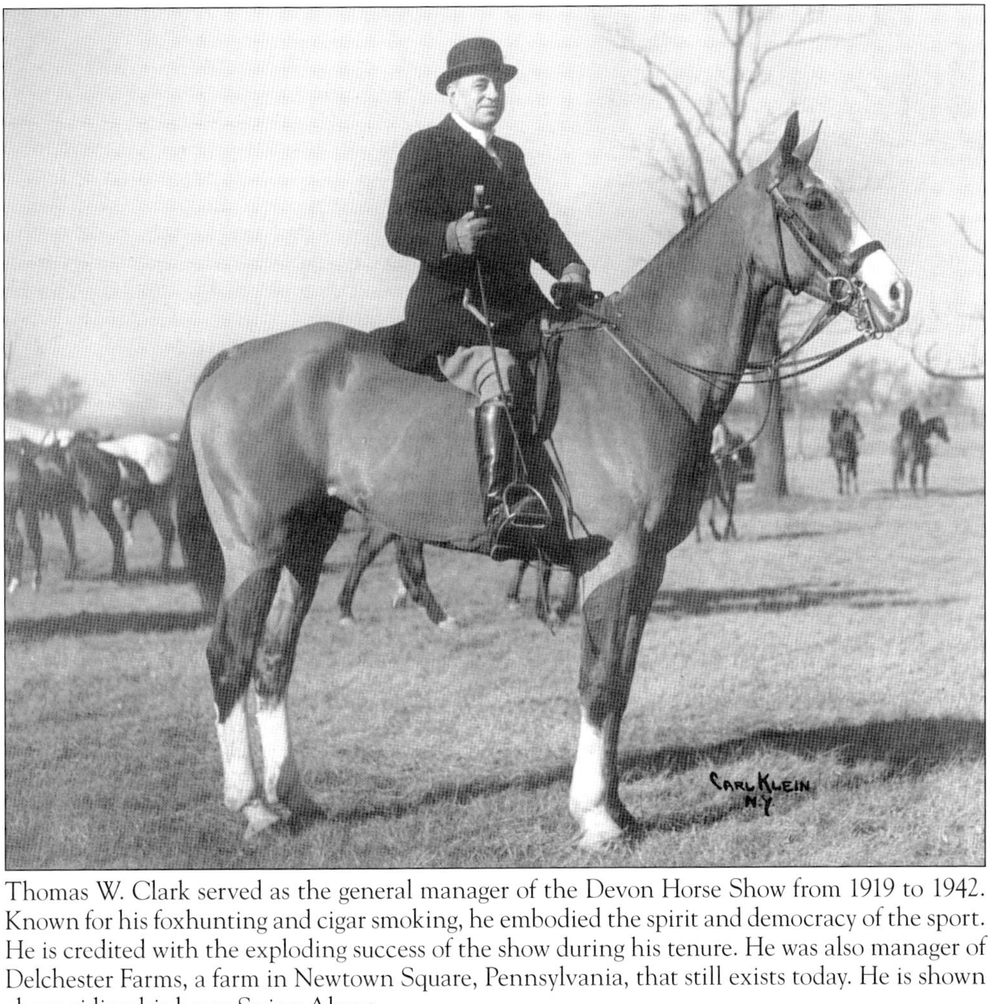

Thomas W. Clark served as the general manager of the Devon Horse Show from 1919 to 1942. Known for his foxhunting and cigar smoking, he embodied the spirit and democracy of the sport. He is credited with the exploding success of the show during his tenure. He was also manager of Delchester Farms, a farm in Newtown Square, Pennsylvania, that still exists today. He is shown above riding his horse Swing Along.

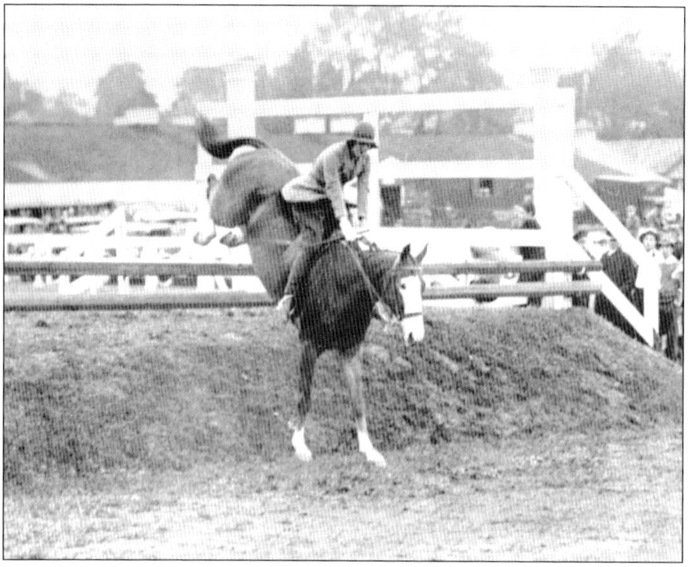

Prominent Philadelphians and socialites Charlotte Ives Montgomery, shown here, and her sister Helen Hope Montgomery Scott retired undefeated in Devon's Hunter Pair Division, and in the 1930s, both competed in the Open Jumper and Confirmation Hunter Champion classes. The Charlotte I. Montgomery Memorial Perpetual Trophy for the Regular Conformation Hunter Championship is presented each year in her honor.

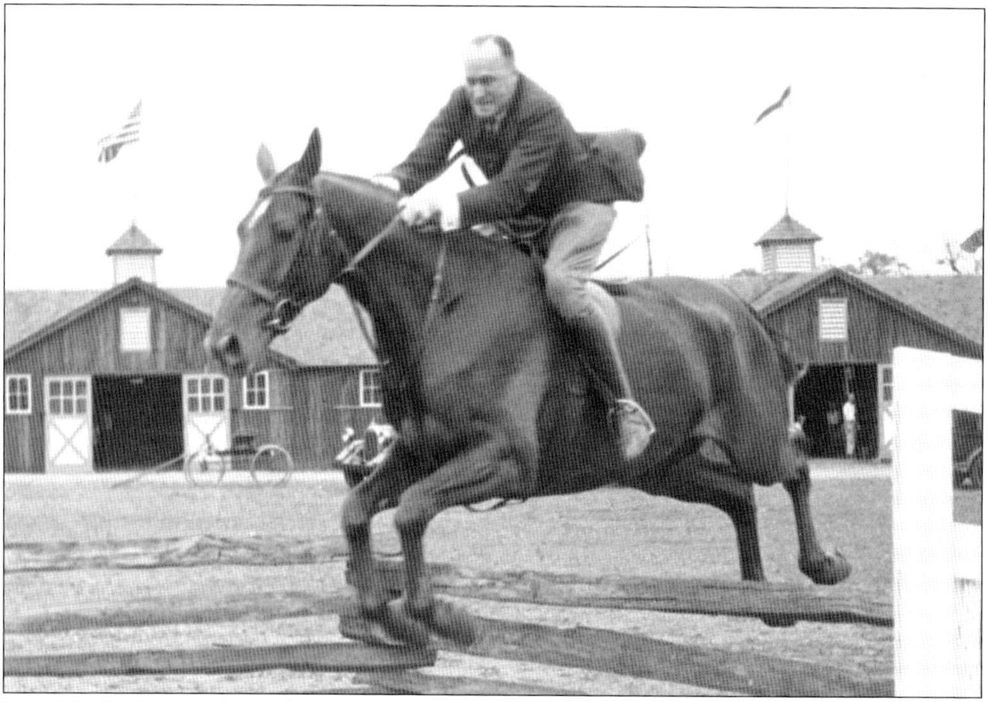

Isaac H. Clothier Jr., shown here in 1934, was truly a sportsman, having shown horses throughout most of his 85 years at all major competitions in the United States and Canada. He was Devon's ambassador at all the large shows. Clothier held the distinction of being the only lifetime director on the board of the Devon Horse Show and Country Fair. Without his efforts and devotion, there would be no Devon today.

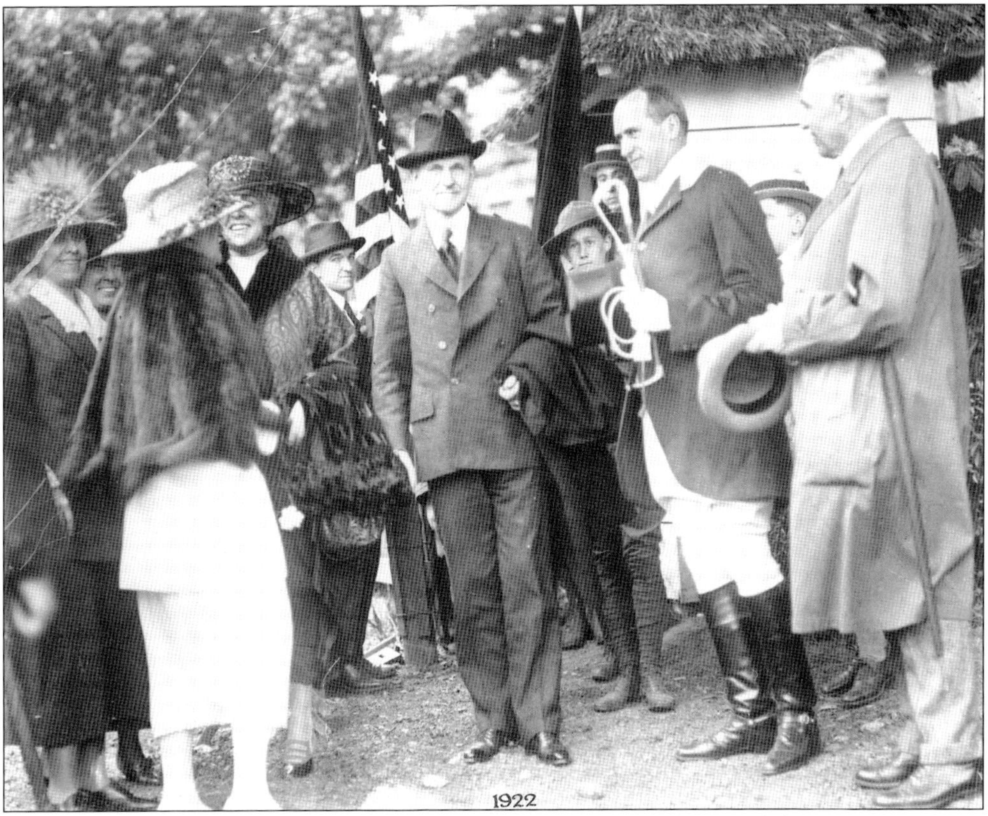

Devon has attracted many national figures, including Vice Pres. Calvin Coolidge on May 30, 1922. Pictured here are, from left to right, Grace Coolidge, Isabel Armstrong Barklie, Charlotte Fisher Pepper, Vice Pres. Calvin Coolidge, Isaac Clothier Jr., and Samuel D. Riddle. Fourteen months after his visit, Coolidge was sworn in following the death of Pres. Warren Harding. He made a return to the show in later years. (Courtesy of the SCRC, Temple University.)

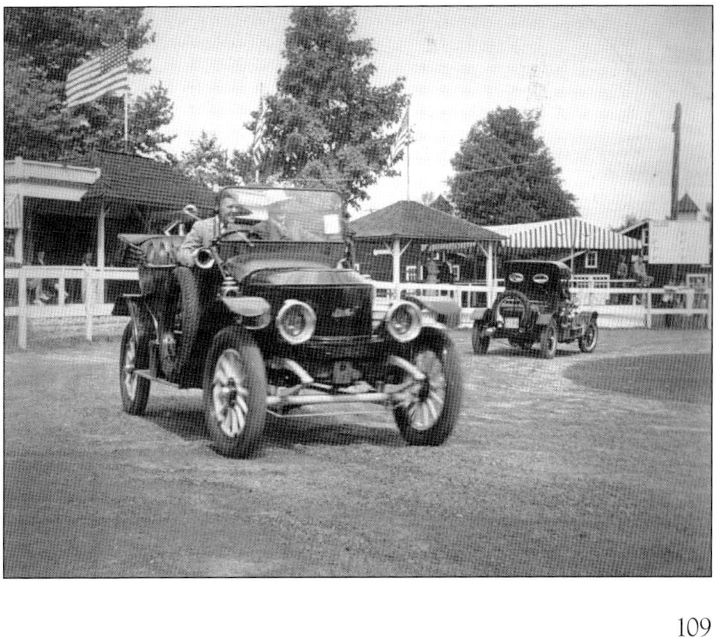

Following the conclusion of Devon week, the showgrounds were used to host an annual car show in the 1940s. Cars were put on display for viewing and also raced around the show ring.

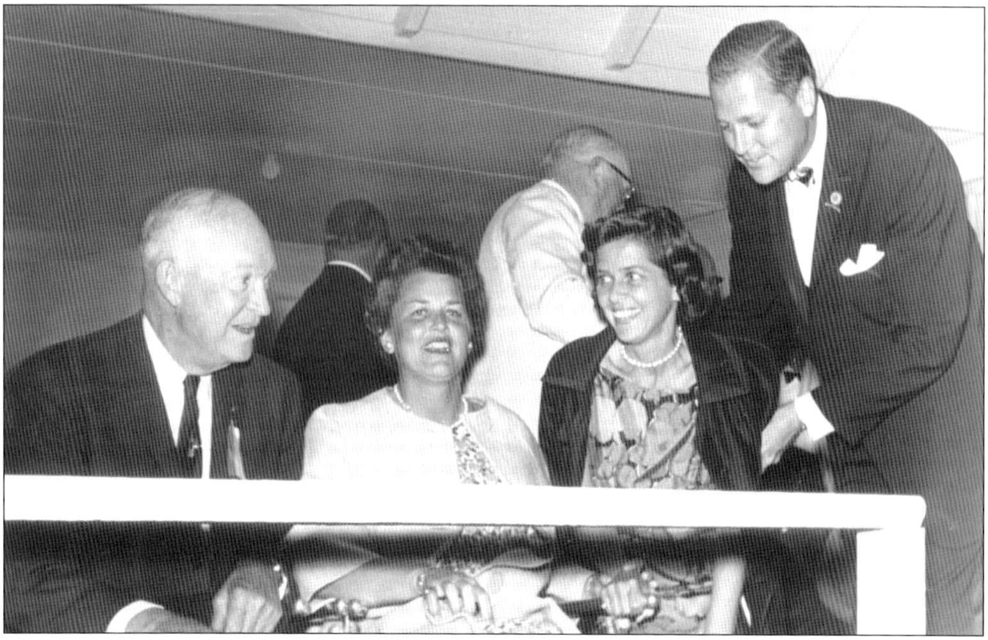

Pres. Dwight D. Eisenhower reportedly slipped into the Committee Stand to watch the Devon Horse Show and Country Fair in 1964 virtually unnoticed. He was escorted to Devon by his good friend Lt. Gen. Milton G. Baker, superintendent of Valley Forge Military Academy, to enjoy the cadets' dragoon ride and band concert. Pictured in the photograph above from left to right with the president are Gay Robinson and Thomas and Margaret Bright. Two years later, Eisenhower visited again, and the entire audience in the grandstands stood to honor him.

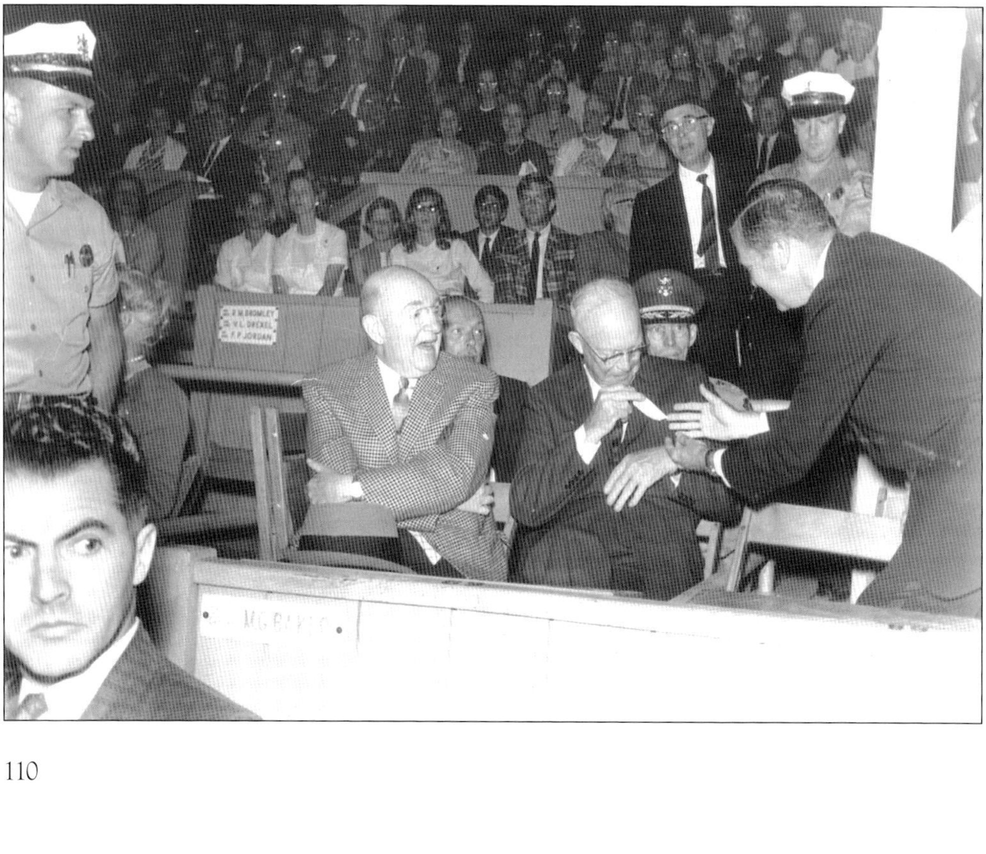

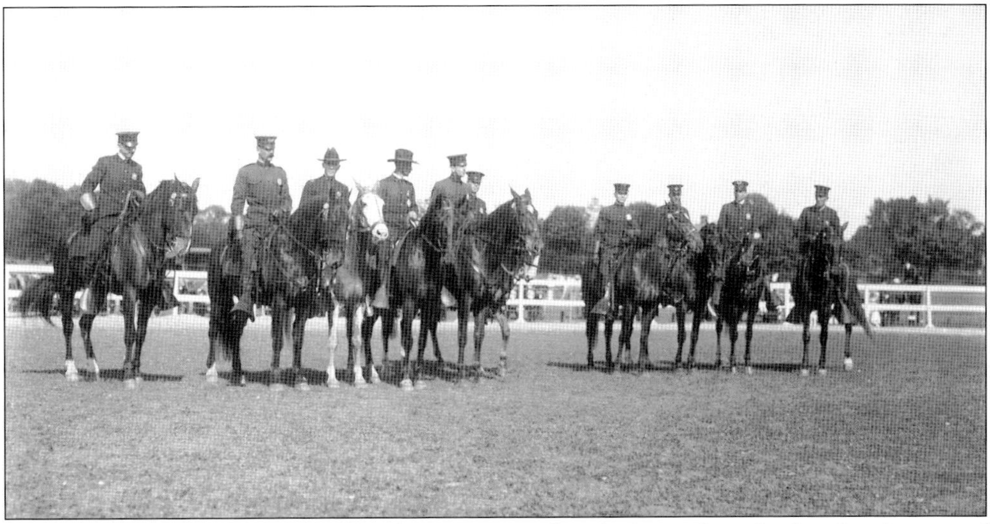

The Royal Canadian Mounted Police have performed at the horse show for decades. A troop of 32 horses and riders performs the "musical ride," a form of cavalry drill including intricate figures and movements demanding control, timing, and coordination.

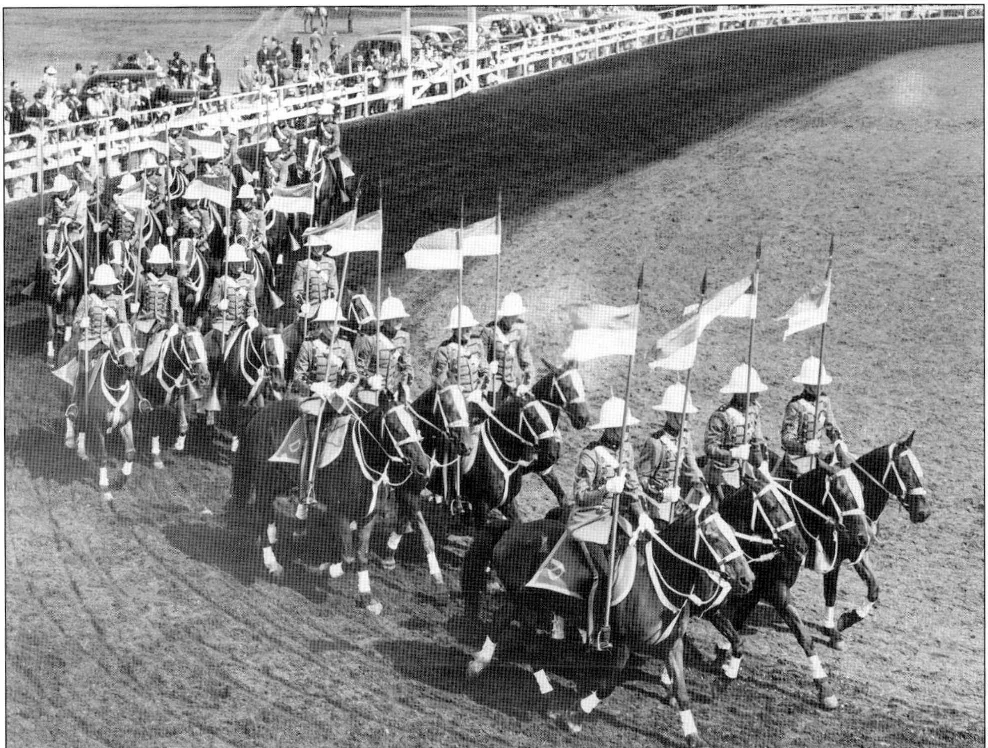

The Valley Forge Military Academy D Troop traditionally appeared at Devon. Shown here in 1940, the troop performed its musical ride before closing ceremonies at the show. Lt. Gen. Milton G. Baker, head of Valley Forge Military Academy in Wayne, served as designated chairman of Armed Forces Day, when cadets displayed flags in formation. At the 50th anniversary of the show on Memorial Day, the troop played taps. (Courtesy of the SCRC, Temple University.)

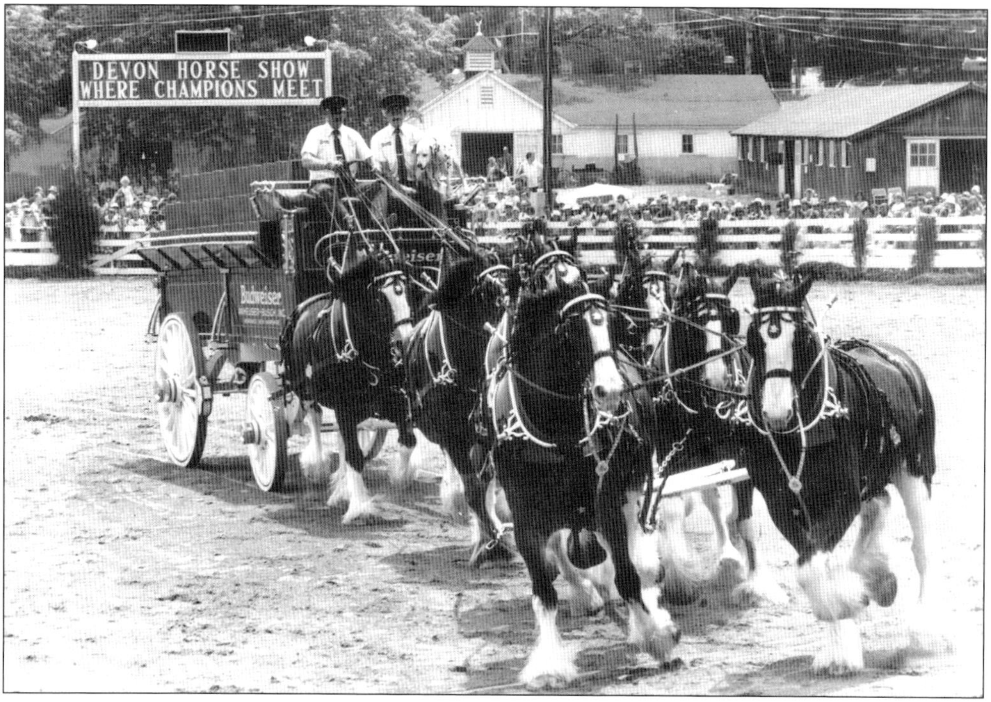

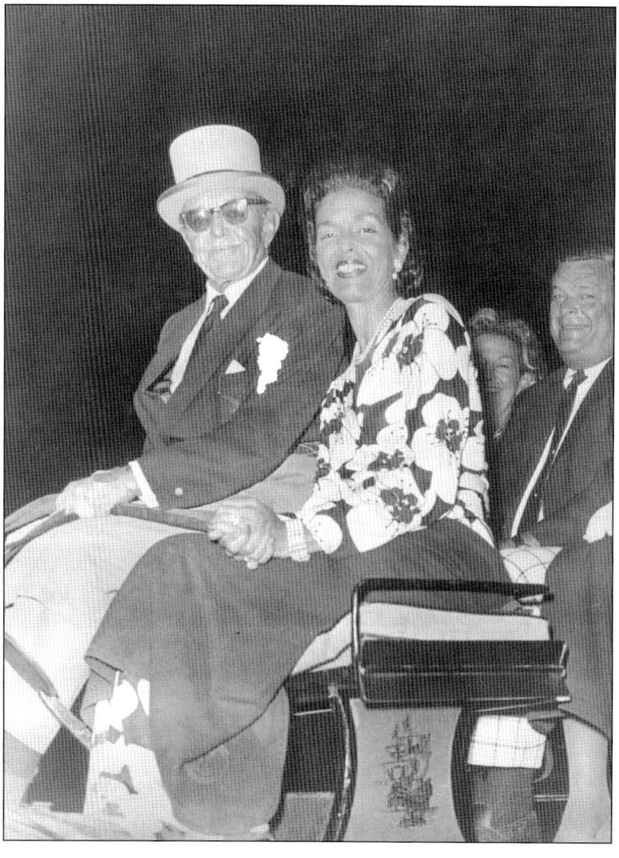

The famed Budweiser Clydesdales bring the lost art of brewery wagon driving to Devon. Shown here in 1976, the Clydesdales eight-horse team pulls a 3.5-ton wagon in a series of intricate maneuvers. The driver holds eight separate reins laced through the fingers of both his hands to individually control each horse. Dalmatian mascot Bud joins the drivers atop the wagon.

The Budweiser Clydesdales made their first-ever appearance in the United States in 1933 and were a gift from American brewing magnate August Anheuser "Gussie" Busch Jr. to his father in celebration of the repeal of Prohibition. Busch, pictured here with his niece Sallie (Kenneth) Wheeler, traveled from St. Louis, Missouri, to participate in a driving class at the 1975 Devon Horse Show.

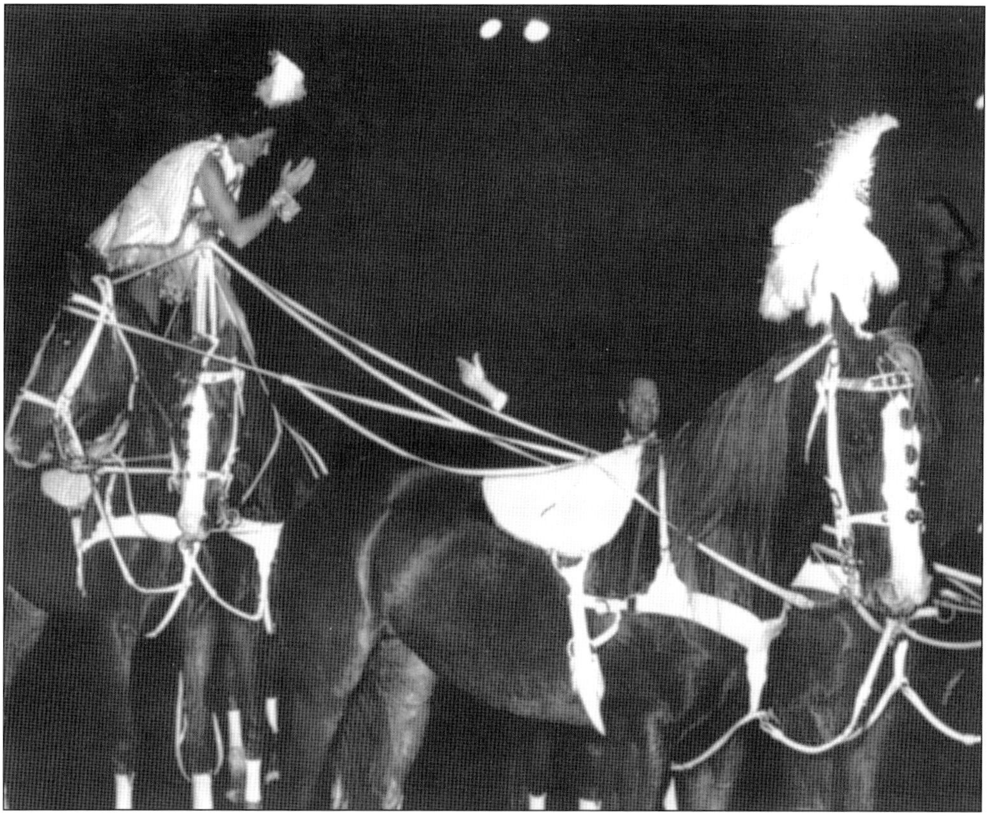

During the 1950s and 1960s, many celebrities were invited and made appearances at the show. Thomas Bright (right), the horse show president, added new classes for publicity and advertised the show as a spectator's event. Pictured with Bright is Gypsy Rose Lee (left), the infamous American burlesque entertainer, who presented a trophy.

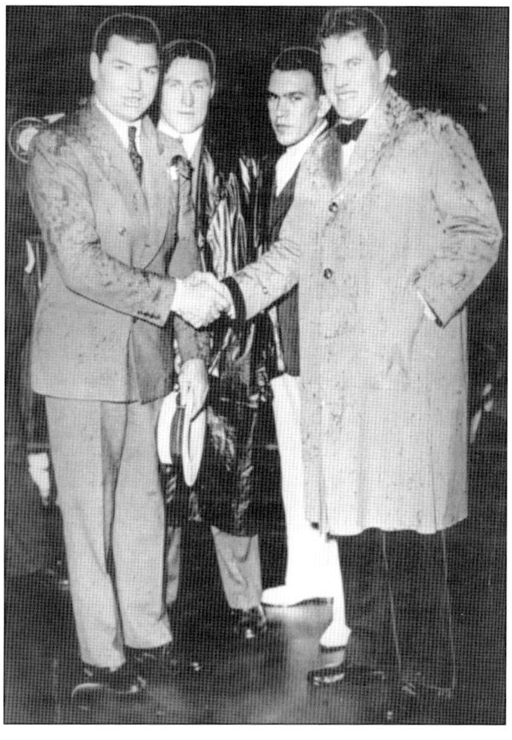

American professional boxers and world heavyweight champions Jack Dempsey (far left) and Gene Tunney (far right) attended the show in 1933. They were there to referee at the amateur boxing matches staged at the show that year on Saturday, May 27. Admission was $1. (Courtesy of The Engraver.)

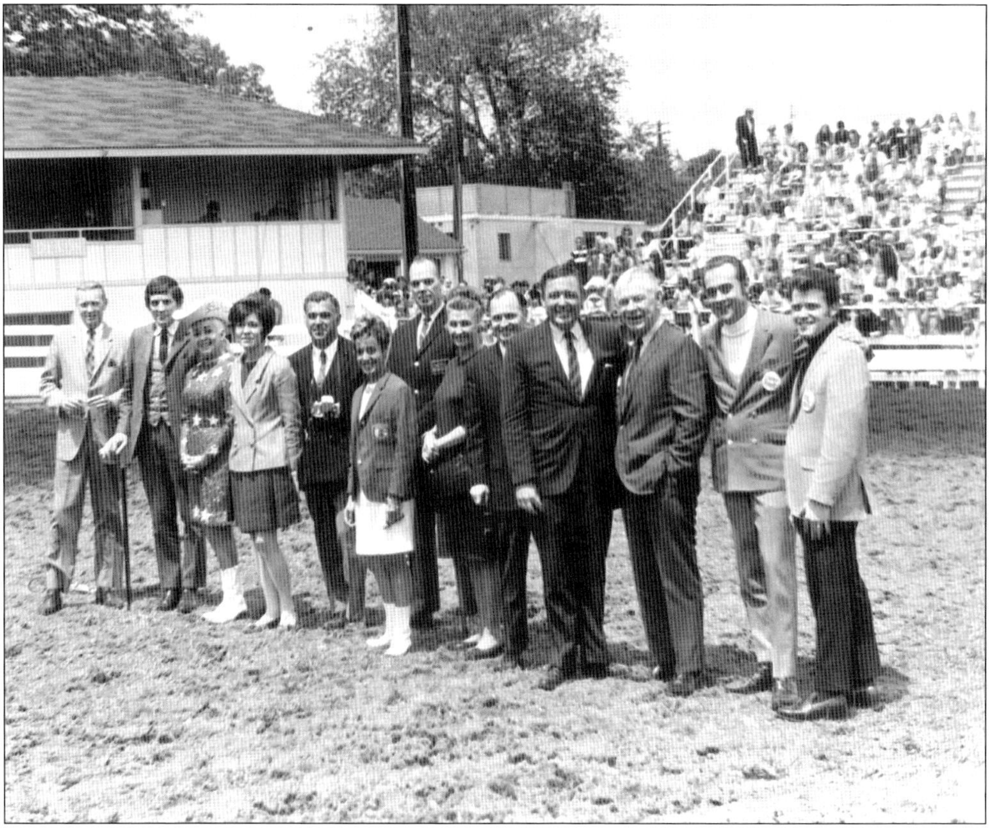

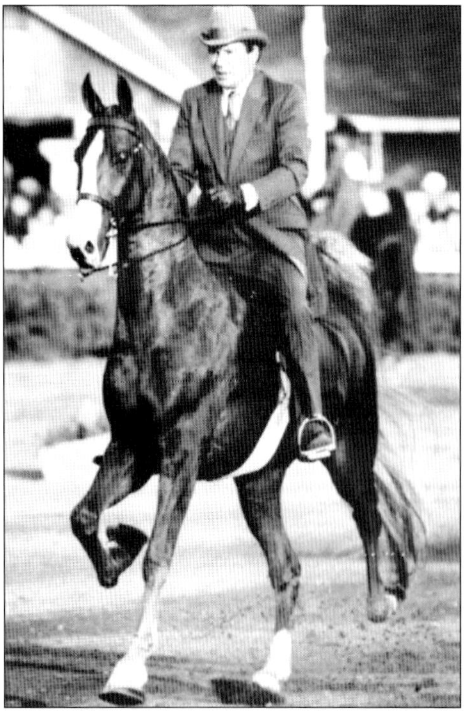

Jonathan Frid (second from left), Sally Starr (third from left), and Gunner Back (third from right) visited the Devon Horse Show and Country Fair. Frid portrayed Barnabas Collins in the popular 1960s vampire serial *Dark Shadows*. At his first appearance in 1968, he drew more than 20,000 visitors. Sally Starr was a prominent 1950s celebrity television personality for local Philadelphia station WFIL-TV (now WPVI). Gunner Back was a WFIL-TV, CBS, and ABC news anchor.

William Shatner, known as Captain Kirk in *Star Trek*, was a top amateur rider who competed at Devon from 1988 to 1990. He is pictured at left on Talent Contest, competing in the Amateur Championship Three-Gaited Saddlehorse class. Other celebrities who have visited or competed in Devon include William Boyd, also known as Hopalong Cassidy, James Cagney, Carson Kressley, and Chubby Checker. Paul Newman, Joanne Woodward, Joan Lunden, and Bruce Springsteen have all had their children compete at the show.

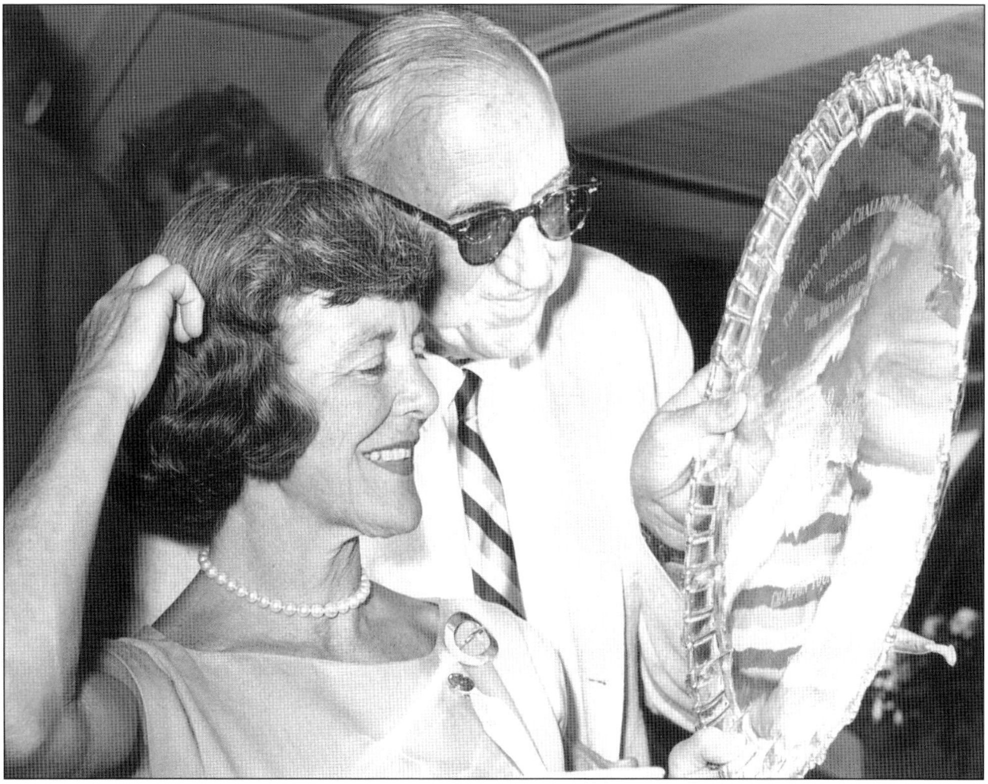

Philadelphia socialite and philanthropist Helen Hope Montgomery Scott was a lifelong devotee of the Devon Horse Show and Country Fair and Bryn Mawr Hospital. She served as an executive director and chair for the Devon Horse Show and Country Fair and had a great respect and understanding for the tireless volunteers of the organization. She began competing in jumping classes at Devon when she was 13 years old. In the 1950s, she was champion of both the Open Jumper and Conformation classes. Scott was the inspiration for the movies *The Philadelphia Story* and *High Society*. She brought grace and free-spirited elegance to Devon. "Devon is a show for the public," Hope Scott has been quoted. "It's important to the riders that there is a big audience. I felt that way, too, when I competed. I wanted a big hand when my horse went well." (Right, courtesy of Alix Colman, photographer.)

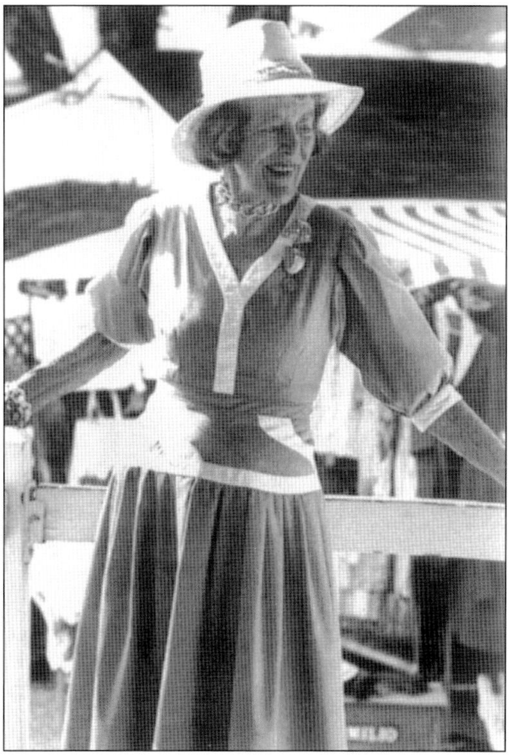

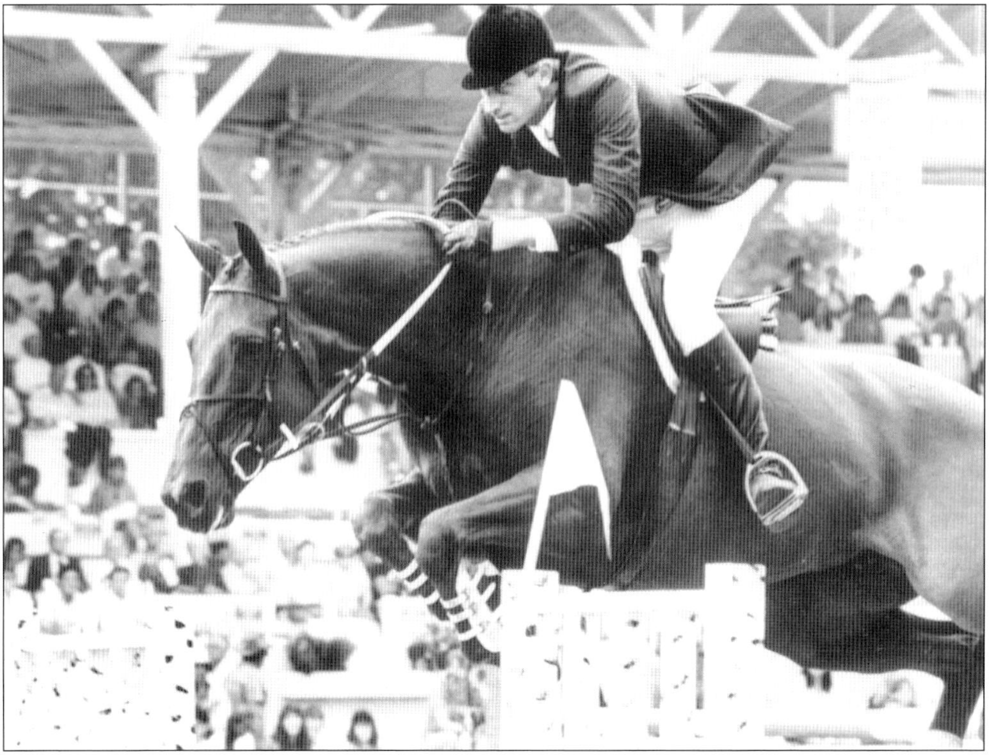

Joe Fargis, shown here on Mill Pearl, frequently competed in the Devon Grand Prix. An Olympic double gold medalist in 1984 and team silver medalist in 1988, he rode Mill Pearl to the best score to win team silver for the United States at the Seoul Olympics. The Devon Horse Show was a selection site for the 1992 Summer Olympics in Barcelona.

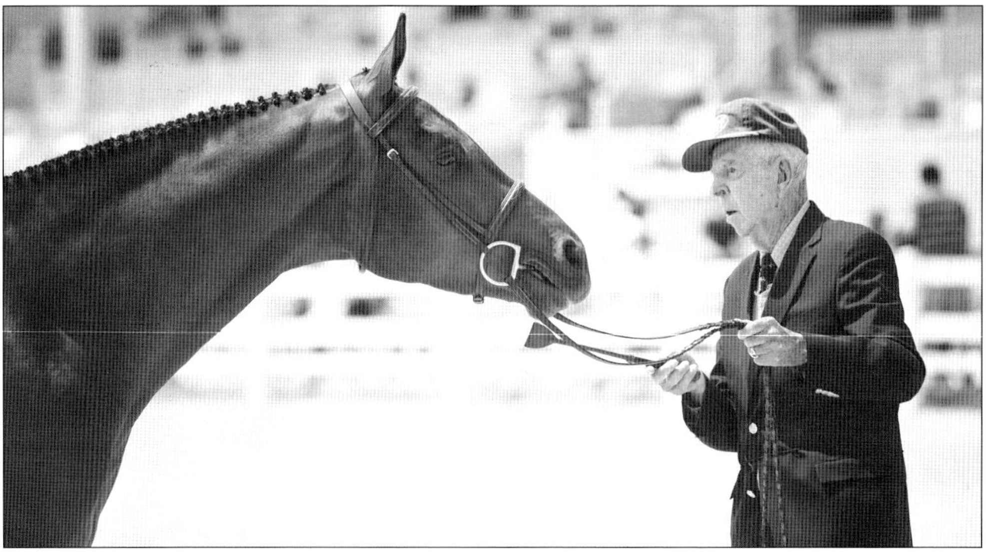

The name Wheeler is well known at Devon. Three generations of Wheelers, including Kenneth Wheeler Sr., shown above, have competed and won at Devon. Kenny Wheeler and his wife, Sallie, have long been supporters of the show and have ridden and trained top hunters and Saddlehorses. Devon renamed the Gold Ring in the Wheelers' honor. (Courtesy of Brenda Carpenter Photography.)

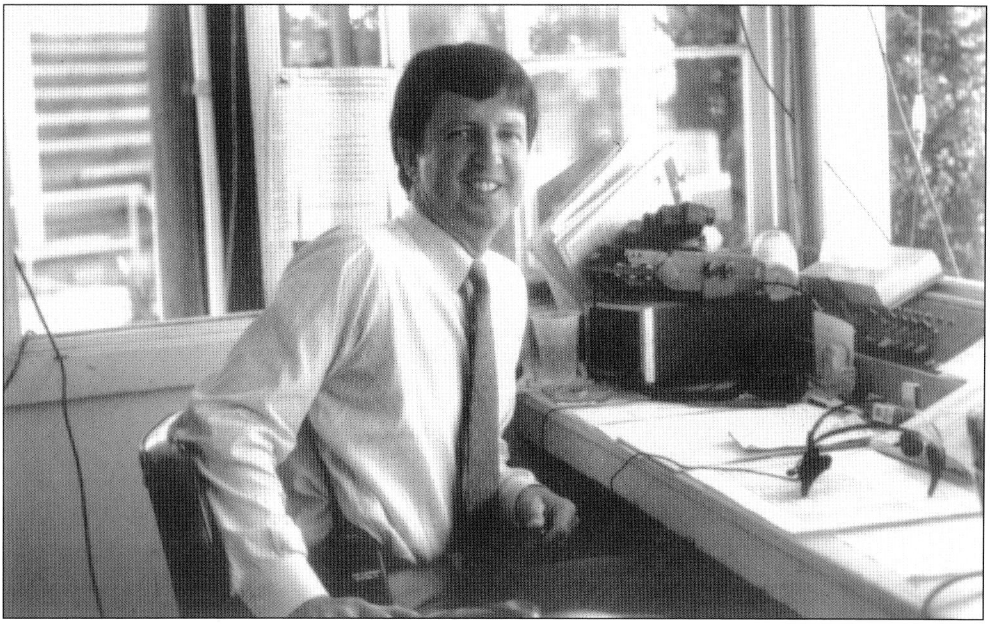

Peter Doubleday is the comanager and announcer of the show. As "The Voice" of Devon, he brings the show to life over its 11 days. Since 1975, he has announced every major horse show, including international events such as the Fédération Equestre Internationale (FEI) World Cup finals, Pan American Games, FEI World Equestrian Games, and the Olympics. He was elected to the Show Jumping Hall of Fame in 2019, where he serves as chairman.

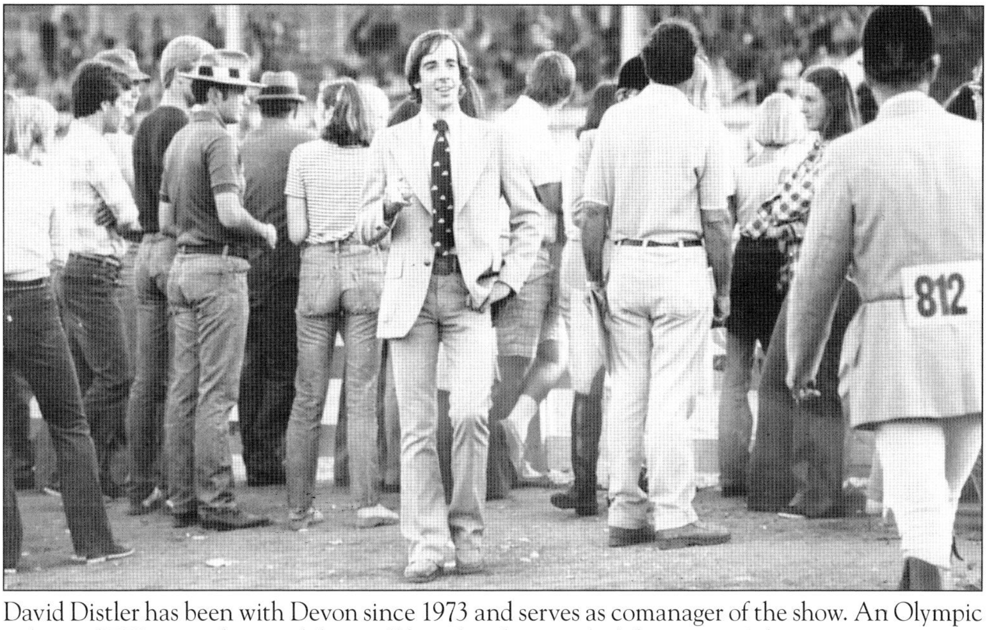

David Distler has been with Devon since 1973 and serves as comanager of the show. An Olympic judge and FEI steward general, he is affiliated with several of the country's biggest competitions, including the USET Show Jumping Olympic Trials, Washington International and National Horse Shows, Winter Equestrian Festival, and United States Equestrian Federation (USEF) Show Jumping Talent Search. He is highly respected for his encyclopedic knowledge of the rules. He was elected to the Show Jumping Hall of Fame in 2020.

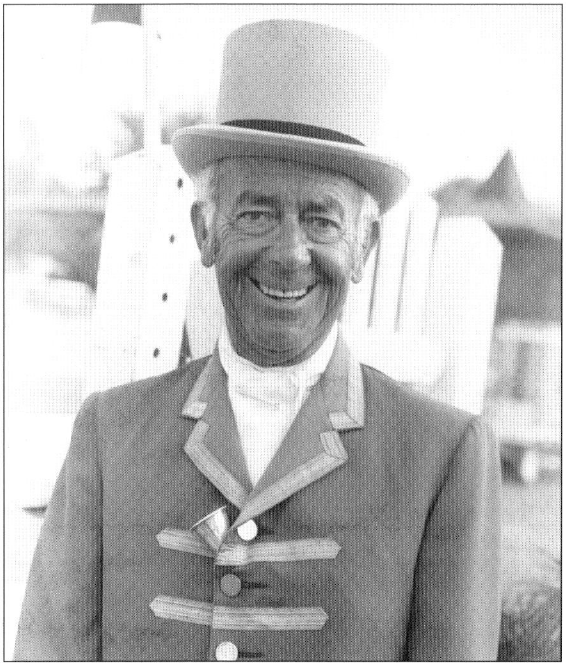

Ringmaster Clarence "Honey" Craven oversaw the organization of the entire Devon Horse Show as manager and manager emeritus from 1976 until his passing in 2003. Although he officiated at over 30 annual prestigious shows in the United States, Devon remained a favorite since his hunter competition win in 1925. He returned to Devon the following year, riding a pony around barns calling various classes so exhibitors could get into the ring on time. Recipient of the US Equestrian Lifetime Achievement Award, he was endeared by horse show committees, officials, exhibitors, and the entire equestrian community.

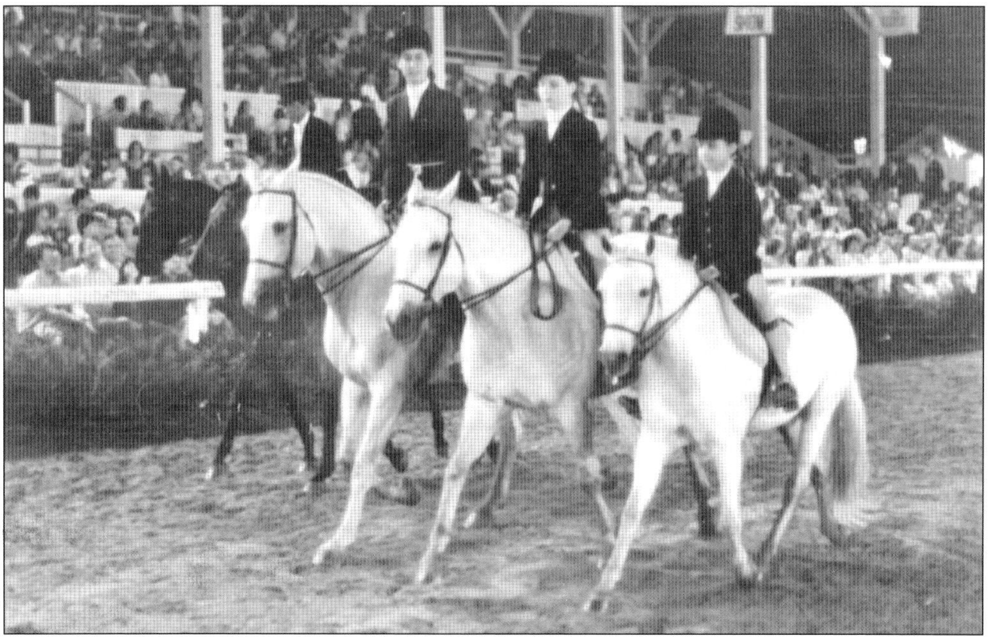

The Chapot family has excelled at Devon and on the international circuit for decades. Winning the Family Class at Devon in the late 1970s are, left to right, Mary Mairs Chapot on her Thoroughbred stallion Good News Joe; Wendy Chapot Nunn on Joy Slater's homebred pony Poconutsmoke; and Laura Chapot on Millbrook Farm's Welsh pony Snowgoose. Laura Chapot has won over 100 Grand Prixs, represented the United States on several winning national teams, and won the Leading Rider Title and the Open Jumper Champion Trophy at Devon numerous times. Her mother, Mary Mairs Chapot, was the first woman to ride for the United States in the Olympic Games in 1964, teaming with husband Frank Chapot as the first husband-wife combination to ride for the USET.

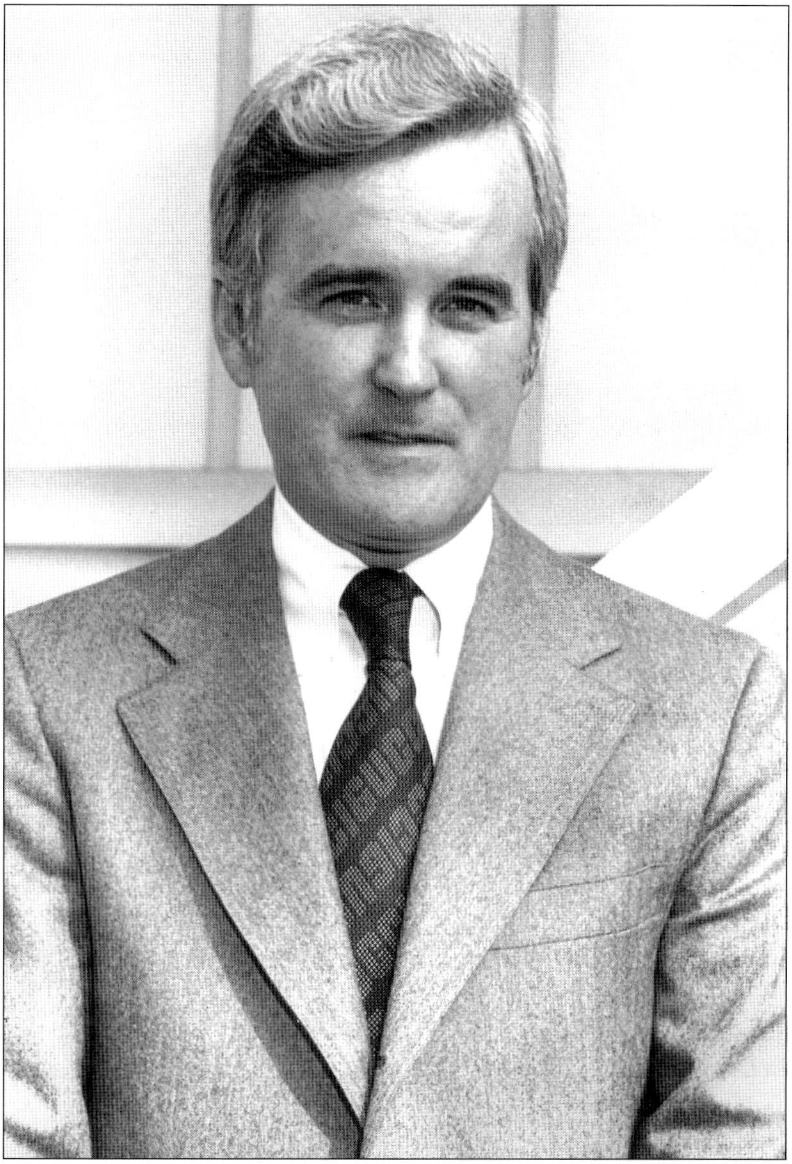

Leonard A. King Jr. devoted over half his life to Devon, leading as president from 1995 to 2005, chairman from 2005 to 2012, and chairman emeritus until his passing in 2015. One of his greatest accomplishments was the implementation of the Directors Executive Committee in 1996, uniting the organization by bringing six members each from the Devon Horse Show and Devon Country Fair Executive Committees to serve as Devon's leadership. This strategy laid the groundwork for Devon's current organizational structure and success. His capital campaign enabled Devon to purchase the showgrounds from Bryn Mawr Hospital, ensuring the show's financial stability. He also served as the manager of the American Gold Cup, both at JFK Stadium and at Devon. King was a founding member of the American Grand Prix Association and introduced a marketing plan for corporate sponsors and media. He was a member of the US Equestrian Team's board of directors and was inducted into the Show Jumping Hall of Fame in 2010. His legacy at Devon is indelible and his diplomacy and dedication irreplaceable. The schooling ring behind the Dixon Oval is named in his honor.

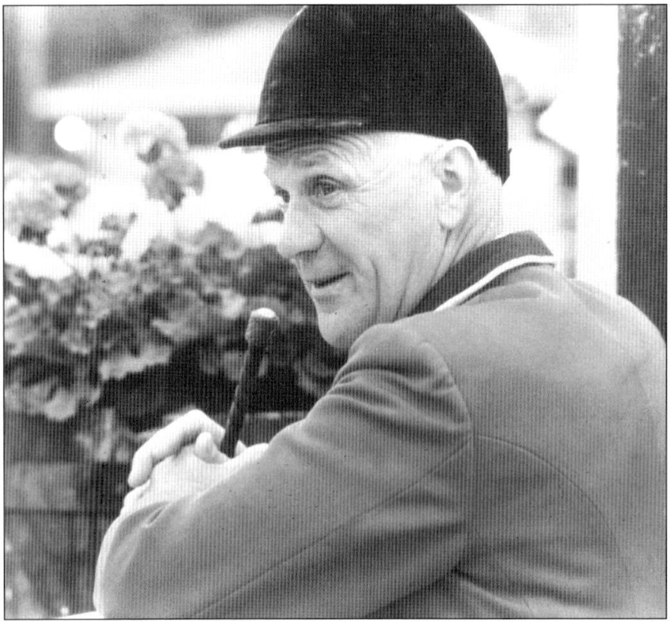

Harry de Leyer was known as the "Galloping Grandfather." He rescued his championship horse Snowman from the slaughter truck, and the duo went on to make history in 1959 when they won the Open Jumper Championship two years in a row. In 1983, de Leyer represented the United States at the World Championships at age 55 on Dutch Crown after winning the Devon Open Jumper Stake. A crowd-pleaser on the circuit, his victory signal was the tossing of his hat into the air and into the laps of the audience.

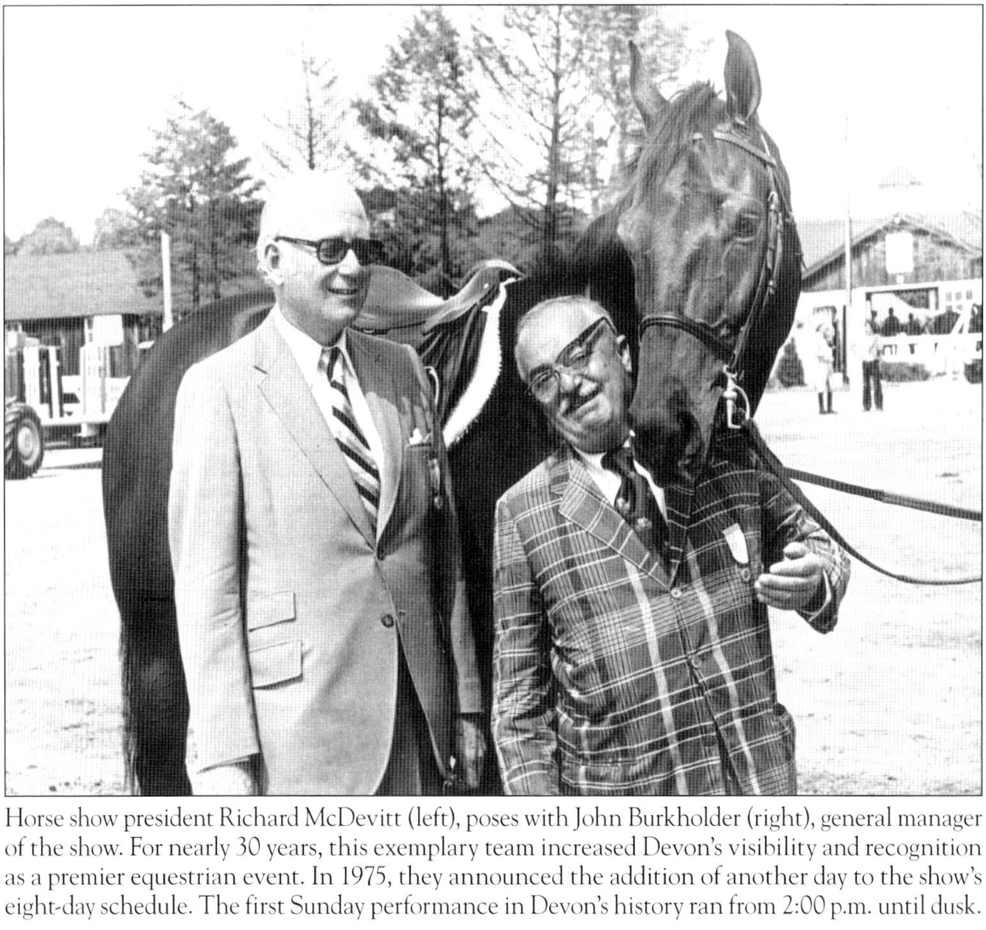

Horse show president Richard McDevitt (left), poses with John Burkholder (right), general manager of the show. For nearly 30 years, this exemplary team increased Devon's visibility and recognition as a premier equestrian event. In 1975, they announced the addition of another day to the show's eight-day schedule. The first Sunday performance in Devon's history ran from 2:00 p.m. until dusk.

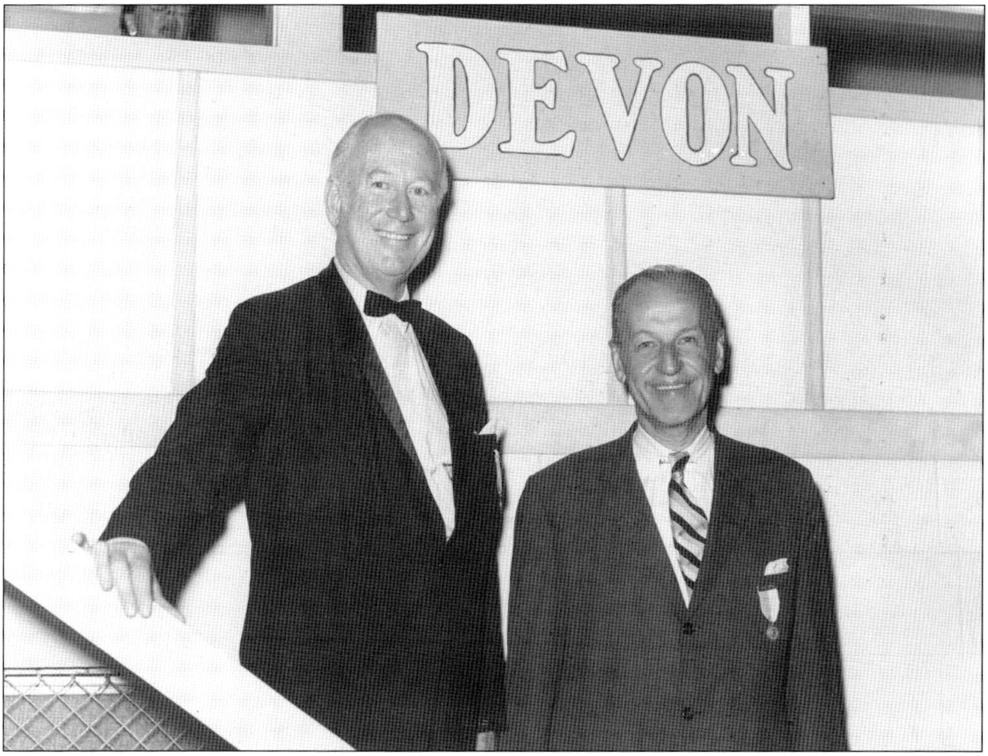

Richard McDevitt (left), president of Devon, and James K. Robinson Jr. (right), chairman of the board, were two legends who served Devon from the 1950s through the 1990s. Both were lifelong respected horsemen known for their integrity and vision. Their families have served Devon for generations, with McDevitt's son Wade continuing the proud tradition and serving as Devon's president in the 2000s. They are credited with expansion, acquisition, and development of the show grounds, including the East and South Grandstands and Gold Ring. Devon's success today is due in large part to their dedication, loyalty, determination, and influence.

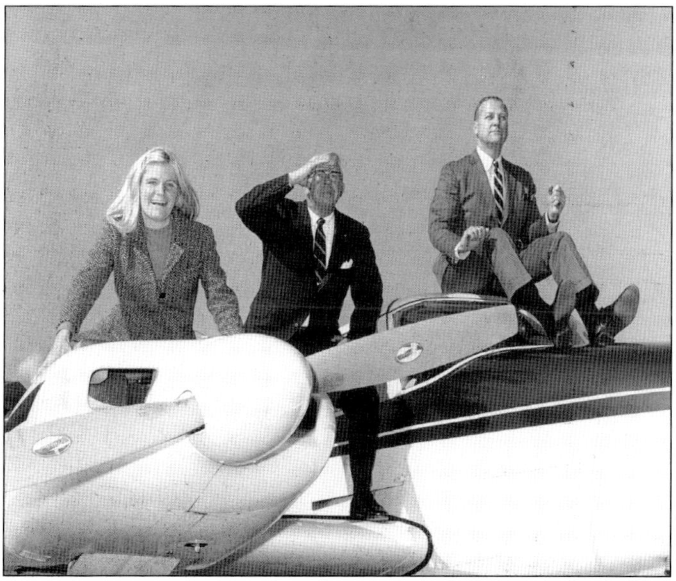

Thomas Foster Bright (right) served as Devon president in the 1960s and 1970s. As a public relations executive, he propelled Devon into the media age, recognizing the value of event promotion to increase attendance and donor support. He and his wife, Margaret Biddle Bright, were killed in July 1971 when his twin-engine crashed. The Mr. and Mrs. Thomas Foster Bright Perpetual Trophy is given in their honor for the Four-in-Hand Coaching class.

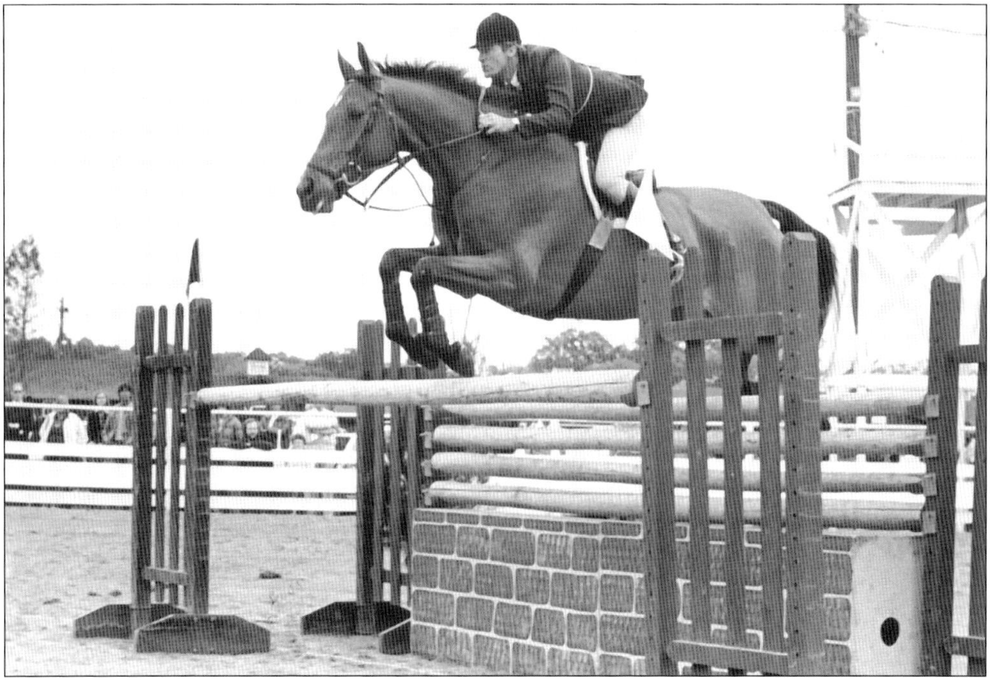

A three-time Olympian, Michael Matz competed in the 1976 Montreal, 1992 Barcelona, and 1996 Atlanta Games, where his fellow athletes honored him by selecting him as closing ceremonies flag bearer. In 2005, Matz was inducted into the Show Jumping Hall of Fame. Among his many accomplishments, he is renowned for his training of Thoroughbreds for racing, including legendary Kentucky Derby winner Barbaro. Matz won the Grand Prix of Devon twice and the American Gold Cup at Devon. With the support of Fitz and Edith Dixon of Erdenheim Farms, he partnered with memorable mounts Jet Run, Rhum IV, Mighty Ruler, and pictured here at Devon in 1977, Blue Line.

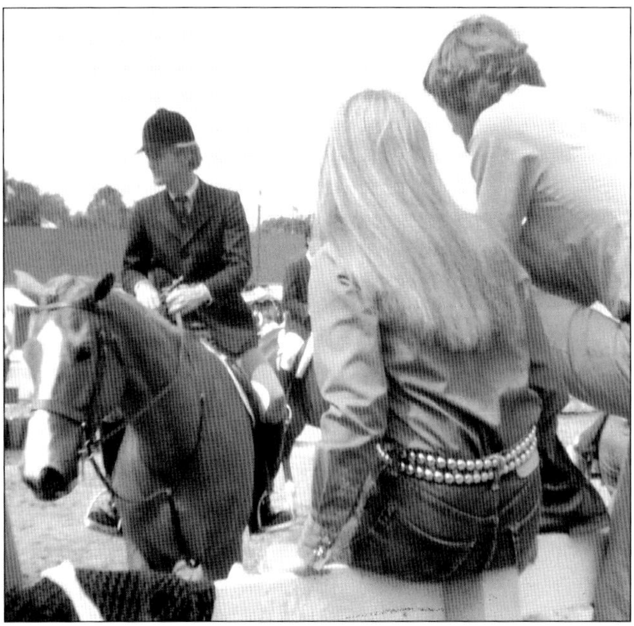

In 1974, Rodney Jenkins won the Grand Prix open jumper competition on Memorial Day weekend, taking three of the top four places while on Idle Dice, owned by Harry Gill of Collegeville. He was a five-time leading rider at Devon. Jenkins dominated the horse show ring in the 1960s, 1970s, and 1980s and retired as the winningest rider in the history of US show jumping. A member of the Show Jumping Hall of Fame, Jenkins won silver at the 1987 Pan American Games in individual and team jumping. Jenkins was given the nickname "The Red Rider" because of his red hair. (Courtesy of The Engraver.)

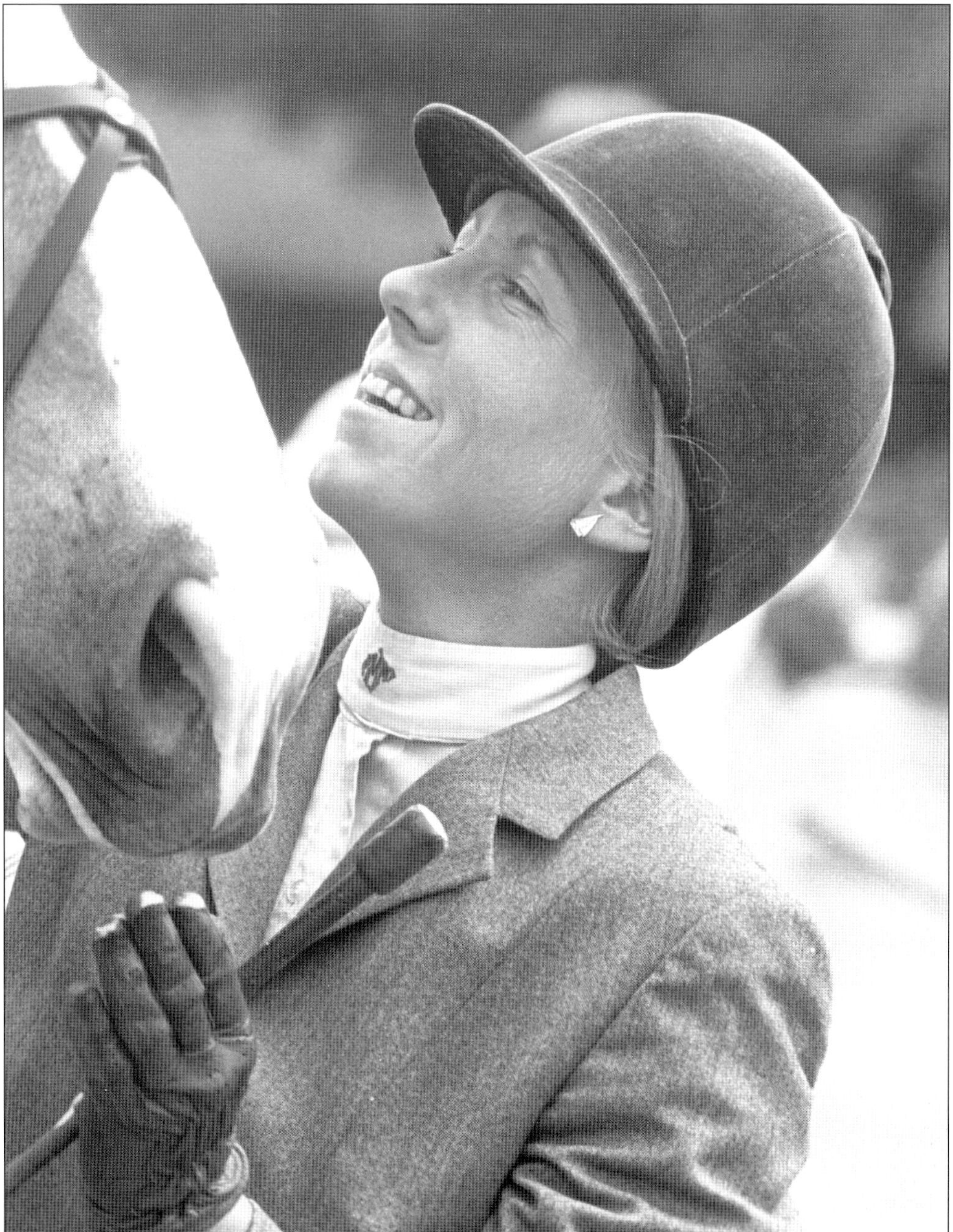

Katie Monahan Prudent was a leading contender in both the hunter and jumper divisions at Devon. A lifelong rider, she rode to dozens of Grand Prix wins across the United States and was selected to the 1980 US Olympic Team but was denied the chance to compete because of the US boycott. Prudent has successfully trained young riders for top competition, including her son Adam Prudent; two-time Olympic gold medalist Beezie Madden; and Reed Kessler, the youngest show jumping rider to compete in the Olympic Games. In 2000, Prudent was named Coach of the Year by the US Olympic Committee, and in 2015, she was inducted into the Show Jumping Hall of Fame.

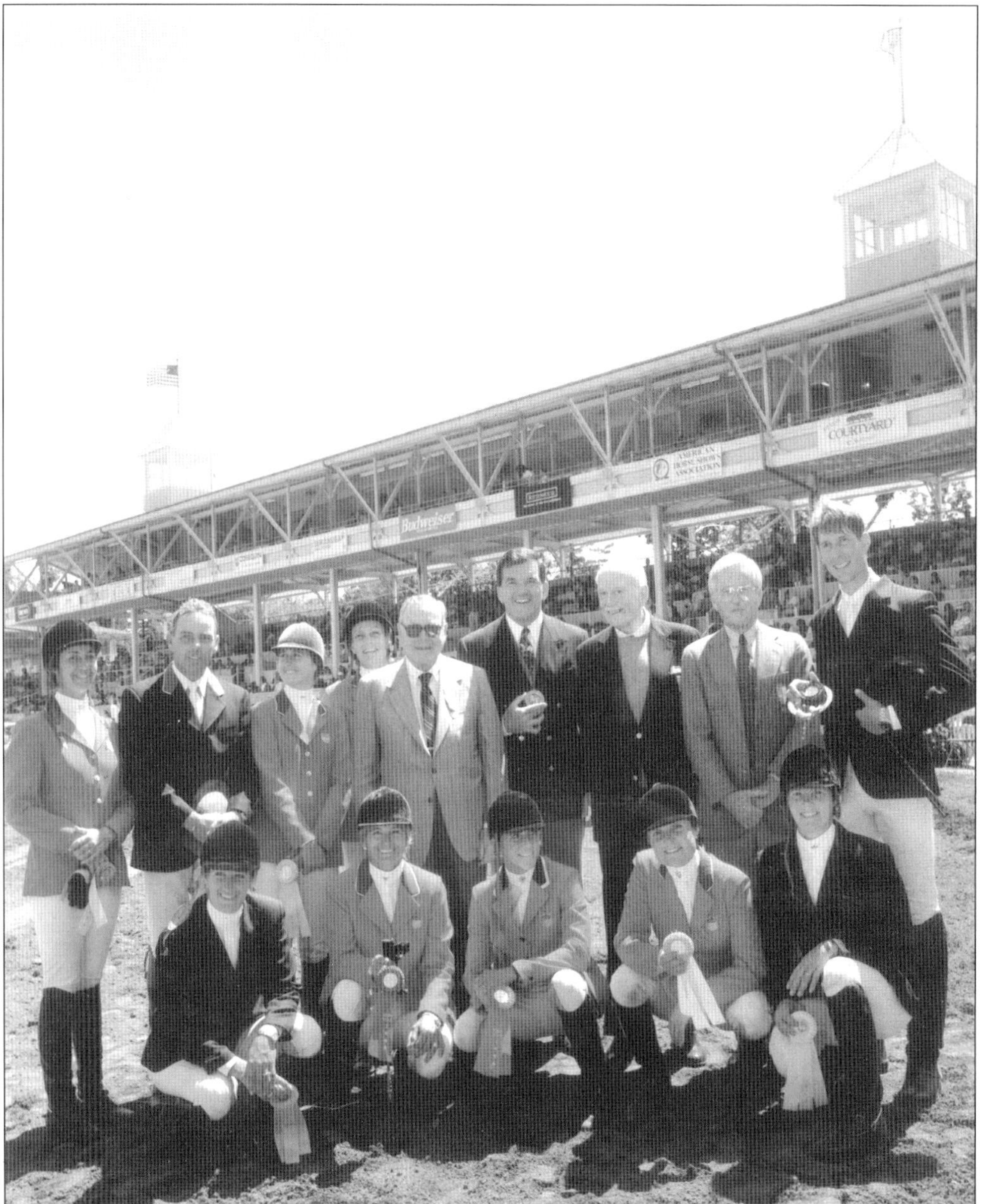

Horseman, educator, and philanthropist Fitz Eugene Dixon Jr. (center) was a major supporter of the Devon Horse Show and USET. He owned some of show jumping's greatest horses, including Jet Run and Rhum IV, which were trained at his Erdenheim Farm in Pennsylvania. His daughter Ellin Dixon Miller won the United States Dressage Federation (USDF) Grand Prix National Championship and served as USDF president. Dixon was owner of or investor in Philadelphia sports franchises, including the Philadelphia 76ers, Flyers, and Phillies in the 1970s and 1980s. Dixon served on the board of the Devon Horse Show and was closely associated with the American Gold Cup when it was held at the showgrounds. In 1990, Devon's main ring was renamed the Dixon Oval in his honor. In this photograph, he and Gov. Tom Ridge (fourth from right) welcome the 1996 US Equestrian Team to the Dixon Oval.

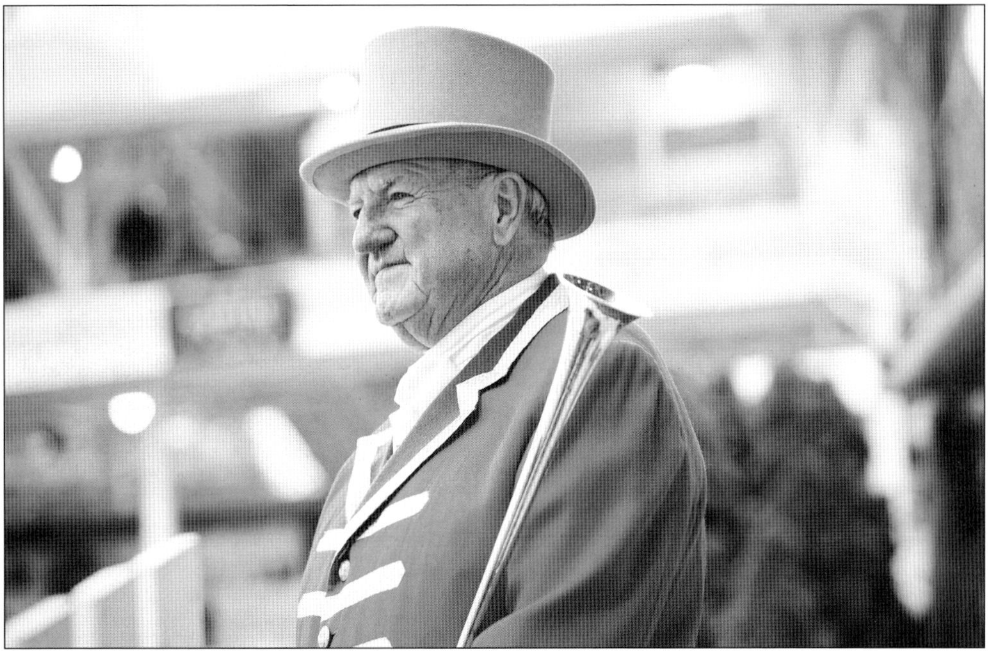

The ringmaster is the chief safety officer of the show and ensures that it runs smoothly for exhibitors, spectators, owners, trainers, and management. The spectrum of duties includes the iconic sounding of the call, which signifies to the riders what is happening in the arena, as well as managing the awards presentation, providing the perfect photograph to sponsors, and serving as the eyes and ears in the ring to assist when needed. Shown above is John Franzreb III and below is Alan Keeley, two of Devon's iconic ringmasters. (Both, courtesy of Brenda Carpenter Photography.)

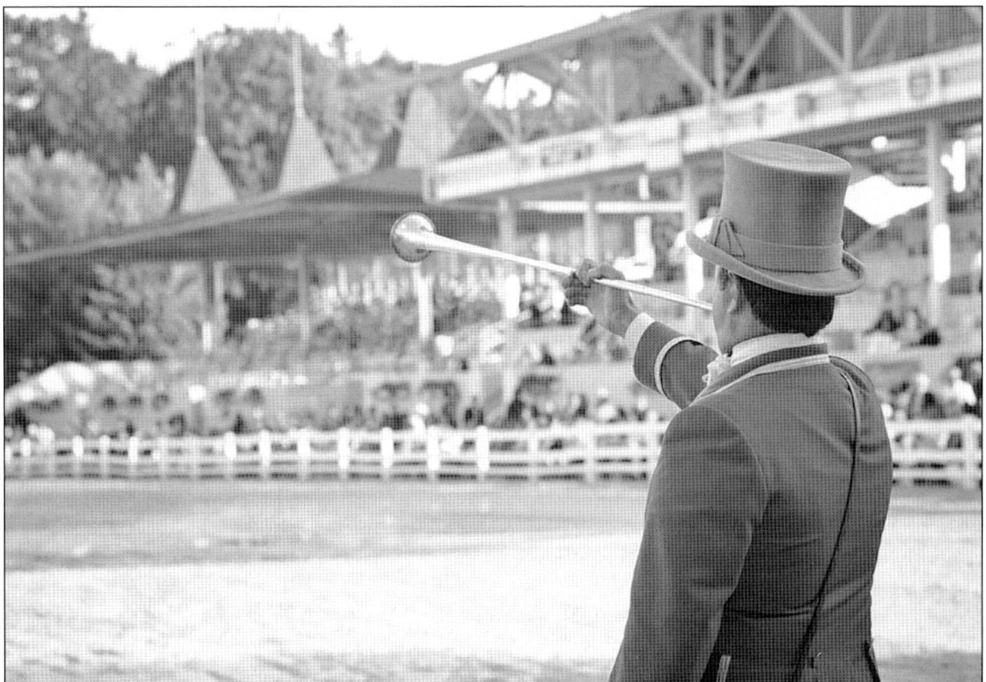

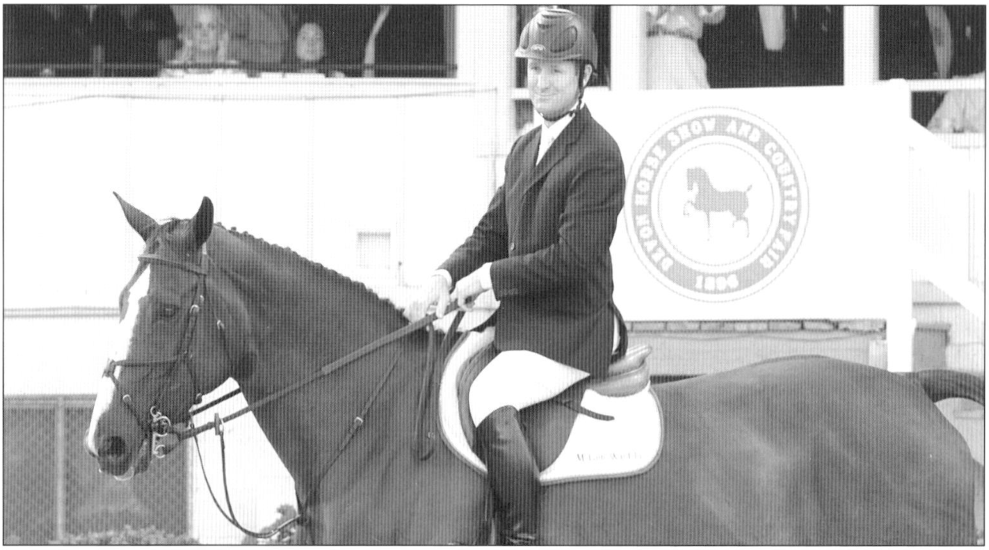

Fan favorite McLain Ward is known as "The King of Devon." To date, he has won the Devon Grand Prix a record 11 times. Winning at Devon has always been very special for Ward, and the Grand Prix is named after his legendary Olympic mount Sapphire. At the 2004 Olympic Games in Athens, Ward and Sapphire won the gold medal as part of the US team in team jumping. At the 2008 Beijing Olympics, Ward, aboard Sapphire, won team gold for show jumping along with Laura Kraut, Beezie Madden, and Will Simpson. In 2012, Sapphire was retired at the Devon Horse Show and Country Fair in an emotional and heartwarming ceremony. (Courtesy of Brenda Carpenter Photography.)

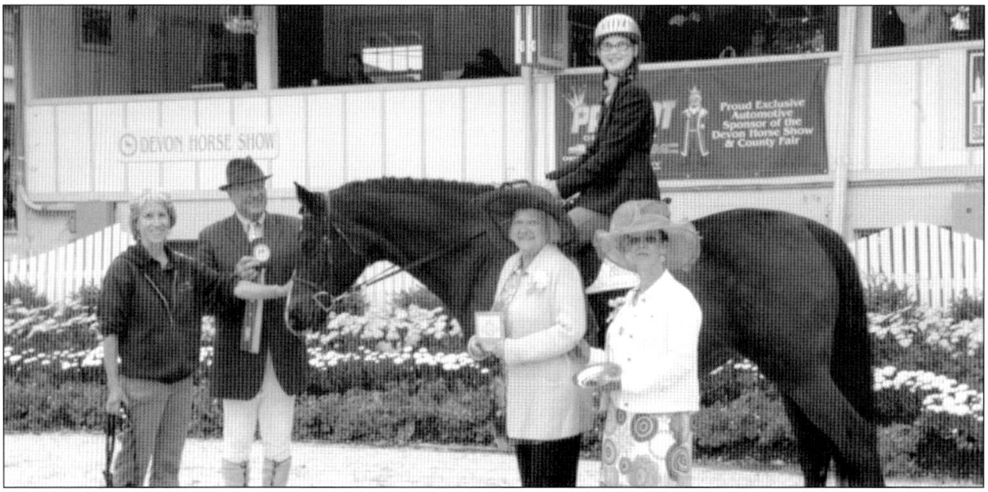

Jane C. MacElree, a fierce Devon philanthropist, hails from a family with a long and storied history in equestrian sport. A nationally recognized sport horse breeder, MacElree is the recipient of the USEF Ellen Scripps Davis Memorial Cup for her contributions to the sport horse industry. Her nationally renowned stallion farm is the sponsor of the Hilltop Trophy, awarded to the champion of the Therapeutic Riders Division of the Devon Horse Show. This event brings together 175 riders with special needs to compete in a variety of classes including equitation and dressage and culminates with the award ceremonies for the championship classes at Devon. In this 2018 photograph, MacElree and her daughter Ann Hill (right) award the Hilltop Trophy to Brynn Barnhart of Special Equestrians at the 39th annual Therapeutic Riders Division of the Devon Horse Show. (Courtesy of Thorncroft Equestrian Center).

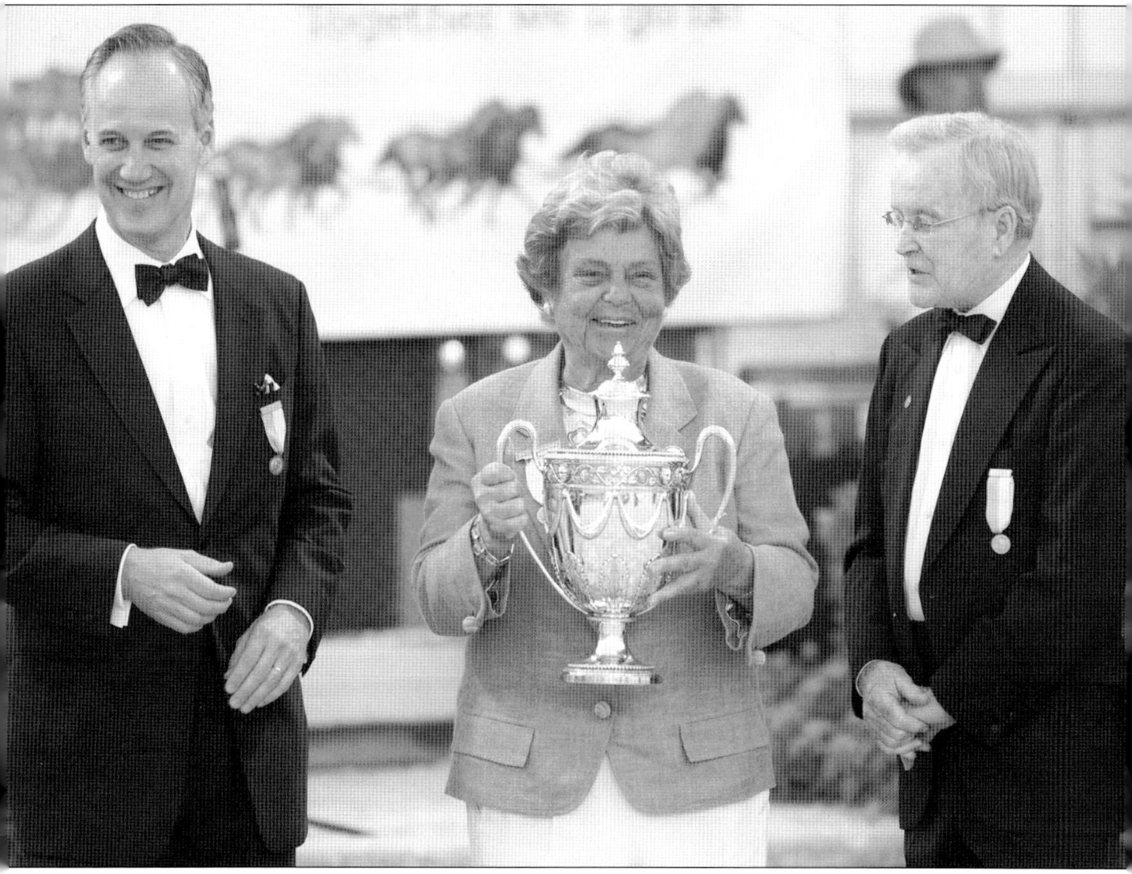

There are many people in the Devon family who have spent a good part of their lives volunteering with and supporting the Devon Horse Show and Country Fair. The first Devon Horse Show and Country Fair Lifetime Achievement Trophy was presented to Betty Moran (center) by Devon president Wade McDevitt (left) and Devon chairman Leonard A. King Jr. (right) in 2012. An avid horsewoman, Moran was a member of Devon's board of directors, an active Devon Country Fair volunteer, and the most generous supporter of the many events that promoted and unified the Devon community. She enjoyed great success as a Thoroughbred owner and breeder as proprietor of Brushwood Stable in Willistown Township, Chester County. Her wit, drive, and devotion remain an inspiration. Moran's personal motto resonates within the Devon community, "Be kind, considerate, charitable and fierce." (Courtesy of Brenda Carpenter Photography.)

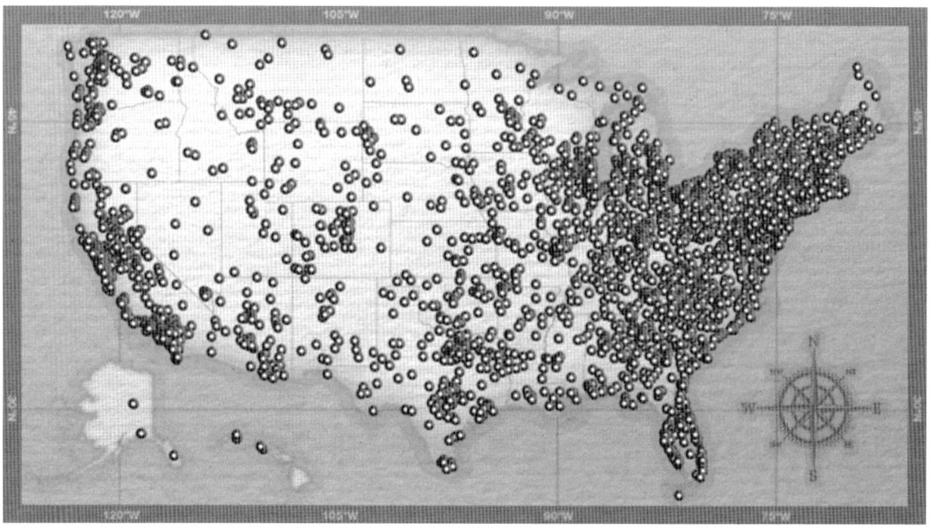

Consistent with our mission to preserve history on a local level, this book was printed in South Carolina on American-made paper and manufactured entirely in the United States. Products carrying the accredited Forest Stewardship Council (FSC) label are printed on 100 percent FSC-certified paper.

MADE IN THE USA